Understanding Corporate Life

Understanding Corporate Life

The Warwick Organisation Theory Network
Edited by **Philip Hancock** and **André Spicer**

Los Angeles | London | New Delhi
Singapore | Washington DC

© The Warwick Organisation Theory Network 2010

First published 2009

SAGE Publications Ltd
1 Oliver's Yard
55 City Road
London EC1Y 1SP

SAGE Publications Inc.
2455 Teller Road
Thousand Oaks, California 91320

SAGE Publications India Pvt Ltd
B 1/I 1 Mohan Cooperative Industrial Area
Mathura Road, Post Bag 7
New Delhi 110 044

SAGE Publications Asia-Pacific Pte Ltd
33 Pekin Street #02-01
Far East Square
Singapore 048763

Library of Congress Control Number: 2009922676

British Library Cataloguing in Publication data

A catalogue record for this book is available
from the British Library

ISBN 978-1-4129-2383-5
ISBN 978-1-4129-2384-2 (pbk)

Typeset by C&M Digitals (P) Ltd, Chennai, India
Printed by CPI Antony Rowe, Chippenham Wiltshire
Printed on paper from sustainable resources

CONTENTS

NOTES ON CONTRIBUTORS

Martin Corbett works at Warwick Business School and has done for quite some time. He has written quite a bit of stuff on the psychological and cultural aspects of technology, although his more recent research interests include neuro-scientific management and the role of the unconscious in organizational behaviour.

Christopher Grey is Professor of Organizational Behaviour at the University of Warwick. He was previously Professor of Organizational Theory at the University of Cambridge and has held posts at Leeds and Manchester. He has wide-ranging research interests including the sociology of management and management education, professional socialization and identity, and the organization of intelligence agencies.

Philip Hancock is an Associate Professor (Reader) of Organization Studies at the Warwick Business School. His research is concerned with a critical appraisal of organizational aestheticization and embodiment, space and place, and the managerial colonization of everyday life, all of which inform his current fascination with the organization of Christmas. He has published in the usual selection of internationally recognised journals and has co-authored and co-edited a number of books, the most recent of which is *The Management of Everyday Life* (Palgrave). He is currently joint editor-in-chief of the Inderscience publication, *The International Journal of Work, Organization to Organisation*.

Chris Land lectures in management at the University of Essex. His research on 'community' has included a two-year project on Communities of Practice with the Innovation, Knowledge and Organization Networks (IKON) research unit at Warwick Business School, living in a commune, and working for a Community Interest Company. He sees in 'community' the possibility of moving beyond the idea of 'resistance' in critical management studies to explore instead the many and varied forms of non-capitalist organization found in daily life around the globe and throughout history.

Karen Legge is Professor Emerita of Organizational Behaviour, Warwick Business School. Prior to her retirement in 2007, Karen held posts at Manchester Business School, Institute of Work Psychology – Sheffield, Imperial College Management School, Lancaster University Management

School and Warwick Business School. She was a long serving Joint Editor of *Journal of Management Studies* and also served on numerous editorial boards, including *British Journal of Industrial Relations, Industrial Relations, Human Resource Management Journal, Gender, Work and Organization* and *Organization*. Karen's research interests lie in the area of applying post-modern and critical organization theory to HRM, change management, the development of learning organizations and in organizational ethics. She has published widely in these areas, a well known publication being *HRM, Rhetorics and Realities* (Palgrave/Macmillan, 1995), an updated anniversary edition of which was published in 2005.

Nick Llewellyn is Associate Professor (Reader) of Organization Studies at Warwick Business School (IROB group). His research focuses mainly on work and interaction in organizations and in public settings. He has published on this research in journals such as *The British Journal of Sociology, Sociology, Organization Studies, Human Relations* and *Discourse Studies.*

Glenn Morgan is Professor of Organizational Behaviour at Warwick Business School, University of Warwick. He is one of the Editors in Chief of the journal *Organization: the critical journal of organization, theory and society.* Recent publications include *Images of the Multinational Firm* (2009: edited with Collinson) and *Changing Capitalisms?* (2005 edited with Whitley and Moen) as well as articles in various journals. He is Visiting Professor at the International Centre for Business and Politics at Copenhagen Business School as well as an associate of the Centre for the Study of Globalization and Regionalization at the University of Warwick.

Maxine Robertson (BSc, MA, PhD) is a Professor of Management at Queen Mary University of London and Director of Research in the School of Business and Management. Her research interests include the management of knowledge workers and knowledge intensive firms, networked innovation and the management of knowledge in organizations. She has published extensively in all of these areas. She is also co-author of *Managing Knowledge Work and Innovation* published by Palgrave (2009). Recent research includes a comparative UK/US study of biomedical innovation. Her current research focuses on the management of clinical trials in the UK.

André Spicer is an Associate Professor (Reader) of Organization Studies at the Warwick Business School and a visiting research fellow at Lund University, Sweden. His research focuses on political dynamics in and around organizations. He has studied these dynamics in the media, ports, libraries, and social movements. His work has appeared in journals such as *Organization, Organization Studies, Human Relations* and *Journal of Management Studies.* He is also author of *Contesting the Corporation*

(Cambridge University Press) and *Unmasking the Entrepreneur* (Edward Elgar).

Andrew Sturdy is Professor of Organisational Behaviour at Warwick Business School. He has a longstanding interest in the production and use of management ideas such as customer service. His research has explored this in various contexts including training, business school education and management consultancy. Most recently, he led a 'fly-on-the-wall' study of consultancy projects, from which a book (with Handley, Clark and Fincham) was published in 2009 by Oxford University Press – *Management Consultancy: Boundaries and Knowledge in Action*.

Emma Surman lectures in marketing at Keele University. After completing her PhD at Keele in 2004, Emma was a research fellow at the University of Exeter and subsequently a lecturer at Warwick Business School before returning to Keele in August 2007 to join the marketing department. Prior to her career in academia, she held marketing posts in a variety of organizations that encompassed the private, public and charity sectors. Her research interests include: telework, emotion in the workplace, the production and consumption of organizational space, and gender, identity and power relations.

Jacky Swan is Professor of Organizational Behaviour at Warwick Business School, University of Warwick. She holds a first degree in Psychology and completed her PhD at University of Wales, Cardiff. Jacky is co-founder of IKON – a research centre based at Warwick on *Innovation Knowledge and Organisational Networks* (http://www.warwick.ac.uk/go/ikon). Her interests are in linking innovation and networking to processes of managing knowledge across different industry sectors and national contexts. She is currently researching the processes through which knowledge is translated from scientific discovery into changes in clinical and healthcare practice, focusing on the management and organizational of clinical trials. She is a Senior Editor for *Organization Studies*, co-author of *Managing Knowledge Work and Innovation* and publishes in organization theory, innovation and management journals.

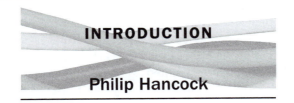

INTRODUCTION

Philip Hancock

Here you will find a collection of essays concerned with the understanding of corporate organization and its management. It has been written at what appears to be a time of almost unprecedented economic upheaval that will undoubtedly have significant consequences for such organizations and the people who work both in and for them. As such, it might be fair to say that a collection such as this is already verging on irrelevancy, dealing primarily as it does with an organizational landscape that no longer exists. Well, possibly. Yet despite the turmoil that currently surrounds us, it seems unlikely that the changes we have seen in the world of work and its organization over the last 30 years or so will be easily reversed. The globalization of the marketplace, the expansion of information communication systems, and the expectations of an increasingly educated and demanding consumer body will all continue to place fresh demands on the corporate world to innovate and expand its interests and operations. And while capitalism is undergoing one of its inevitable lurches into crisis, it cannot simply be viewed as the same beast that it was during its last period of major decline and recession. As Thrift (2005) has observed, capitalism is now a much more sophisticated system. It is one that has arrived at a state of virtual self-consciousness, learning not only from its own innovations but also those ideas, and indeed criticisms, that are circulated about it, often turning them to its own advantage. It is has succeeded in embedding itself deeper into our cultural psyches than ever before, providing not only the backdrop to practices of work and consumption but also to our leisure activities, our moments of familial togetherness, and even our most intimate experiences of ourselves and each other (cf. Tyler, 2004). As Thrift (2005: 1) himself expresses it: 'Capitalism has a kind of crazy vitality. It doesn't just line its pockets. It also appeals to gut feelings. It gets involved in all kinds of extravagant symbioses. It adds to the world as well as subtracts'.

Not that all diagnoses of the current condition of capitalism share quite such a breathless optimism. Hardt and Negri (2000), for instance, have argued that while capitalism has indeed achieved a new stage in its development this must largely be understood in terms of its colonization of both global difference as well as personal values and individual aspirations. In particular, corporations are required increasingly to 'incorporate' nearly every aspect of their employees' everyday lives into their operations in order to maximize 'creativity, free play and diversity in the corporate workplace' (Hardt and Negri, 2000: 153), as well as their own socio-cultural legitimacy. Another critical perspective on such developments is that offered by Boltanski and Chiapello (2005), who have pointed to the emergence, over the last 20 years or so, of what they describe as a new spirit of capitalism. This is a spirit which is concerned with the continued ideological legitimacy of capitalist economic and social relations, and places a priority on the cultural and moral engagement of employees in general, and managers in particular. Corporations engage employees not simply as units of labour, therefore, but as invaluable assets who must be encouraged to exercise initiative and creativity within a framework of flexibility, the promise of self-development, and a contribution to the idea of a common good.

Now none of these are, I would argue, developments that will depart the scene very quickly, whatever the character of the current market. They define contemporary capitalism today and will for a number of years to come. Yet, however one conceptualizes or theorizes the nature of capitalism and the quality of corporate life that extends from it, what is of particular interest to us here is to what extent has the study of corporate organizations shifted in order to engage this contemporary landscape? Certainly from the perspective of what one might term 'mainstream' textbooks on the subject, it would seem that the answer is hardly at all. Open any such text and what you will tend to find are chapters on topics such as structure, leadership, motivation and culture which, while often updated in terms of empirics and perhaps more topical case studies, could have been found in any similar textbook published over the last 30 years or so. This is not to suggest that there are no good textbooks in the field of organization theory available – far from it. Offerings from the likes of Clegg et al. (2008), Knights and Willmott (2006) and Hatch and Cunliffe (2006), amongst a number of others, do ask difficult questions of corporate organizations and often engage with highly novel aspects of their activities and practices. As textbooks they often remain restricted, however, by both the format expected of such books and the requirements of their readership, leaving little opportunity for the reader to encounter and engage with the ideas and experiences of the authors behind the writing.

The book you have in front of you is, as we hope you will notice, somewhat different to the usual textbook, however. First and foremost it isn't a textbook as such, not as one might understand it anyway. It contains few, if any, diagrams, thinkboxes, suggestions for further reading or indeed case studies or sample essay questions. Nor does it cover what one might term the usual suspects of organization theory as suggested above. Subjects such as culture, power, leadership, and even motivation, are present of course, but just not as explicitly as one would encounter in a standard student textbook. Rather, they might live beneath the surfaces of the chapters you will encounter here, providing the background against which certain topics are discussed. For instance, motivation inevitably provides the context in which discussions of identity, aesthetics and a host of other topics take place. Alternatively, traditional subjects might surface quite explicitly in chapters such as those concerned with knowledge or technology, but be presented in a very particular and often personal manner.

In fact this is what really sets this book apart from the more established textbook genre in that it is a very personal book for each of its contributors. For not only do these chapters each discuss an area of contemporary corporate life that has been largely ignored or at best marginalized in most mainstream textbooks, they do it from the very particular perspective and interests of their author or authors. As such, what you won't find here are particularly standardized formats or claims to exhaustivity in the treatment of the material under consideration. Rather, what you are offered is a series of essays that will introduce you to topics that, in the view of the individual authors, characterize the experience of corporate organizational life today. Furthermore, these topics are addressed and delivered in line with what these authors consider to be their most pertinent and important features, and in terms of how they would discuss them with their own students. As the title of the book suggests, therefore, the aim of this collection is not simply to record the features of contemporary corporate life, but to promote an understanding of what characterizes the everyday experience of work in and around such corporations as they adapt to the changing face of capitalism.

Now, having made such an apparently strong claim for the value of the insights that the authors of this book can bring, it is perhaps somewhat incumbent on me to say something about the team of academics who produced this collection. Or, to put it more directly, just what, or indeed who, is the Warwick Organisation Theory Network? The authors collected together here either serve, or have served, as members of faculty at Warwick Business School (WBS), part of the University of Warwick, and are affiliated to the Warwick Organisation Theory Network (WOTNet). Formed in 2004, WOTNet aims to support and promote the critical, interdisciplinary and expansive study of organization amongst WBS faculty members through a range of events, publications and other activities. The Warwick Business School has a long and celebrated history at the forefront of developments in organization theory and related fields, and it is the ambition of WOTNet to continue this tradition. Its members are widely recognized as leading scholars in the various sub-fields of organization theory in terms of both their research and their contribution to teaching and scholarship. They have long-standing links to some of Europe's premier journals in the field, including

Organization Studies and *Organization,* as well more specialized publications such as *The International Journal of Work, Organisation and Emotion.*

The Warwick Organisation Theory Network is also centrally involved in the design and delivery of the WBS masters programme in Management and Organizational Analysis. Drawing on a range of social science disciplines, this is a programme that seeks to challenge managerial orthodoxies and contribute to a forward view of how organizations are evolving, and indeed pushing the ideas of organization and organizing beyond traditional boundaries towards ideas of organizing as a fundamental activity of social life. All of the topics covered by the chapters here have at one time or another, therefore, constituted part of the teaching curriculum of each of the authors. Similarly, the training and supervision of PhD students is also a core activity of the majority of members of WOTNet, ensuring that each of us remains tightly integrated into a culture of collaborative learning with our students, exploring new avenues and pushing boundaries in terms of what constitutes knowledge and an understanding of organization.

Having broadly outlined the ethos of the collection and the qualifications of the authors it is perhaps time to turn to a brief description of the contents of the book itself. In the first of the chapters, Martin Corbett offers a discussion of technology and corporate life which offers a rethinking of the relationship between technology and the cultural and human dimensions of organizational activity. As he notes, while from the earliest days of the industrial revolution technology has represented a vital corporate resource, it has tended to be viewed as a distinct and quite discrete aspect of organizational life; one largely ignored by the field of organizational theory until around the mid-point of the twentieth century. Since then, however, technology has emerged as something of a contested terrain, viewed in terms of a range of competing dualities such as human/non-human and, in terms of an ethical orientation to the questions it frequently poses, good/evil. In contrast to this, however, Corbett seeks to argue in favour of a more aesthetic conceptualization of technology by which it is viewed not so much as a separate dimension of organizational life, but as something integral to each and every aspect of it. Thus, utilizing the popular image of the cyborg he argues that human agency, organization and technology have become mutually indispensable to one another, a proposition that challenges us to rethink the vary basis of our humanness perhaps as much as it does the ways in which we think about the relationship of technology to the structuring of corporate working life.

Following on from Corbett's opening intervention, we have Chris Grey's reflections on what without doubt has become one of the corporate world's overriding operational priorities, that of speed. Opening with a nod to the ghosts of Karl Marx and Friedrich Engels and their observation regarding capitalism's insatiable need to constantly change and revolutionize itself, Grey situates the 'need for speed' at the heart of contemporary corporate life. While, as noted above, the pursuit of speed has always been integral to the very nature of capitalist business, it is an operational quality that has taken on even greater significance with the rise of a culture of globalization, itself in part driven by the accelerating consequences of modern computer technologies. Despite what at first sight might appear to be the advantages such a prioritization of speed might entail for organizational competitiveness, however, for Grey a fixation on the celebration of speed at all costs is one that is not without its dangers. Inspired in part by the unlikely ideas of Luddism, he suggests that the way in which speed has become an end in itself is potentially destructive not only to the possibility of capitalism operating with at least some reference to the idea of the common good (see for instance some of the critiques levelled at the finance markets and their contribution to the recent economic crisis), but that it destabilizes the very fabric of people's everyday lives. In contrast then, he turns his attentions to the possibilities offered by the increasingly popular 'slow movement' and how this might inform a revalorization of speed in order to serve the creation of a more just and human set of both social and organizational arrangements.

While the chapters by Corbett and Grey are clearly linked by a concern with technology, the following chapter by Philip Hancock shares another related concern, that of aestheticization. While Corbett refers to an aesthetics of technology and Grey, if albeit implicitly, to the subjective experience of acceleration and the particular aesthetic associated with it, Hancock's chapter presents the aesthetic as something which is in and of itself an increasingly significant corporate interest. Taking it to refer to knowledge acquired through one's pre-reflective and sensual exposure to the materiality of the world, what is presented in this chapter is a critical reflection on the ways in which corporate organizations are increasingly managing their aesthetic dimension in order to secure competitive advantage. This process, which he terms organizational aestheticization, is illustrated through a discussion of a range of contemporary corporate practices. These range from the presentation of management as an art-like activity, through the stylization and landscaping of organizational environments, up to and including the manipulation of the bodies of employees in order to render them aesthetically congruent with the aims and aspirations of the employing corporation. And while open minded to the possible benefits such an interest in the aesthetic qualities of work and its organization might bring to both employers and employees, Hancock maintains a wary eye on the idea that the aesthetic can continue to thrive under the aegis of corporate rationality, reminding us that the line between liberation and colonization is often a rather narrow one.

The importance of architecture to corporate image building, an issue touched upon in Hancock's chapter, is expanded and refined by André Spicer in his following chapter on corporate space and its production and design. Noting the almost inevitable ubiquity of spatial relations to understanding corporate life, for Spicer the social construction and individual and collective experience of such spaces – ranging from the mundane environment of the office to the grandiosity of the corporate headquarters – play a central role in the formation of identities, both of corporations themselves as well as those who occupy such corporate spaces. Deploying a tripartite analytical framework that concentrate on the production of space through physical distance, patterns of understanding, and the materialization of control, he charts a path through the various spatial histories and landscapes of the corporate world from the factory floor, through the open plan office, to the supermarket checkout. In doing so he interrogates a series of questions such as how is corporate space produced, who serves to benefit from its design and management, and how and why do individuals frequently become attached to the corporate spaces they inhabit? In doing so, Spicer evokes an image of corporate organization which is both material and imagined, productive and produced; leaving us in little doubt that in order to understand the conceived and lived experience of corporate life, space is, and must remain, an integral contributor to that endeavour.

Charles Lamb, the nineteenth-century English essayist once commented that nothing troubled him more than time and space and yet nothing troubled him less 'as I never think about them'. Despite the rather contradictory quality of this observation what is significant, however, is that he recognized the inescapable relationship between the spatial and the temporal qualities of human existence. We are creatures that exist within both these dimensions, however much we might to try to deny at least the latter of the two. Thus, it may perhaps come as no surprise that following Spicer's consideration of space and spatiality we next turn our attentions to the temporal and the relationship between time and an understanding of corporate life. In this chapter Karen Legge considers the relationship between objective time – namely that characterized by formal systems of calculation such as industrial 'clock time' – and its subjective counterpart; that which flows from our individual experiences and personal mental constructions of time which lacks the homogeneity and equivalency of its objective other. At the heart of Legge's argument is a belief in the need to recognize time and its competing modes as a vital terrain of, to use her own words, 'commodification, compression, control and colonization', whereby corporate organization seeks to reconfigure subjective time in line with its own 'formal' imperatives. In order to resist this, both theoretically, and indeed practically, Legge evokes a range of far more dialectical orientations towards the temporal world such as the 'timescape', or 'spiral time', both of which emphasize the interrelatedness of differing conceptions of time, resisting their easy assimilation into one variant or the other.

It is difficult these days not to encounter the proposition that we are, in one way or another, both living and working in an increasingly globalized environment. Indeed one of the most popular explanations of this process is that this is a consequence, taking us back to the previous two chapters, of the compression of time and space brought about by the almost unlimited reach and speed of information communication technologies (Harvey, 1989). In the sixth of our chapters Glenn Morgan tackles this question of globalization and how it impacts on our understanding of contemporary corporate life. He commences by sketching out a conceptual framework within which contemporary processes of globalization are defined in relation to a series of increased interdependencies between social actors over a global scale. From this starting point Morgan is then able to offer a richly illustrated analysis of how people's everyday experiences of work and life directly reflect such processes. In particular, he explores the role played by global economic forces in the production of the conditions of everyday corporate life via, for instance, the restructuring of firms, processes and consumption as well as the ways in which it has created new global migrations of labour. In particular, he considers how such migrations have created both new pressures and new opportunities in terms of the appearance of transnational communities who are increasingly central to the global circulation of finance. Contributing as they do both to the criminal laundering of money on the one hand, and the support and welfare of the vulnerable members of the global community on the other; both represent a true challenge to how we conceive the nature and role of multinational organizations.

While Morgan's chapter is primarily concerned with the apperance of a form of globalized community born of a sereis of interdependencies, in the next chapter Chris Land tackles the issue of community and its implications for corporate life head on. As he rightly acknowledges, corporate life increasingly extends well beyond the formal parameters of the workplace and nor should it always be reduced simply to the expereince of the buisness organization. Nonetheless, as he explains, community has long had its associations with the realm of the corporate business organization. It has been posited, for instance, as the antithesis of such organizational forms, grounded as they are in a far more instrumentalized set of social relations in comparison to the more substantivie rationalities of traditional community. Yet despite this apparent tension with the idea of community, as Land observes, much organizational effort even today is concerned with attempting to reclaim the values of community associated with its apparent dissolution in the face of the mass industrialization and urbanization of the nineteenth and twentieth centuries culminating in the contemporary organizational ideas of communities of practice and the marketing category of brand communities. Yet despite all this, Land continues to identify the ways in which the ideal of the community continues to provide a focus for those opposed to the influence of corporate ideology both within, and external to, the sphere of the formally constituted work organization.

While community continues, in Land's analysis, to represent a contested terrain, both conceptually and politically, it is clear that how one is orientated to the idea can have a notable impact on the sense of identity one constructs for oneself. And it is to the subject of identity that Nick Llewellyn turns his

---

7

attention to in the next of our chapters. In what is an empirically rich piece of writing, Llewellyn explores some of the ways in which young people learn to occupy an identity position of worker even before they enter the corporate labour market. Explaining the evolution of identity as a profoundly social process, the chapter locates identity and the question of its formation and regulation as a problem that sits at the heart of contemporary organization theory. This understanding is then relocated in the ways in which, through the discourse of transferable skills so beloved by the current UK government, young men and women are encouraged and resourced to constitute an identity for themselves as an employable worker from an increasingly young age. That is, within the transferable skills framework, young people are encouraged to view and represent even the most mundane of activities – ranging from playing sport to going on holiday – as the building blocks of a corporately oriented identity, evidence of perhaps yet a further incursion of corporate interests into the everyday lives of those increasingly subject to them.

Our penultimate chapter directs our attention to a theme touched upon not only in Land's chapter via the theme of communities of practice, but in its own way in Llewellyn's reflection on identity. I refer here to Jacky Swan and Maxine Robertson's chapter on knowledge and knowledge management. While critical of much of the hype that has surrounded the idea of knowledge as a vital corporate resource, at the heart of this essay is a realization that organizations are increasingly seeking to tap into or harness the knowledge of its employees as well as the formal and informal networks they inevitably belong to. Drawing on research into the biotechnology industry, a knowledge rich environment if ever there was one, Swan and Robertson explore the various mechanisms by which not only the organization attempts to exploit both professional as well as personal and friendship based networks in order to maximize access to and retention of knowledge based resources, but also how these so-called 'knowledge workers' are quite prepared to utilize their interpersonal relationships in order to achieve corporate objectives. What is particularly interesting, they conclude, is how many of the judgement calls made by employees in terms of who to cooperate with and trust in what is in fact a highly competitive environment often comes down, to return to Hancock's chapter, to aesthetic judgments based on intuition and gut feelings.

This leads us to the final chapter of the collection, which is by Emma Surman and Andrew Sturdy. Here the theme resonates with the final observation of Swan and Roberstson regarding the importance of non-rational judgements in the corporate sphere in that its topic is that of emotion. While much research has been conducted into the role emotion increasingly plays as a mediating agent between employees and customers, most notably in the service industries, the authors of this chapter take a somewhat different perspective. Drawing on various studies of emotion within organizations and some of the author's own research, this chapter explores managerial efforts to appropriate emotional experiences with particular reference to what they term the emotional arena of *fun and friendliness*. Rather than focusing on the interface between the corporate organization and the consumer then, what is unpacked here are the ways in which managerial efforts have turned to the emotions generated within organizations and between colleagues. The incorporation of activities one might normally associate with life outside the workplace such as games, quizzes, dressing up, raffles, etc., are thus explored directly in relation to attempts to establish work as a 'fun' and 'friendly' place to be, distinct from the rational traditions of organization, in order to bolster employees' identification both with each other and, ultimately, with corporate agendas of enhanced productivity and quality of service. The study of emotionality, and more importantly the ways in which emotional attachment is engendered through the promotion of fun and friendless within the workplace is, as with all the topics considered in this collection, presented as a vital element in our renewed attempts to understand contemporary corporate life.

1

TECHNOLOGY

J. Martin Corbett

Introduction

Perhaps it is because of its ubiquity and taken-for-grantedness in everyday life that Organization Studies (OS hereafter) has never really quite got to grips with the world of machines and technology. Whatever the reasons for this hesitancy, the historical trend in OS reveals a tendency to insist on a distinct epistemological separation of the social/cultural from the technological, and the pursuit of an understanding of how these two realms interact at the organizational and societal level. For well over 100 years, the same mantra has been chanted: culture is concerned with people, agency and desire whilst technology is to do with all things non-human and mechanical. Thus, in the early twentieth century, the Futurists and capitalists enthusiastically embraced technology, believing it would change the social world for the betterment of all. On the other hand, the Romantics feared that new industrial technologies were alienating people and forever changing human values. As the twentieth century 'progressed,' this debate between the technophiles and the technophobes was re-problematized within a debate cast in terms of technological determinism versus strategic choice. As far as OS was concerned, technology did not really exist as a subject of serious empirical enquiry until about the 1960s and within 25 years technology disappeared once again as it became wrapped up within newly formulated approaches based on social constructivism. Today, technology has all but disappeared from the OS curriculum (although it has been readily embraced by technophiles allied to other Business and Management School disciplines). Technology, it would seem, is nothing, and does nothing, unless human agents make it so. Nevertheless, the efforts of a small band of social constructivists notwithstanding, the epistemological dualism remains intact.

The first part of this chapter will review these debates in which technology is seen as a prosthetic *extension* of social capabilities and agency. For example, a microscope extends the capability of the eye to see objects too small for the unaided human eye to register. Whilst this is a useful way of conceptualizing technology, and enables researchers to examine the important political aspects of technology, it overlooks the way in which technology can act as an aesthetic *intension* within the human (for elaboration, see Danius, 2002). In other words, as technologies change the way we make sense of, and perceive, the world, the world also changes. Returning to the example of the microscope; once microscopic things became visible to scientists, the very way these things are represented and theorized by scientists also tends to change. 'It is said that modern technology is something incomparably different from all earlier technologies because it is based on modern physics as an exact science', suggests the philosopher Martin Heidegger. 'Meanwhile, we have come to understand more clearly that the reverse holds true as well: modern physics, as experimental, is dependent upon technical apparatus and upon progress in the building of apparatus' (1977: 295–6).

Like Heidegger, McLuhan (1962) argues that we interiorize technologized ways of perceiving ourselves and the world. It is for this reason that the epistemological dualism of technology–human is unsustainable. This perspective heralds a new mantra: we are all cyborgs (and have been for at least a millennium). Whilst mainstream OS research has tended to align itself with a technology-as-prosthetic epistemology and the analysis of the production of technological effects on people, the second part of this essay examines how research based on an epistemology of technology-as-aesthetic reveals how the technological and the social are mutually implicated and inextricably interlinked in organizational and everyday life. Rather than viewing technology as an object which only becomes knowable once it is placed in front of an ontologically distinct subject, we should regard it as a *nobject* (Macho, 2000) – something that is not in front of us but completely surrounds us in everyday life. The chapter ends with a consideration of the implications of such a reconceptualization for OS research.

'Prosthetic' Theories of Technology and Organization

One of the first problems to be faced in exploring the role of technology in everyday corporate life is deciding what we mean by 'technology'. After all, most aspects of the organizing process involve extending the abilities, competences and actions of individual actors. In this sense, a business organization is a technology for producing objects and services that 'society' demands. Job design, organizational structure, payment systems, rules and regulations, and decision-making procedures are essential technological elements of this process. The sociologist Alan Fox (1974) argues that this broad definition of technology encompasses what he calls 'social technology' – the organizational methods and structures which order and shape the behaviour of people. The problem with such a broad definition of technology for OS researchers is that it becomes to difficult to think of any organizational process that is *not* a social technology.

Fox suggests an alternative conceptualization of technology as a 'material technology', by which he means the physical tools, equipment and machines used within an organization to achieve its objectives. The main bulk of empirical OS research on technology has employed this more restricted definition as it enables the relationship between material technology and other aspects of organizational behaviour to be analysed in a more systematic way. In such research, material technology becomes the key independent variable – the factor that is controlled or changed by the researcher to discover the effect it has on another factor or variable (such as job design, skill or communciation).

An additional problem associated with the study of technology and organization relates to the different levels of analysis employed by researchers. At the macro level of analysis, one can conceptualize technology as the process undertaken by an entire organization. For example, a university is a social and material technology which produces knowledge and provides education. However, at an organisational level of analysis it is possible to see that different technologies are used by different departments and functions within the same university. A micro-level analysis of technology would involve the study of a particular technology in a specific university department or work setting. In practice, of course, research is conducted at all three of these analytical levels. However, as Hatch (1997) contends, researchers inspired by a prosthetic approach to technology and organization 'typically simplify the organisation-level conception by downplaying the diversity of technologies within a given organisation and emphasising the core technology for producing the organisation's primary output' (1997: 129).

An exploration of the philosophical, theoretical and empirical studies of the social impact of technology at all levels of analysis is well beyond the reach of one short essay (see McLoughlin, 1999, for an overview). For this reason, we will restrict our embrace to studies explicitly concerned with the impact of core technology – technologies used in the production of goods and services within an organization – on everyday life in organizations. We begin by considering the provenance of prosthetic theories of core technology and organization as this has an important bearing on the ideational development of such theories within OS.

A surprisingly large number of scientific disciplines, whether ostensibly 'natural' or 'social', seem to develop by a working through of oppositional theoretical formulations – nature versus nurture, wave versus particle, mind versus matter, universalism versus relativism – and the study of technology within OS is no exception. The development of the vast majority of prosthetic theories of technology can be traced through debates centred around two dualisms which have

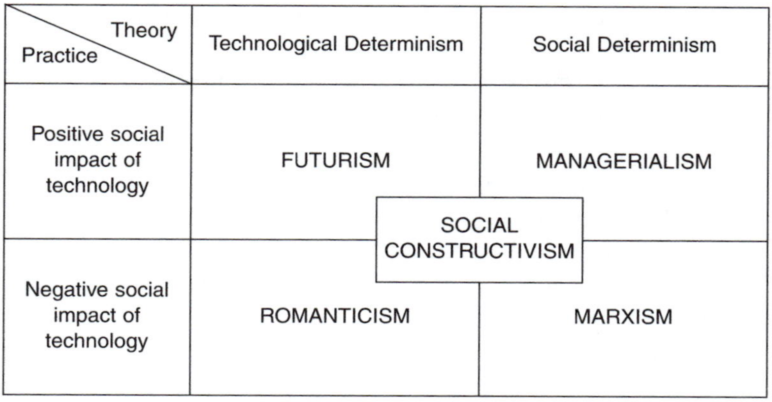

Theory / Practice	Technological Determinism	Social Determinism
Positive social impact of technology	FUTURISM	MANAGERIALISM
Negative social impact of technology	ROMANTICISM	MARXISM

SOCIAL CONSTRUCTIVISM

Figure 1.1   Prosthetic theories of technology and organization

been occupying philosophers and social theorists for over 2,000 years. First, there is the dualism of determinism and voluntarism (free will): is the impact of technology on organization determined by characteristics of the technological apparatus itself or by choices made by the adopting social organization? Second, we have the dualism of good and evil: is technology a 'good thing' or a 'bad thing' for members of the adopting social organization? Although theorizing about these dualisms has become more sophisticated within the social sciences, prosthetic theories tend to locate themselves close to one of the two poles that make up such dualisms. As we shall see a little later, one notable exception is actor network theory which tries to attend to both poles of both dualism simultaneously without inhabiting either. Nevertheless, in the time-honoured tradition of scientific 'typologizing', it is possible to locate a number of theoretical traditions around the intersections of the two dualisms (see Figure 1.1). Although such typologies are inevitably an over-simplification, they at least enable us to tease out the assumptions, themes and findings within OS theorizing about technology. The reader will find a more extensive guide to the research findings which underpin this typology in Table 1.1.

Futurism

The label 'Futurism' is most commonly associated with the early twentieth-century European art movement which saw a huge potential in the new technologies of cinematography, radio, phonography, telegraphy, transport and manufacturing machinery for the improvement of society in general and artistic expression and culture in particular. For the Futurists, the characteristics of the technological apparatus itself heralded fundamental changes to everyday life. Crucially, they saw these changes as bringing almost uniformly positive benefits for all – freedom from the drudgery of work and labour, better communication, material wealth, freedom of expression, and a better understanding, and mastery, of the world. Within OS, there are numerous researchers who share Futurist leanings (although they rarely, if ever, make this connection explicit).

Writers such as Davidow and Malone (1992), Woodward (1980) and Forester (1985) argue that organizations must change the way they function on a day-to-day basis in order to reap the benefits of technology. We are told that new technologies enable organizations to achieve higher quality, higher productivity, faster communication, flexibility, happier customers and lower costs. In the 1970s the normative prescription to 'automate or liquidate' pervaded the Western manufacturing world, and 30 years later we were told that computer-based Enterprise Resource Planning (ERP) systems will enable a complete 're-engineering' of organizations through adherence to the 'best practice' encapsulated within them. Futurist OS does not deny that we have some choice in how we use technology, but they make it clear that the only truly rational choice is to embrace it and take full advantage of its benefits. Here is a typical example.

> The tangible benefits that accrue due to ERP include: reduction of lead time by 60 per cent, 99 per cent on-time shipments, increased business, increase of inventory turns to over 30 per cent, cycle time cut to 80 per cent and work in progress reduced to 70 per cent. The intangible benefits include: better customer satisfaction, improved vendor performance, increased flexibility, reduced quality costs, improved resource utility, improved information accuracy and improved decision making capability. (Siriginidi, 2000: 381)

Here, Fox's distinction between material and social technologies collapses as it is assumed that the business corporation itself is, or should be, perceived as a technology. More efficient or flexible machines mean a more efficient or flexible organization. As we will see shortly, Futurist OS offers little empirical evidence to support such optimism, and its position is seen by many as both untestable and untenable. Nevertheless, as Grant et al. (2006) point out, the discourse of technological determinism continues unabashed in the prescriptive writings of management consultants and technology providers. Perhaps it is the development of the internet that has added the freshest impetus to the Futurist project, with many writers arguing that all traditional forms of organization are rapidly becoming obsolete to make way for the 'virtual' organisation (e.g. Davidow and Malone, 1992; Grenier and Mates, 1995).

The Futurist perspective represents what Jaques (2002) terms a *cypto-utopia* in that it contains utopian ideals which are concealed within the language its supporters use. While crypto-utopianism purports to communicate the truth about the future, Milojevic (2003) argues that such realistic futures also subtley promote implicit assumptions about the nature of future society – for example, that it should exploit all the benefits of high technology – and impose these views on other perspectives.

Romanticism

The term Romanticism usually refers to a secular and intellectual movement in the history of ideas that originated in Western Europe during the late eighteenth century. It stressed the importance of nature and human emotion, and the individual imagination as a critical authority. Inevitably, as technology was culturally coded as 'artificial' and 'unnatural', Romantics were strongly technophobic, and, within OS, a discernible anti-technology Romanticism is evident among some researchers. Whilst sharing the technological determinism of the Futurists, the Romanticists have a far more pessimistic outlook.

The Romanticist critique of technology stems from a perception that modern technology undermines certain core 'natural' human values and abilities – particularly the ability to act autonomously in the making of life choices. Technology, Jaques Ellul argues,

> itself, *ipso facto*, and without indulgence or possible discussion, selects the means to be employed. The human being is no longer in any sense the agent of choice. He [sic] is a device for recording effects and results obtained by various techniques. He does not make a choice of complex and, in some ways, human motives. He can decide only in favour of the technique that gives maximum efficiency. But this is not a choice. (1964: 84)

This negation of human choice is made possible, according to Marcuse, because political interests are 'not foisted upon technology "subsequently" and from the outside; they enter the very construction of the technological apparatus' (1968: 223). In other words, ideological choices are made by designers and these decisions overly constrain (determine) choices available to organizational members, and these choices inevitably 'dehumanize' everyday life (see Noble, 1984).

Managerialism

This approach, like the term itself, has a briefer history than the previous two theoretical positions. Managerialism is less a theory than a framework of values and beliefs about organizations which emphasize behaviour oriented to efficiency and economy, market responsiveness, and the control of employee behaviour towards these ends by senior and executive managers (Trowler, 2001). As far as the technology–organization relation is concerned, managerialism stresses the key role played by management's strategic choices of how best to employ core technologies to achieve the desired economic ends (Child, 1997). From this perspective, 'technology has no impact on people or performance in an organisation independent of the purposes of those who would use it and the responses of those who have to operate it' (Jones, 1982: 199).

In enthusiastic terms similar to those used by Futurists, managerialists talk of technology as 'enabling' organizational change and improvements (e.g. Bessant,

1991; Buchanan and Boddy, 1983; Mathews, 1989). To be sure, there may be employee resistance to any perceived abuses of managerial power such that technological 'choice' may be the outcome of localized bargaining and negotiation, but technology itself remains a pawn in such power games. The rules of the game are managerialist nonetheless.

Marxism

Although some Romanticist OS theorists share a certain affinity with the early writings of Karl Marx (which some have argued betray a romantic view of pre-capitalist society), theorists who share a Marxist approach to technology and organization explicitly take their starting point from Marx's major work, *Capital*. In this later work, Marx argued that the economic conflict inherent in capitalism produces social relationships which are unstable. Capitalist organizations are built upon the economic contradiction between the use value of labour (what owners must pay to procure labour) and its exchange value (the revenue received for the goods or services produced by that labour). Marx reveals how capitalist society relies upon the former always being lower than the latter so that surplus value (profit) can be extracted. Class conflict is played out between the owners of capital who control the means of production and who desire to maximize profits, and the workers who rely on them for employment and who seek higher wages in exchange for their labour. But, because higher wages threaten to reduce surplus value, owners must use their power to minimize labour's use value.

Marxist OS theorists see a key role for core technology in this class conflict. From this perspective, exemplified by the work of Braverman (1974) and the labour process theorists he inspired (e.g. Knights and Willmott, 1988; Thompson, 1989), capitalists will employ core technologies in such a way as to control and deskill labour. This strategy enables capitalists to reduce both labour's bargaining power (as skilled knowledge can be displaced into intelligent machines) and its use value (lower skilled work reduces training costs and commands lower wages), and thus increase profits. In other words, technology is employed as an extension of capitalist's power to exploit and degrade workers. The deskilling hypothesis is not without its detractors (e.g. Beechey, 1982; Zimbalist, 1979) but continues to generate a wealth of empirical research highlighting the deeply political nature of technological change (see below).

Social Constructivism

A constructivist approach insists that we no longer talk about technological apparatus as if it were distinct from the social realm. Rather than making an *a priori* distinction between the technical and the social, Bijker suggests the use of the term 'socio-technical ensemble' to stress how 'the technical is socially constructed and the social is technically constructed' (1995: 273). Technology is 'society made durable' (Latour, 1991) although any distinction made between the technical and the social is contingent upon economic, social, historical, cultural and political circumstances. For this reason, social constructivists are relativists who do not regard 'socio-technical ensembles' as necessarily either good or bad. Their interests lie in how networks of people, materials and practices become stabilized over time, and numerous studies of technology have explored these processes. However, a majority of these studies examine the social dynamics involved in the design of technologies (e.g. Bijker, 1995; Callon, 1986), with far fewer studies exploring the everyday use of technologies in production (e.g. Bloomfield et al., 1992; Saetnan, 1991).

The constructivist position attempts to overcome the dualisms underpinning the other four sets of theories, and to offer a corrective to their one-sided technology-as-prosthetic epistemologies. However, in some accounts (e.g. Grint and Woolgar, 1997) technology loses all materiality to become an exclusively social and semiotic phenomenon. In this way social constructivists, whilst claiming to be epistemological relativists, often follow a strong social determinist line in their insistence on the interpretative flexibility associated with any given technology. The notion that technology may have certain social impacts is replaced by the notion that social discourse determines what is commonly defined as technology. Because organisations are rarely semiotic democracies, this approach allows the political dimensions of technology to be examined through the ways meaning is managed and contested (see Brigham and Corbett, 1997).

Prosthetic Theory: Research Findings

So what and where is the evidence to help us make sense of the differing claims put forward by these OS theories? As with other scientific disciplines grounded in dualisms, the 'truth' seems to lie somewhere in-between the poles. Much of the research on the impact of technology and organization falls quite neatly into three areas of corporate life; namely, job design, organization structure and organization culture. Unfortunately, the results are frustratingly inconclusive (see Table 1.1).

Technology and Job Design

Research on technology and job design received a huge impetus from the publication of *Labour and Monopoly Capital* (Braverman, 1974), and a flurry of case studies were published subsequently in response to Braverman's deskilling hypothesis. Some researchers, whilst closely aligned with the Marxist

Table 1.1   Research findings on the relationship between technology and organization

Job Design	Organization Structure	Organization Culture
Enskilling (Currie and Procter, 2005)	Decentralization (Mathews, 1989)	Faster work rate (Collins, 2005)
Empowerment (Womack et al., 1990)	Flexibility (Piore and Sabel, 1984)	Workflow efficiency gains (Kidd, 1994; Siriginidi, 2000)
Deskilling (Braverman, 1974)	Increased centralisation (Bain et al., 2002; Ritzer, 1996)	Increased stress (Montreuil and Lippel, 2003)
Empowered machines, disempowered users (Cooley, 1987)	Increased bureaucracy (Frenkel et al., 1999; Grant et al., 2006)	Increased surveillance (Robins and Webster, 1986; Sewell and Wilkinson, 1992a)
	Patriarchy (Barker and Downing, 1985)	Impersonality/Isolation (Mann and Holdsworth, 2003)
Skill twisting (Zuboff, 1988)	Power shifts (Lash and Urry, 1987)	Amplification of existing tensions (Brigham and Corbett, 1997)
Technological effects shaped by local contingencies (Wilkinson, 1983; Wood, 1989)	Any structural changes shaped by local contingencies (Clark, 1995; Fry, 1982)	Any cultural impact shaped by local contingencies (Baruch, 2000; Jackson, 1999)

approach (e.g. Wilkinson, 1983; Wood, 1989) found evidence that employees were often able to resist management's deskilling strategies. Other researchers (e.g. Cockburn, 1983; Wajcman, 1991) found some support for the hypothesis but argued that gender (and ethnicity) as much as class relations of power were involved, and found a male gender bias in the social construction of skill. 'When a white man developed manual dexterity, it became a skilled trade; when a woman or black developed manual dexterity it was a natural characteristic and defined as unskilled' (Game and Pringle, 1983: 7–8).

Managerialist researchers regard the Marxist distinction between 'Capital' and 'Labour' as overly simplistic and the former's case studies tend to reveal how employees are often enskilled or upskilled once technologies were introduced by managers much keener to improve product and service quality, market share and product innovation, than they were to increase their control over the labour process (e.g. Mathews, 1989).

Although the vast majority of job design researchers ground their theoretical assumptions with reference to the dualism of determinism versus voluntarism, many conclude that, regardless of whether jobs were deskilled or enskilled, the role of technology was not a simple one-sided affair. That said, a remarkable number of job design studies implicitly or explicitly offer technological determinism as the theoretical position to be disproved, and the methodology of choice is the case study. Case study research in a variety of organizations typically shows similar technologies being used in different ways and associated with different operating job designs. In explaining these findings researchers have examined the mediating role of organization size, culture, politics, environment, management concerns, employee concerns and other non-technical variables. Very few have closely examined the particular technology under scrutiny, preferring to treat it as a constant or controlled independent variable. In 'black boxing' technologies in this way the technological determinist position is virtually impossible to prove. This is all the more surprising when you consider that even managerialist researchers confess that technological design choices may constrain subsequent job design options. For example, the psychologists Hackman and Oldham, founding fathers of the highly influential Job Characteristics Model of job redesign (1980), argue that 'if work is to be meaningfully redesigned in an organisation either (1) the technology must be of the type that provides at least moderate employee discretion or (2) the technology itself must be changed to be compatible with the characteristics of enriched work' (1980: 122). Similarly Child admits that 'a given technological configuration ... may exhibit short-term rigidities and perhaps indivisibilities, and will to that extent act as a constraint upon the adoption of new workplans' (1972: 6).

With the notable exception of studies such as Noble's examination of the development of computer numerically controlled (CNC) machine tool technology (1984), case studies of core technologies tend to exclude any examination of the social factors and choices which influence and shape the design of the technology being studied. This failure even to differentiate between different types and makes of CNC machines (and they vary from user-friendly shopfloor programmable machines through to paper tape controlled machines with retro-fitted CNC controllers which have no shopfloor part programming facility) suggests that researchers have simply assumed the neutrality of CNC as a generic, homogenous technology before embarking on their job design study.

Technology and Structure

Managerialists are quite adamant that organizational structures should be adapted by executive decision-makers to exploit the benefits of new technologies, and offer numerous case study examples in support of this position. However, in reviewing 140 of these studies, Fry (1982) notes that they employ confusing, often contradictory conceptualizations of the two variables. His review shows that six different definitions of technology have guided the empirical research, that three different organizational levels of analysis (organizational, group and individual) were examined, and a mixture of objective and subjective measures were deployed. This makes it difficult to reach any firm conclusions regarding their interrelationship. Where measurement has been applied (and quantitative methods certainly dominate the managerialist studies) it often fails to disaggregate technological and organizational variables. On the one hand, this is understandable given the widespread development and use of organization-wide systems technologies which blur the distinction between technology and organization. On the other hand, given these technological developments, Fry (1982) maintains that researchers must fine tune their empirical and analytical instruments if the dynamic relationship between technological and organizational variables is to be understood.

Romanticist and Marxist research, in contrast, favour more qualitative research methods, and the examination of broader structural issues such as patriarchy, democracy and power (see Table 1.1). However, such research tends to focus on the socio-political dynamic between management and labour, and to downplay the socio-political dynamic between different (often competing) managerial and professional levels and functions. As Scarbrough and Corbett (1992) have noted, such broad emphases may do little to convey the uncertainties and interactions of the relationship between technology and everyday corporate life, nor do they account for the role played by groups and individuals in resisting or reshaping the impact of technology on organization structure. 'Indeed, on occasions the transformational power of technological knowledge may escape the intentions of the powerful and undermine, and not simply reproduce, existing social and economic structures' (Scarbrough and Corbett, 1992: 23). This is one reason why so many early technology-led knowledge management initiatives failed. Recent research on knowledge management informed by a less managerialist 'community approach' (see Swan and Robertson, this volume) emphasizes the role of informal social networks and relationships in the shaping and diffusion of technology and technological knowledge. Whilst it may suit the egos of executive managers to believe that top-down technology-led initiatives will produce the desired changes in corporate structure, in reality the control of technology is not exerted quite as easily as that – technology is everywhere subject to political processes in which different groups seek to place particular elements of technology under their own control.

Technology and Corporate Culture

The concept of corporate culture came to prominence within OS following the publication of the managerialist bestseller, *In Search of Excellence* (Peters and Waterman, 1982), but it wasn't really until the 1990s that the role of technology in the shaping of culture was seriously studied within OS. Its impetus seems to have stemmed from the emergence of company-wide information and planning intranet systems, and the rapid proliferation of electronic mail systems which suddenly started to appear on the computer screens in the offices of academic research staff. Research on Enterprise Resource Planning (ERP) systems (e.g. Grant et al., 2006), and on computer-based distance working (e.g. Baruch, 2000) reveals a complex picture and suggests that such technologies are a 'double-edged sword' bringing both benefits and costs to organizations. However, as Dery et al. (2006) have observed, the literature on the impact of ERP on organizational behaviour is heaviliy dominated by managerialist discourse such that the definition of 'costs' is phrased almost exclusively in terms of efficiency and overall business performance rather than in socio-political or psychological terms.

Perhaps the most researched variable is the electronic surveillance of work which is often desired by management (Sewell and Wilkinson, 1992a) but not always successfully implemented (Timmons, 2003). Romanticists see particular problems with information and communication technologies designed for electronic surveillance of employee behaviour. For example, a survey of 900 large US companies by the American Management Association (reported in Huczynski and Buchanan, 2007: 81–2) revealed that over two-thirds of the sample admitted to employing electronic surveillance of their staff. Monitoring of email traffic, telephone conversations and internet use is relatively easy where machines are connected to a central server, and closed circuit television cameras are an increasingly common sight both inside and outside of business organizations. Romanticists such as Zuboff (1988) suggest that the use of an electronic panopticon – the all-seeing eye – is a very tempting one to over-worked managers, and especially to managers responsible for the performance of distance workers. Indeed, the case studies of call centres conducted by Bain et al. (2002) suggest that managerial utilization of targets to impose and measure employee performance via technology enables the continuation of the application of Taylorist methods into the twenty-first century.

The development of the internet has introduced more complexity into the new technology–organization culture relation as it enables corporations to influence the external perception of its culture more easily than the internal culture can be changed. As Ogbonna and Harris observe, 'given that the Internet may become the only source of contact between many customers and certain organisations, external (web-based) perception of organisational culture may become more important than actual physical contact and inter-action with an organisation' (2006: 172). Their case study of a financial corporation reveals how executives within the company viewed the introduction of internet operations as an opportunity to change the culture of the organi-zation so that the entire organization 'embraced the values and assumptions defined by the executives as critical to maintaining competitive advantage'

(2006: 168). Ogbonna and Harris note that, in practice, this managerialist social determinism was undermined owing to the existence of competing and diverse sub-cultures within the case company.

Nevertheless, social determinist approaches dominate research on the cultural impacts of technology. However, in exorcizing the 'ghost' of technological determinism many of the analyses of the research data fall back on a rather simplistic model of organizational behaviour – especially when it comes to the notion of management choice. Technological impact is conceived as a negotiated process carried out primarily between a dominant coalition of organizational decision–makers (i.e. management) and labour. However, as noted above, this research tends to overlook the possibility of competing corporate sub-cultures or that management does not represent a homogeneous group of decision-makers. Research by Armstrong (1984, 1985) and others indicate that accountants, personnel managers, computer experts, engineers and marketing/sales managers may themselves have conflicting interests and differential influences on the design and ultimate configuration of organizational control systems such as factory automation systems (see Scarbrough and Corbett, 1992). The concept of 'strategic choice' tends to overlook this dynamic. It also assumes that choice is a rational process – a questionable assumption, at best, in the light of research on the irrationality inherent in much organizational decision-making (e.g. Cohen et al., 1971; Todd and Gigerenzer, 2003).

In concluding this brief overview of the diverse research findings on the impact of core technologies on job design, structure and culture, we should consider why no clear picture of the relationship between technology and everyday corporate life has emerged in the OS literature. One obvious reason lies in the huge variety of technologies being studied. The computer numerically controlled (CNC) machine tool was the technology of choice in the 1970s and 1980s, whilst the networked computer information system became the focus by the beginning of the 1990s. However, as we have seen, the lack of clarity may stem from the epistemological assumptions of the researchers and the way in which the empirical data is collected, collated and analysed.

In an effort to move beyond this impasse, researchers such as Orlikowski (1992) have emphasized the need to place core technology in its context and to analyse the linkages between action and structures. Based on Giddens's structuration theory (1984) she recognizes the fundamental duality of any technology: technology shapes and is shaped by the organizational context in which it is adopted. In other words, technology should be seen as both a material entity and a social construct. This is not the same distinction as the one made by Alan Fox between material and social technology we discussed earlier in this chapter. Rather, we are talking here about technology having a real physical presence but one which is open to different interpretations by different actors. We have already seen such interpretative flexibility in the different interpretations of the impact of technology offered by Futurist, Marxist, Romantic, and managerialist commentators and researchers. A key point is that the way a technology is socially constructed plays an important part both in shaping technology's ultimate impact on organizational behaviour and in shaping actors' reactions to this impact. For this reason social constructivists are keen to question the distinction between technology and organization, and especially to question the need to consider technology as anything other than a social construct. In this way the content of the 'black box' of technology can be opened up to enable the context of its development and use to be placed under scrutiny (see McLoughlin, 1999). However, when aesthetic theories of technology and organization open the 'black box' they do so from the inside. It is to these theories that we now turn.

'Aesthetic' Theories of Technology and Organization

Aesthetic approaches to an understanding of the relationship between technology and everyday corporate life often utilize the cyborg as their basic epistemological category and they consequently reject any straightforward notion of technology (as object or other) having an impact on the social (as subject or self). Rather, technologies are conceived as *nobjects* (Macho, 2000) that are so implicated in social organization that you can no more set them apart than you can actually separate the mind and the body. As Gilles Deleuze (1992: 6) argues, 'types of machines are easily matched with each type of society – not that machines are determining, but because they express those social forms capable of generating and using them'. Whilst empirical case studies predominate in prosthetic theory research, researchers sharing an aesthetic approach often take a more longitudinal, historical perspective and criticize the former for its lack of reflexivity. Hollway (1991) and Townley (1992), for example, stress the active role played by work psychologists and human resources specialists in the construction of the organization as a technologically-based order in which the employee becomes a component in a collective enterprise that connects technical means with productive ends. As Hill (1988: 39) opines, 'the world and our experience of it is enframed by technology, and revealed only within the ongoing dynamic of order that this frame implies, and not within the aesthetic that is humanly constituted in everyday action and individual control'. In other words, the meaning of organizational behaviour derives from what technologies can do to it. We are everyday cyborgs, not occasional 'users' of technology. We are not like people from the Middle Ages who happen to watch television or travel in aeroplanes. Our entire outlook on the world has been shaped by technologies which have become so commonplace that we take them for granted. This is why philosophers such as Heidegger (1977) and Ihde (1990) argue that any understanding of technology requires an understanding of the everyday cultural practices and 'mindset' which technology reflects and reinforces. In a sense, we are all inside the 'black box'.

Take, for example, what is probably the most taken-for-granted technology of modern times – the mechanical clock. The word clock derives from *clocca*, the Latin term for a bell. In twelfth-century Europe, everyday life in Christian monasteries was regulated by the manual ringing of a bell to mark the beginning and end of different collective activities (prayer, reading, eating, sleeping, etc.). By the fourteenth century innovations in time-keeping design heralded the development and diffusion of mechanical clocks out of the monasteries and into towns and cities. These clocks were capable of displaying equal hours on a clock face and were to have two profound consequences for the European mentality (Corbett, 2003).

First, the mechanical clock symbolized a decisive step in the appropriation of time away from the heavens and from God (especially the liturgical practices of the Church) to humanity; from eternity to the here and now. Fourteenth-century money changers and lenders, tax officials and industrialists were the groups eager to appropriate this new time standard. In the churches of the Byzantine East and Greek Orthodoxy the installation of mechanical clocks was forbidden lest eternity became contaminated with time. The Roman Church in Western Europe, by contrast, embraced the new technology and turned its back on eternity and the mystical interpretation of numbers. Before long Roman church bells were ringing secular, mechanical time – a process started by King Charles V of France in his 1370 decree requiring all public clocks in Paris to be synchronized to his own palace clock. Thus, as Mumford (1934: 17) notes: 'The bells of the clock tower almost defined urban existence. Time-keeping passed into time-saving and time accounting, and time rationing. As this took place, Eternity ceased gradually to serve as the measure and focus of human actions'. Furthermore, as Boorstin (1983) argues, the newly-calibrated equal hour was a declaration of humanity's independence from the sun, new proof of our mastery over ourselves and nature.

The second consequence of the encroachment of public clock-time into everyday urban life was equally profound. Historians tell us that the medieval populus were innumerate as well as illiterate. How much reckoning could a person do in a world that knew no uniformity of measurement? Units of distance were linked to physical characteristics that varied as people do (the English *foot*, for instance), whilst weights typically were converted to volume standards (a *bushel* of grain) that inevitably varied from place to place. Landes (1983) argues that with growing trade in the twelfth and thirteenth centuries came the need to calculate and reckon. Roman numerals were displaced by the now familiar Arabic numerals during this period and these made calculations easier. It was the urban commercial populations that seem to have been the quickest to learn the new language and techniques of reckoning:

> Arithmetic was the province above all of the unlettered speakers of the vernacular (as opposed to Latin). Many of these learned arithmetic in the shop or on the road, but even before they entered trade, they learned to count the bells of the clock. Not by the old church bells ringing the canonical hours; these did not mark equal units and hence did not lend themselves to addition and subtraction. But the new bells and the calculations they made possible (how long until? how long since?) were a school for all who listened and began to organise their lives around them. (Landes, 1983: 78)

So, in the towns and cities of late Medieval Europe, it became possible to keep appointments fixed by points on the face of the mechanical public clock. The punctuality demanded of the monks was enforced by the ringing of the cloister bell, whilst, in secular life, punctuality was the quality of being *on the point* which was read from the mechanical clock face. As Ihde (1990) argues, such secular time discipline was to intensify with the refinement of the portable clock and the personal watch; with the growth of a civilization even more attentive to the passage of mechanical time and hence to productivity and performance. Today, of course, clock-time is so fundamental to the vast majority of organizing practices that it is difficult to conceive of organization without it (see Legge, this volume, for elaboration).

Along with many other everyday technologies, such as the mechanical printing press (McLuhun, 1962) and the flat-glass mirror (Mumford, 1934), the mechanical clock illustrates how technology has enframed our relationship to the world for at least 500 years, how machines and humans have a common cultural history. It is in this sense that we are cyborgs and our organizations are cyborganizations. Our identities are inextricably bound up with timetables, mirrors, electricity, clocks, calculators, books and photographs, and we have learned to trust these technologies more than our own bodies. Similarly, within business organizations there is often unquestioning reliance on the technology of the company balance sheet in understanding everyday corporate activities and 'performance'.

According to Seltzer (1998), it is not so much that the application of technology to human organization has led to a mechanization of the human; rather humans have come to rely increasingly on technology to understand themselves. This, in essence, is the thrust of technology-as-aesthetic theory. There are no essential characteristics attributable solely to the human, the social or the technological. All four of the conventional prosthetic theoretical positions share an essentialist epistemology in that they regard human nature as something shared by all humans (regardless of colour, creed, gender or culture) and quite distinct from technology. Deleuze and Guattari (1984) employ the term *mechanique* (mechanic) to describe this view of technology–organization relations.

Although the binary choice between technology as either good or bad offered by most prosthetic theorists is rather bleak, some aesthetic theorists have not entirely given up hope – Grint and Woolgar's (1997) argument for 'anti-essentialism' in technology studies, for example. If we take a properly symmetrical approach to such anti-essentialism, and question the common organizational content of both technology and of the human, then it might provide a way out of the impasse in conventional theorizing about technology and organization. Such an approach might draw upon the insights of actor-network theory (Callon, 1986; Hassard and Law, 1999; Law, 1992), proximal organization theory (Cooper, 1992; Cooper and Law, 1995) and post-humanist cyborgology (Haraway, 1991; Wood, 1998) to productively deconstruct the dualistic oppositions of human – machine, and organization – technology. Deleuze and Guattari (1984) employ the term *machinique* (machinic) to describe this notion of the cyborganization which

> is never stable at all: it incessantly creates and recreates itself. It also accepts that the relationship between self and non-self is quite vague: it works as Massumi (1992: 192) points out, by dint of contamination than by dint of isolation. Even more importantly it is not subordinated to a master pulling the strings but rather loses itself in a continuous play with its environment. The machinic machine is an open-ended process. (ten Bos and Kaulingfreks, 2002: 25)

Yet such a move towards *nobjectivism* may prove threatening to the discipline of OS. As Land and Corbett (2001) suggest, any attempt to take technology seriously is too readily interpreted as an attempt to privilege the technical mastery of the engineering disciplines over the humanities. But such a reading is the result of an inability to think outside the oppositional dualism of organization and technology. Rather than questioning the premises upon which this dualism is constructed, such thinking can only succeed in overturning it, leading to the privileging of one or the other of its terms. While there have been numerous analyses of the ideologies hidden within seemingly neutral technologies, too rarely has this analysis been turned back upon the humanistic social theories conducting these analyses.

Spicer (2002) observes that as soon as the question of technology passes our lips it attaches itself to the points of good and evil. This is as true for prosthetic theorists of technology as it is for everyone else. Yet, aesthetic theorists counter-argue that the relationship between technology and organization cannot be deduced and evaluated so easily. Ultimately, if we truly are cyborgs, then it is equally valid to ask ourselves if we are good or evil. 'Perhaps questioning our tools tells us more about ourselves, our society and our desire for moral quandaries than even post-humanists like Haraway suspect' (Spicer, 2002: 82).

2

SPEED

Christopher Grey[1]

Corporations cannot survive without constantly revolutionizing both the technologies they use and the way that people work, which of course in turn impacts upon the whole of society. In the past, business was very much about stability, doing the same old things in the same old ways. The modern world is distinguished by constant change and uncertainty. Fixed ways of doing things based on habit or prejudice are being swept away, and new ways of doing things change again even before they become routine. Things which used to be unchanging and taken for granted must be eradicated: there can be no 'sacred cows'. That is the reality of modern businesses and those who work in them have no choice but to become aware of it.

These could be the opening words of just about any volume you might pick at random from the business section of a bookshop. But in fact they are a paraphrase of something written a long time ago – in 1848 – and by people with very different intentions to that of the typical business writer. The authors were Karl Marx and Friederich Engels, and the original text comes from *The Communist Manifesto*:

The bourgeoisie cannot exist without constantly revolutionizing the instruments of production and thereby the relations of production, and with them the whole relations of society. Conservation of the old modes of production in unaltered form was, on the contrary, the first condition of existence for all earlier industrial classes. Constant revolutionizing of production, uninterrupted disturbance of all social conditions, everlasting uncertainty and agitation distinguish the bourgeois epoch from all earlier ones. All fixed fast-frozen relations, with their train of ancient and venerable prejudices and opinions, are swept away, all new-formed ones become antiquated before they can ossify. All that is solid melts into air, all that is holy is profaned, and man is at last compelled to face with sober senses his real conditions of life and his relations with his kind. (Marx and Engels in Freedman, 1962: 14)

The theme of this chapter is speed, and this remarkably prescient writing, which continues with an account of globalization which also has much contemporary resonance, serves to remind us that in one sense there is nothing new about the idea that speed is a defining feature of society. But it reminds us of something else as well. Marx and Engels were pointing to the enmeshment of speed and constant transformation with the imperatives of capitalist ways of organizing production and society. Whether or not their explanation is compelling, it was animated by a radical critique and a sociological theory: they were not engaged in some kind of conservative lament for a more stable world. This is important if we are to understand speed analytically, rather than through the lens of nostalgic sentimentality.

As a concept, speed is clearly intimately related to that of time, discussed elsewhere in this book by Karen Legge, for speed denotes a change or motion that happens over time. My focus is on that notion of change and more precisely with the idea of doing things quickly; and with the consequences of the demand for quickness on people's lives. We could say that somehow speed and quickness are inherent in 'business', a word which is, of course, an elision of 'busy-ness'. Being busy, being active, doing things quickly, speeding things up; these are the related notions that I will explore. And I want to do so 'critically' in the sense of suggesting that there is something deeply problematic about speed; that there are enormous prices to be paid for it by individuals, by organizations and by society; and that it connects with an important malaise within contemporary Western society.

Speed is not just related to time, however. The modern concern with doing things fast and then faster is embedded, precisely, within the modern condition and links to a wide array of technological, organizational and sociological issues: 'Power, speed, motion, standardization, mass production, quantification, regimentation, precision, uniformity, astronomical regularity, control, above all control – these became the passwords of modern society in the new Western style, (Mumford, 1967: 294). Whilst speed was but one of the terms invoked by Mumford in his account of modernity, more recent social theorists have understood it as being *central* to what is now sometimes called 'liquid modernity' (Bauman, 2000) or 'hypermodernity'. Foremost amongst these theorists is Paul Virilio (1997) who coined the term 'dromology' to denote the analysis of the compulsive logic of speed. For Virilio, the speed at which something happens has the capacity to change its character and in this sense the speeding up of contemporary life is not just 'modernity but faster', but rather denotes a qualitative change in social relations – hence the term 'hypermodernism'.

The use of this term is significant in being different to the more familiar term 'postmodernism'. There are various debates about this distinction in relation to Virilio's thought (Armitage, 2000) but for present purposes the key issue is the suggestion that it represents an extension of, rather than a break with, modernism. That is to say it remains consistent with Mumford's account and there is one particularly important link in terms of understanding organizations. The emblematic organization of modernity was, as Max Weber, showed, bureaucracy. According to Weber (1978), bureaucracies displaced other forms of organizations because of their technical efficiency, and this included the speed with which they could function. In an analogous way, Virilio claims that the faster always dominates the slower.

There is nothing new about seeing speed as a defining feature of society. However, in Virilio's work, and that of others to be discussed in this chapter, there is an emerging sense that the present time is characterized by an increased emphasis upon speed and perhaps a speeding up of speed itself. Such claims are difficult to evaluate, not least because they recur. For example, when railways emerged in nineteenth-century Britain there was a widespread fear that the speed of movement would be socially destabilizing and even physically damaging to travellers. Indeed it was the case that trains reconstructed nineteenth-century understandings of space and time (Schivelbusch, 1980) in ways which, as we will see, have some contemporary echo. Or, to take a completely different example, one of the most influential cultural and aesthetic movements in the first half of the twentieth century was Futurism. This movement celebrated speed, and linked it to the benefits of technological advance and progress (Humphreys, 1999).

It is difficult, then, to say whether at a general level speed is more important or more significant now than in the past. What has changed, however, is arguably the decoupling of both the fear and the celebration of speed as being linked to *progress*. Within the modern narrative, speed was getting 'us' somewhere. Within hypermodernism it might be said that speed has become an end in itself. This enables us to ask questions about whether speed is, in and of itself, indeed desirable. There is also a second distinctive feature of the contemporary celebration of speed, and this lies in the way that it forms a part of the process identified by Nigel Thrift (2005) in which twenty-first-century capitalism has become ever more preoccupied with, and sophisticated in, giving accounts of itself. In this sense capitalism has, for Thrift, become 'knowing capitalism' in that it is not simply the subject of analysis by social scientists and political commentators. Through, for example, management gurus and academics and the business press, contemporary capitalism provides an ongoing commentary upon *itself*. This social 'reflexivity' is distinctive if not in its nature then at least in its intensity and proliferation, and central to it is an account of capitalism that stresses speed, change, flexibility and agility.

It is against this general backdrop that I will seek in this chapter to explore, explain and critique the way that speed dominates corporate life in the early twenty-first century. I will do this by pursuing three main themes. First I will explore how speed is linked to the nature of the contemporary economy and, within that, organizational practices. I will suggest that what has variously been called fast capitalism, hypermodernity, supermodernity or disorganized capitalism feeds an ideology in which 'speed is good'. Using examples including Capita, the NHS, private equity firms, Enron and ICI,

I will indicate how this ideology works in practice and identify some of the difficulties it gives rise to. In the second section of the chapter, I develop the explanation of the problems of speed by reference not so much to organizations but to people and society. Drawing upon a range of recent 'popular' academic texts dealing with happiness, wealth and choice, as well as speed, I suggest that a great deal that is good in life is lost by an excessive preoccupation with speed. This then leads to the third main section in which I consider alternatives to this preoccupation, focusing in particular upon the emergent 'slow movement'. Despite its limitations, this movement does open up important questions about whether hypermodern speed is inevitable, which I attempt to address in the conclusion to the chapter.

Fast Capitalism and Corporate Life

From the standpoint of the early twenty-first century, it is easy to see that speed remains as central to social relations and, within that, to corporate life as it was in Marx and Engels' day. Gee et al. (1996) write persuasively of the 'fast capitalist story' in which constant transformation of organizations, and constant speeding up of work within those organizations, is mandatory to organizational survival. In calling it a 'story' they do not mean that it is untrue but rather that it is an ideology with real effects: that is, to the extent that the story is accepted and acted upon then the consequences for organizations and individuals who are not 'fast enough' will be *punitive*. Gee et al.'s analysis is consistent with a rash of related observations made by several influential commentators on the nature of contemporary society and capitalism. Notable amongst these are the sociologists Lash and Urry (1994) who identify a shift from the organized capitalism of stable bureaucracies, mass manufacturing markets and national corporations to what they call the 'disorganized capitalism' of constant change, organizational flexibility, globalization and an economy based upon symbols (e.g. brands) rather than material goods. In a somewhat related way, the cultural geographer David Harvey (1989) has suggested that a combination of cultural, technological and economic changes have fed a 'time–space compression' in which traditional conceptions of distance and speed have been dramatically telescoped.

Central to the fast capitalist story is the notion of a rupture between 'old' and 'new' capitalisms. This appears in a variety of guises within both social scientific accounts of capitalism, such as those just cited, and also amongst the kind of self-reflexive ways that capitalism now produces theories about itself, identified, as mentioned earlier, by Thrift (2005). Such accounts have proliferated since the 1980s, and a typical example from that period would be Piore and Sabel's (1984) characterization of the first and second industrial 'divides': the former based upon stable mass markets and bureaucratic work practices, the latter on rapidly changing mass markets and flexible working practices; the former slow, stable and *lumpen*, the latter fast, transformational and dynamic. There is a need for caution here, in that, as Jacques (1996) has pointed out, such distinctions have a very long lineage, and one can find similar claims being made in, for example, the early twentieth century. Moreover, it is contradicted by the way that, at least for Marx, capitalism was *always* a social form that precipitated and required radical change. Arguably what has happened is a further speeding up of this change but, even if not, the extent to which invocations of fast capitalism are widespread and ideologically potent and therefore real in their effects remains important.

From that point of view, there seem to be good reasons to think that the significance of speed in organizations has increased in the recent past. Under the impact of technological developments, deregulation of national and international markets and the erosion of trade union power there has been an increasing emphasis on the necessity for ever faster transformations in the workplace. Elsewhere I have described this as the 'fetish of change' (Grey, 2003) which appears as the unquestioned common sense of corporate life. From the waves of 'downsizing' and 'delayering' in the 1980s through the 're-engineering revolution' of the 1990s there has been an almost unchallenged insistence that rapidity is mandatory for organizational survival. At the same time, the adoption of 'lean production techniques' introduced the practice of 'just-in-time management' with its accent upon immediacy. Sennett (2006: 37–41), in his discussion of 'the new capitalism', locates these and similar developments in the unleashing of huge amounts of investment capital following the collapse of the Bretton Woods agreement (the system which had regulated international trade and currency movements since the end of World War Two) in the 1970s. This in turn led to an era of massive restructuring through mergers and acquisitions; investors became much more powerful than corporate managers, and became increasingly demanding of short-term share price growth rather than long-run organizational performance. Stability, indeed, came to be seen as a sign of weakness and companies had 'to look beautiful in the eyes of the passing voyeur [by] demonstrating signs of internal change and flexibility' (Sennett, 2006: 40). One might say that the display of this beauty became one of the 'symbols' of the economy of the disorganized capitalism identified by Lash and Urry (1994), and flexibility the defining feature of businesses within 'liquid modernity' (Bauman, 2000).

In the last few years one of the fastest growing 'industries' in the UK and elsewhere has been dealing in private equity. Private equity firms specialize in buying up companies and subjecting them to drastic reorganizations, usually involving large-scale redundancies and work intensification, designed to generate very rapid returns before selling the companies off to new owners. To critics, this amounts to asset stripping – simply squeezing money out of a business with no thought to long-term considerations, to customers or to employees. Whether or not this is the case, what is more to the point is that private equity firm activity represents no more than the latest, if perhaps most intensive, phase in the ratcheting up of the speed of organizational change and working lives. This ratcheting up of organizational speed is explored in an innovative way by Hancock (2006) who studied a range of organizational documents, and in particular visual images. These range from the explicit lionization of speed as a central aspect of business, for example the delivery firm Fedex which boasts that 'everything happens at breakneck speed' (Hancock, 2006: 632), to the more subtle invocation of 'vitality', for example in the case of global professional services firm PriceWaterhouseCoopers (PWC). These kinds of images embody what Hancock, with a nod towards the words of Marx and Engels quoted at the start of this chapter, calls the 'glorification of the world of melting solids' (2006: 631).

This glorification is an important aspect of the ideological impact of the fast capitalist story. Widespread acceptance of the inevitability of that story is a very powerful way of securing employee compliance with constant changes to, and intensification of, their work practices. There is nothing new in attempts to speed up work rates, and indeed these have been central to industrial disputes for centuries. The classic examples of struggles over attempts literally to speed up the moving assembly line of Fordist production are well documented in the labour process literature and elsewhere (e.g. Delbridge, 1998; Edwards, 1979). What is distinctive about the fast capital-ist story, though, is precisely its ideological power. Instead of overt struggle over very visible speeding up, the idea of speed as necessary, obvious, incon-testable and perhaps even desirable becomes inserted into the very fabric of people's everyday lives and self-understandings. Indeed it is noteworthy that some of the examples discussed by Hancock (2006) are clearly designed to appeal to, for example, graduate recruits. In this sense it is not just that the fast capitalist story may be regarded as inevitable, but that it is actually seen as desirable. Speed can be seductive, so that rather than a manager standing aside from us, speeding up the assembly line, we ourselves have internalized speed as a taken-for-granted, even desirable, imperative (Hochschild, 1997).

In this way, as has been suggested throughout this book, there is no very clear line to be drawn between people's work and non-work lives. We live in a world of speed dating; of TV programmes with ever faster camera cuts, or where some task such as cooking a meal must be done against the clock; where the quicker our internet connections and processor speeds are the better we think it; where food is fast food, and so on. The anthropologist Philip Augé (1995) argues that we now live in 'supermodernity' – a very similar notion to Virilio's 'hypermodernity' – in which cultural life has speeded up to the extent that the very frame of history has changed, with the very recent past becoming immediately a subject for historical reflection and the present being immediately evaluated for its historicity. For example, in the UK at the time of writing, Tony Blair was stepping down as Prime Minister, but before he had even done so there were lengthy TV 'retrospectives' of his time in office and assessments of his historical standing and legacy. This may be taken as a particular instance of the telescoping of time entailed in Harvey's notion of time–space compression. It is also consistent with Richard Sennett's (2006: 127) observation that contemporary organizations are almost completely uninterested in the past, but instead value only present, and more importantly future, achievements.

These developments have a profound impact upon organizational practices and, therefore, upon work in ways that would have surprised our parents and grandparents. It is noteworthy that for much of the twentieth century the expectation was that the fruits of greater prosperity and mechanization would be a more leisured and reflective existence (Russell, 1935/2001). This continued to be a cardinal assumption in, at least, Western societies, right up to the 1970s. What in fact has happened is that we have a much more frenetic and pressurised world. In the 1980s an expression which defined the period was that 'greed is good'. Perhaps the expression that defines our own time is that 'speed is good'. A clear illustration of this can be found in the following example: 'The millionaire businessman Rod Aldridge … boasts that his company Capita takes seven hours to make a decision reached in seven weeks by the civil service' (*The Guardian*, 15 February 2003, chrisafis: 13). If we examine this quotation, it contains several implicit and explicit themes, all of which are typical of the fast capitalist story. The most obvious is the suggestion that the private sector is superior to the public sector by virtue of the agility of its decision-making. Nested within that is an implication of the deficiencies of bureaucratic ways of organizing. How are these deficiencies made manifest? In terms of speed: quickness denotes flexibility and agility. Why is this important? Because change is rapid and organizations which cannot keep up are doomed. Finally, this business*man's* boast sound like an exercise in untrammelled masculinity, conjuring a world in which hard, no-nonsense decisiveness is vastly to be preferred to soft, vacillating, consultative consideration. This is all of a piece with the macho images which dominate much of the theory and practice of leadership (Sinclair, 2007)

But is speed really good? Although Capita is a hugely successful company with a turnover in 2006 of around £1,700 million (albeit no longer headed by Rod Aldridge, who resigned in 2006 over allegations that government contracts were linked to his donations to the Labour Party), it has presided over a string of abject failures. Capita is one of the companies of choice for the British government for the privatization and/or sub-contracting of what had hitherto been state provided services. The long list includes Individual Learning Accounts (which collapsed amidst fraud allegations); criminal records (which failed to vet teachers in time to allow the school year to commence on time); housing benefits (system collapsed) and television licences (system collapsed). Capita has taken over the running of a huge series of public functions, from driving tests and defence contracts to the leasing of ambulances, and in many cases the service has either failed or been mired in scandal and controversy. For this reason the satirical magazine *Private Eye* refers to the firm as 'Crapita'.

The case of Individual Learning Accounts, to take just one example, is revealing. Launched in 2000, the scheme cost £268 million until its collapse in 2002 due to widespread fraud on the part of bogus training providers. The National Audit Office (NAO) investigated what had happened and its head, Sir John Bourn, said: 'the *speed* with which the Department [for Education and Skills] implemented the scheme resulted in corners being cut … which made fraudulent activities possible (NAO Press Notice 60/02, emphasis added). This case also points up the fact that, whatever Rod Aldridge may think, the emphasis on speed is by no means confined to the private sector. On the contrary, the doctrine of continuous reorganization has become a hallmark of public sector management (Clarke and Newman, 1997). The National Health Service is the largest employer in Europe. In 2005 it had an annual budget of over £90 billion. Founded in 1948, by 2005 it had been the subject of a major reorganization on average once every six years, with three such reorganizations, and another seven less major but still substantial reforms, in the 10 years since the election of the Labour government in 1997. The first major change abolished 'fundholding' general practices (the frontline doctors who refer patients to specialists) which had budgetary control and could purchase services for their patients on an internal market. The third major change, amongst other things, re-introduced a virtually identical system called 'practice-based commissioning'. Reviewing this third change, which occurred in July 2005, the Health Select Committee, which is independent of government, concluded that 'the cycle of perpetual change is ill-judged and not conducive to the successful provision and improvement of health services'. Nevertheless, at the time of writing another major reorganization is underway.

At the beginning of this chapter I pointed to the irony of the way that today's business books echo *The Communist Manifesto*. A related irony is the way that modern management in both the private and public sectors apes the Trotskyist and Maoist doctrines of 'permanent revolution'. Yet there is a conundrum in this. The Marxist account of capitalism and speed suggests that there is a functionality about continuous change – that it is necessary. Attempts to boost productivity through speeding up the assembly line are obviously an example of this logic. Yet I have suggested that speedy decision-making at Capita is linked with poor performance, and that the NHS changes are not a recipe for better healthcare. So this would be to say that there is a dysfunctionality in speed.

This dysfunctionality is, indeed, one of the reasons why the private equity boom has attracted so much criticism. Whereas the speeding up of work and change is typically justified by the need for corporate survival, the criticism of private equity is that it simply sucks value out of a business leaving it unfit to last in the long-term. The purpose of speeding up is not to create business efficiency as traditionally understood, but to allow complex financial engineering strategies which generate potentially huge short-term rewards for investors, as well as substantial fees for advisers (see Folkman et al., 2006 for a detailed explanation).

Whether linked to the activities of private equity firms or not, there is no doubt that the contemporary workplace in the UK and elsewhere is characterized by an emphasis on speed. The UK has at various times been described as a manufacturing economy, a service economy, a post-industrial economy or a knowledge-intensive economy. Now, it has been suggested, it is an 'economy of permanent restructuring' (Froud et al., 2006). The implications of such an economy for organizations are profound. Drawing upon the work of Paul Virilio, mentioned earlier in this chapter, Roberts and Armitage (2006) explore the now infamous case of the US company Enron. They depict Enron as having developed, since its foundation in 1985, from being a 'modern' organization, specializing in gas distribution to a 'hypermodern' organization by the end of the twentieth century. As a hypermodern organization, its business became ever more diversified and moved away from being based upon tangible assets, such as gas pipelines, to being a complex web of financial engineering and brand management. In this way, Enron may be said to exemplify Lash and Urry's insights into disorganized capitalism, in which physicality gives way to an economy of symbolic manipulation. Enron was in a continuous and continual process of reorganization; work practices were constantly changing, staff turnover was massive. And this accent upon speed had its ironic counterpart in the rapidity of its demise for, as Roberts and Armitage point out, having become 'hypermodern' by the late 1990s, Enron collapsed in 2001.

This again may suggest the dysfunctionality of speed in corporate life but, if so, there is no sign of let up, as the continuing rise of private equity companies shows. The respected business journalist Simon Caulkin (2007) discusses developments at ICI, one of the world's leading pharmaceutical companies. He points out that its global dominace was built on investment in long-term – meaning spanning decades – research and development work. Yet now, under the impact of pressure to conform to the business model of hypermodernity, ICI has transformed itself into a company concerned with deal-making – mergers, de-mergers, acquisitions, divestments – and the whole panopoly of what Caulkin calls 'the approved nostrums of financial management … the institutionalised bad management of the kind that ticks all the boxes of the narrow playmakers by whose rules the UK's corporate economy now runs'. In other words, rather than being an organization that allows the gradual, long-term building of real products, Caulkin sees ICI as becoming a shell for the rapid, short-term generation of shareholder value and predicts that this mission will be the 'epitaph' of what was once a world-beating company.

The Problem of Speed

I have already implied that excessive speed can have consequences in terms of organizational functionality, but in this section I want to suggest that, in a more general way, a preoccupation with speed entails the loss of something important. That this might be so is captured in the Woody Allen joke: 'I took a speed reading course and read *War and Peace* in twenty minutes. It involves Russia'.

Over 30 years ago, the economist E.F. Schumacher published the seminal book *Small is Beautiful* (Schumacher, 1973). It was possibly the first book in the post-World War II era to enter the popular imagination that questioned the logic of economic growth. The timing of the book is significant. The assumption of that era had been that ever faster growth and ever-rising prosperity were central to societal well-being. This assumption had two aspects to it. On the one hand, economic growth was vital to avoid the poverty and degradation which had been caused by the 1930s depression, which in turn was seen to have sown the seeds for the political instability that led to dictatorship. On the other hand, and more positively, it was assumed that increased prosperity would not only stave off instability but would also create a more cultured, peaceful and leisured society in which human beings could realize their potential. These two assumptions can be called the *progressive myth*.

That it is a myth is Schumacher's central message. He suggested that the logic of economic growth led systematically to inequality, conflict and environmental degradation. In doing so, he arguably stood within a much older, and now much misunderstood tradition: that of Luddism. I say much misunderstood because the term 'Luddite' now stands for the unreasoned opposition to any kind of technological change. Yet both in its nineteenth century origins, and in its more recent articulation as 'neo-Luddism' (Glendinning, 1990; Noble, 1993; Sale, 1996), Luddism is not anti-technology *per se*, but rather is concerned with the effects of technological change upon individuals and civil society (Mumford, 1934). Rather than assume that these effects – which of course almost always involve a speeding up – are good, Luddites and neo-Luddites want to ask what one might think of as a highly realistic, rather than an idealistic, question: for whom is technological change good and for whom is it bad?

These kinds of questions are almost entirely ignored within the standard literature on business, management and organizations. At best, they are treated as part of the 'irrational resistance to change' that managers must overcome. That phrase has been described as 'an appallingly prejudice-ridden and authoritarian expression' (Boudon, 1986) because it already pre-supposes that resistance is ill-founded. It is quite remarkable that whilst the standard literature purports to be scientific and value-free, it actually consistently presents managerial change initiatives as having a (positive) value. We can and should do better. The fundamental purpose of organizations is, arguably, to enable people to achieve a better life collectively than they could achieve individually. So surely it is right to ask whether our organizational arrangements do in fact achieve this?

If the literature and ideas I have quoted in this section so far seem rather obscure, there has recently developed an accessible body of writing which is saying something very similar about present day life. Like Woody Allen, Schumacher and the neo-Luddites they are saying that there is something fundamentally flawed about contemporary life. Before discussing them it is perhaps worth emphasizing why these flaws are all linked to *speed*. The entire thrust of technological development in the computer age is one of speed: speed of processing power, speed of communication. Images can travel around the world in seconds; people can traverse the globe in hours. Companies have to innovate quickly to keep up with competition; and they need to be flexible and agile to do so. Consumers want more, but they also want it more quickly. The world is accelerating. But what do these truisms really mean for the people affected?

The distinguished economist Richard Layard has broken open the whole question of the relationship between economics and well-being. In his book *Happiness* (Layard, 2005) he shows that increased economic prosperity in the post-World War II era did not make people happier, and may have even made them less happy. In a somewhat related way, the psychologist Oliver James has identified the phenomenon of 'affluenza' (James, 2007) – the way that increased prosperity in the West has led to increasing levels of anxiety, selfishness, unsatisfying consumption and mental illness. A third, again related, text is that of the sociologist Barry Schwartz. In *The Paradox of Choice* (2004), Schwartz says that the huge array of choices we in the West have to face is overloading and leads to dissatisfaction and unhappiness. The very success of economic productivity means that every good and service we consume comes in a myriad of different forms and, moreover, that the range of areas in which we have to make choices, from, say, utility providers and credit card providers to holiday destinations and toothpaste, is ever widening. Thus we are increasingly busy just to keep up with the choices we must make.

Speedy economic growth should, if the progressive myth is right, have led to equally speedy increases in contentment. But Layard (and, in different ways, the others) says that, except for the very poorest people and countries, the opposite is true. Why? Primarily because increasing wealth dilutes social cohesion. In a world where we are all out for as much as we can get as quickly as we can get it, the bonds of community and shared norms get destroyed. An easy illustration is that naked self-interest is quite consistent with, and perhaps indeed encourages, 'anti-social behaviour': why should anyone consider other people's interests if the satisfaction of their own is paramount? This is a very important argument with political implications far beyond those identified by Layard. The growth of an unfettered market economy was the key effect of the neo-liberal governments of the 1980s, especially in the UK, the US and New Zealand, but also more widely. Taking the UK case, the Thatcher governments on the one hand promoted economic liberalism through privatization, but on the other hand promoted social traditionalism in terms of 'Victorian Values' of family and morality. The great irony was that these were incompatible: market values inevitably destroy social traditionalism. If self-interest is primary, then why shouldn't people sell drugs to children? If global markets are all, then why should people feel patriotic allegiance to the nation they happen to have been born in?

That free market economics destroys social solidarity was a fact very well known to the supposed high priest of economic liberalism, Adam Smith. In book V of *The Wealth of Nations* (1776/2000) he pointed out the dangers of markets: that they undermined what he called 'martial virtue', meaning the propensity of individuals to identify with and give service to society at large. Although their ideological perspectives were different, Smith like Marx understood that markets destroyed non-market values. What seems to have happened in recent years, however, is that this destructiveness has multiplied because of the 'speed is good' ideology. As Schwartz says, 'being socially connected takes time' (2004: 110), but the combined pressures of speeded-up work, consumption and choice do not allow time for such connections to be made.

The connections between marketization, individualization and speed are complex and far-reaching. For example, the economics of permanent restructuring is typically conceived of as a response to the ever more discerning and ever more demanding customer. This provokes rapidity in product innovation, redesign and re-branding. Yet this 'response' is itself the cause of the ever widening array of choices that the consumer must make, and the perpetual dissatisfaction which, James says, consumption engenders. Or, to take another connection, the de-regulation and privatization of services like, in the UK, electricity providers is designed to lead to competition which in turn leads to work-intensification as the providers try to get more work out of less people. But it also leads to a new set of choices as consumers are encouraged to switch between providers in search of the best deal (a search which proves elusive in part because one way that service providers protect profitability is to give better deals to new customers than to existing ones).

At the same time, the pursuit of consumption is very much an individualistic one: an image that captures it might be that of a parent sitting downstairs looking for the 'best buy' mortgage in a financial magazine, whilst a child sits upstairs at a computer downloading music.

That this image is becoming typical of the way that people in the West live seems consistent with the influential analysis of Putnam (2000). Looking at data on the United States, Putnam suggests that over the last 30 years North Americans have begun to spend less and less time with friends, and that families eat together or share leisure activities far less frequently. In ways which have clear parallels to the literature already discussed, he says that it is social bonds, rather than prosperity, that lead to well-being, and that the growing erosion of such bonds are a significant cause of ill-health and unhappiness. It seems clear that this declining 'social capital' (as Putnam calls it) is linked to the drive for economic competitiveness and the intensification of work. For whilst I have spoken repeatedly of these issues in terms of 'the West', it does seem to be the case that they are a feature of Anglo-Saxon countries, or those which have adopted the neo-liberal model of work and welfare. Countries such as France, Italy, Spain and, especially, the Scandinavian countries seem to have been less affected. I do not mean to imply that the speeding up of work and life is not an issue in these countries, but surveys of quality of life routinely show them as outperforming the neo-liberal states (e.g. JPC-SED, 2004) and a plausible explanation is that this is because the social bonds that lead to well-being are less eroded in these countries. This kind of material also suggests that what is at stake is not simply a matter of prosperity, for some of these countries, especially the Scandinavian ones, are both more prosperous and more productive than the UK or the US.

What this suggests, then, is that the malaise under discussion is not simply the inevitable consequence of capitalist markets, or of affluence, but is something to do with the way that life, and perhaps in particular work, is organized. It is certainly the case that work demands in the US and the UK are much higher than in the 'happier countries': in 2002 UK and US workers did an average of around 2,000 hours work per year, whereas in Germany, France, Italy, Denmark and the Netherlands the average was around 1,700 hours (Layard, 2005: 50). Being more busy seems to make people less happy and make societies less cohesive.

However, there is a distinction to be drawn between the issues of time and hard work and speed. After all, our grandparents typically worked many more than 2,000 hours a year, yet arguably experienced more robust social bonds and higher degrees of 'social capital'. So it is not, simply, that working hard leaves less time for the cultivation of social relations. It is more to do with the consequences of speed in 'an economy of permanent restructuring'. Richard Sennett's (1999) research is very revealing on this point. Based upon studies of several individuals and groups of workers (including some who he had studied 20 years previously), he argues that it is the radical disorganization of work associated with the 'new capitalism' which has disoriented and even destroyed what had previously been reasonably solid social relations. In particular, the erosion of stable career structures where the work ethic was rewarded and which existed within reasonably stable organizations embedded within communities has been a major factor in eroding trust and well-being. Instead, short-term contracts, geographical mobility and constant change characterize the workplace. As he puts it in a later work, 'a shortened framework of institutional time [i.e. speeding up] lies at the heart of this social degradation' (Sennett, 2006: 181). This is a much more political analysis than that supplied by Putnam, for example, and in a sense brings us back full circle to Marx and Engels: the societal consequences of an economic system in which all that is solid melts into air. Like Woody Allen's speed reader, we lose much that is both significant and valuable when the doctrine of 'speed is good' holds sway.

Alternatives to Speed

In introducing the notion of the 'fast capitalist story' I suggested that the word 'story' does not mean it is untrue, but that it is ideological. The power of ideology lies in it being accepted as inevitable truth; that 'there is no alternative'. The first step in breaking away from ideology is therefore to envisage alternatives.

The development of a (fairly) popular literature about the problems of fast capitalism, introduced above, indicates that this process may already be underway. However, the main way in which theses issues are talked about in organizations and in political debate is in terms of improving 'work–life' balance. The basic idea here is that people are working too many hours and need to find ways of reducing this, so as to rebalance the time they spend with families, on leisure activities, and so on. There are several limitations of such an approach as a way of tackling the problem of speed. First, 'work–life balance' actually addresses the problem of time, not of speed. It may suggest working less time, but not working less quickly. Indeed it may even be compatible with the idea of speeding up 'work' in order to gain more time for 'life'. Certainly to the extent it has been embraced by many businesses as an important issue, this has been because of the proposition that people will actually be *more* productive if they work fewer hours (e.g. Employers for Work–life Balance, 2007).

Second, the notion of work–life balance ignores the fact, alluded to earlier, that the problem of speed is not simply about work, but also about the pace at which consumption proceeds and the burden of choice associated with consumption. In this sense, a better balance of work and life does not necessarily imply a deceleration in the pace of activity. Again, one can draw the comparison with earlier generations who worked longer hours and yet for whom work–life balance was not considered an issue. This is probably partly a matter of changed social expectations – and perhaps especially in those relating to gender and childcare – but also because the speed of consumption and leisure was less intense.

Third, to a great extent work–life balance is presented as a matter of lifestyle – perhaps, in fact, another set of choices to be made – and does not address the political dimension of speed implied by its relationship to neoliberalism. In France, which has sought to avoid the neo-liberal model, the policy of a maximum compulsory working week of 35 hours was adopted in the late 1990s. Whilst not uncontroversial – and at the time of writing under debate – this does at least represent an attempt to deal with work–life balance at the societal rather than the individual level.

Some of the complexities which surround this issue can be seen in the study by Arlie Hochschild, one of the leading sociologists of work, of the firm she calls 'Amerco' (Hochschild, 1997). At the core of her analysis is that, in many cases, work is seen as a refuge from a chaotic and unsatisfactory home life. From this perspective, the re-balancing of work and life can hardly be a recipe for well-being. Moreover, she points to the way that the home sphere is increasingly invaded by work. Under the friendly sounding label of flexible working, and facilitated by new technologies, it has become increasingly common (and much more so in the years since Hochschild's study) for people to use email, virtual private networks and mobile phones to dip into work whilst at home or on holiday. Indeed, this is a major aspect of the more general phenomenon of speed with which this essay is concerned.

The issues of work–life balance and the 'time squeeze' are discussed in more detail by Legge (this volume), but now I want to look in some detail at a far more radical approach to the problem of speed: the 'Slow Movement'. As its name implies, the Slow Movement is explicitly concerned with challenging, negating and replacing what its adherents would call the cult of speed: in other words the problems I discussed earlier in this chapter. The origins of this as a 'movement' (although no doubt the ideas it draws upon are older) lie in the development of the notion of 'slow food' as an antidote to the growth of fast food (Kummer 2002; Petrini, 2001). Whereas fast food is about no more than 're-fuelling' in between activities, slow food is about taking time to savour and enjoy not just the experience of eating but that of preparing food and of sharing it with other people.

To the extent that fast food, in the form of McDonalds, has been treated as the *leitmotif* of contemporary society (Ritzer, 2004), this idea of slow food can be seen as offering a wider challenge to the cult of speed. It also suggests a challenge to that more general ensemble of modern concepts linked to speed identified by Lewis Mumford (1967) which I quoted in the introduction to this chapter. For fast food is not just 'fast' but also industrialized, standardized

41

and de-personalized. It is clear that what are claimed as the virtues of slow food address some of the problems of speed identified earlier. By slowing down, what is gained is the well-being and pleasure that are lost when life is lived at speed. More particularly, slow food offers the possibility of repairing the social bonds that are shattered by speed.

What began as a slow food movement has become a wider set of proposals for alternative ways of living which all share the desire to resist the continual attempt by others to make us do things faster, and our own internalized desire to do so. Although as a movement it is fragmented and still emergent, many of its tenets have been articulated by Carl Honoré (2004). Honoré writes, for example, of slow cities where striding is replaced by strolling; of slow medicine where a quick consultation and drug prescription is replaced by unhurried and holistic healing; of slow parenting where pushing children into a hectic range of high-achieving activities is replaced by more leisured play and emotional connection; and of course slow work. Perhaps most revealingly, he writes of 'slow leisure'. This is significant because it addresses the issue which the work–life balance concept ignores, namely the speeding up of leisure. There is a great deal of difference between a frenzy of 'leisure activity', and a more reflective and contemplative use of time: it is like the distinction between reading and 'speed reading'. Work–life balance is about carving up time differently, but is not necessarily about slowing down. Perhaps, indeed, the idea that we should have it all – work, family, leisure, etc. – actually contributes to the acceleration.

There are difficulties and limitations with this notion of slow living, which I will come back to. But one thing which should be clarified first is that it does not propose that there is no place for speed in life. For example, slow medicine does not offer a good response to a heart attack. Honoré is clear that different people (and at different times) and different activities will proceed at different speeds. The argument is just that the Western world increasingly has only one speed: the maximum possible. Nor is he saying that new technologies should be abandoned, but rather that they should be tamed and controlled. Like at least some of the neo-Luddites I referred to earlier, the issue is about how technology is used and whether it dominates how people live.

The slow movement clearly links with other philosophical and political ideas, notably those of Buddhism and environmentalism. There is a sense that fast living is disruptive to spiritual well-being, and that it links to the ever more rapacious consumption of the world's resources. It also links – most obviously in the case of slow food – to arguments for localism and seasonality. Part of the way that people traditionally related to food was in terms of what was available in the local area at a given time. Now, with supermarkets flying produce from around the world and throughout the year, that relationship is fragmented, with environmental as well as human consequences. Part of the idea of slowing down seems to be to re-connect with more traditional rhythms, rather than the artificiality of the 24/7/365 society.

This, however, is one of the difficulties. Embedded within the slow movement there appears to be assumptions about what is 'natural' and what is 'authentic'. Thus slow food, holistic medicine and slow living in general are somehow more real than the way we actually live. But the way people live is always conditioned by the social standards of their time. Is taking time to eat a meal with your family natural? No, it is a practice belonging to a particular time and place – primarily the mid-twentieth century middle class, at least as regards to the 'nuclear family'. It is impossible to pin down almost any human practice as natural, and even if it was, it would not follow that this practice was desirable. However, this argument cuts both ways, since the speed culture cannot be regarded as natural either: in which case the question becomes what are desirable ways of living?

Perhaps more problematic is the inescapable sense that the slow movement is an expression of a predominantly middle-class, affluent sensibility. If Layard's analysis is right, and prosperity does not bring happiness, then perhaps the slow movement is only an attempt to trade off some prosperity in order to gain some well-being. This is not surprising, in that when individuals become rich, they often opt to slow down, and the slow movement is asking the legitimate question of why it is that in rich societies, a speeding up rather than a slowing down is occurring. Nevertheless, it runs the danger of simply transferring the problem to poorer people. The desire to pick and mix between slow and fast life underscores this: leisurely family meals when you want, but burger and chips always available for when you do not. In that scenario, the working classes are left at the mercy of the speed culture, scurrying to work at the fast food restaurant on a zero hours contract as and when customers turn up to be served. It is also the case, as I have tried to suggest throughout this chapter, that the problem of speed is primarily one that faces highly economically developed, predominantly Western, societies. In other parts of the world, the problem of stasis and stifling traditionalism are much more pressing.

Conclusion

In discussing speed, I have necessarily ranged over a very wide set of issues in this chapter. I have tried to explain that central to capitalism, and especially to the capitalism of the late twentieth and early twenty-first centuries, is an ideology of speed. Organizations try to do things fast, and to do them faster and faster, whether we are talking about work rates or the rate of organizational transformation. This is not just something which applies to the workplace, though. It is a characteristic of Western society more generally: we in the West live life at an ever increasing pace.

Nevertheless, it should be stressed that work and organizations are absolutely central to this speeding up. It is work which, for most people, dominates their time, structures their lives and provides an important source of their identities. It is the radical speeding up of organizational change that most impacts upon careers, identities and communities. And it is this speeding up of production which feeds the speeding up of consumption, so that leisure becomes a frenetic round of activity. It is, indeed, the speeding up of production which transforms education into a kind of force-feeding to prepare students for the labour market. In this respect it is interesting to consider Carter and Jackson's (2005) manifesto for the 'Laziness School' as an alternative to the 'Busy-iness School'. They propose, in a light-hearted but not, I think, flippant article that business schools in particular should adopt a commitment to inaction rather than action. This is a literally revolutionary idea in that it is orthogonal to the dominant image of the fast manager who is central to contemporary accounts of what managers should be (Thrift, 2005: 130–52).

Although one would hardly think it to read most Organizational Behaviour textbooks, the way that we organize is inseparable from the very broadest questions of how we should live. Perhaps it is the case that ever more rapid change and ever more intense work are vital to competitiveness and to rising prosperity. But if that is so then we have to confront the problem identified by Layard, James, Schwartz and others that rising prosperity appears to make people unhappy and unwell. On the other hand, it may be the case that rapidity leads to poor decisions and failure, as the cases of Capita and the NHS suggest. Either way, it is impossible to say that speed is necessarily good. The slow movement suggests that speed is actually bad for us. How can it be desirable, still less healthy, to live in a world in which, as Carrie Fisher put it, 'instant gratification takes too long' (Honoré, 2004: 11)?

Yet what seems to be absent in at least Honoré's articulation of the slow movement is any serious understanding of the relationship between speed and capitalism. The drive to make people work and consume faster and faster cannot ultimately be separated from the capitalism to which, as Marx and Engels explained over 150 years ago, it is endemic. From this perspective, the contemporary nature of fast, new or disorganized capitalism is simply an extension of what has long been the case. The speeding up of work, and the constant reorganization and financial engineering which follows are simply what is needed to deliver the maximum possible shareholder value. If we are to look for alternatives to speed then we have to address this. I believe that we can do so in two ways. One would be the line of argument I proposed earlier: that speed is not necessarily functional to efficient capitalism in that it can lead to poor decision-making and corporate collapse. Roberts and Armitage's (2006) analysis of the Enron scandal, Caulkin's (2007) fears about ICI and Froud et al.'s (2006) studies of financial engineering and private equity, as well as many similar analyses, pose very sharp questions about the sustainability of 'fast capitalism'. Ultimately organizations need to deliver something beneficial in terms of real goods and services, to do so reliably and durably, and to meet the needs of people – both employees and customers – above and beyond shareholders.

This leads to the other, more far-reaching argument, which is to re-pose the question of what the purpose of human collective activity is and whether current social and economic arrangements deliver it. This would be to open up the fundamental question of social philosophy: what is the good life and how is it to be achieved? We need not answer this in binary terms of capitalism or communism, and indeed few would now do so. It is quite possible to envisage systems which retain private property and market exchange but which are based upon local economies and work practices which are supportive of, rather than damaging to, human potential and the environment. Despite the contemporary stress upon shareholder value and free markets as unquestionably desirable, the historical truth is that capitalism has always, to a greater or lesser extent, been subject to, and regulated towards the consideration of, wider concerns about social well-being. If an overwhelming preoccupation with speed at all costs is indeed as deleterious to that well-being as has been suggested by the many commentators on whom I have drawn in this chapter, then that, in combination with the dysfunctionality of speed for, at least some, organizations begins to make out the need for alternatives.

Such alternatives should not imply a retreat to traditionalism and an end to transformation. A world which offered no possibilities for change and which trapped people forever in pre-ordained roles would be stultifying and oppressive. Nor should it be forgotten that, for some, the 'global kinetic elite' (Roberts and Armitage, 2006: 567), speed is desirable, energizing and exciting. But a world which is constantly in flux is surely equally damaging, and for many engenders profound feelings of dislocation and uselessness (Sennett, 2006: 83–130). The contemporary business mantra is that everything must change, and nothing should be considered sacred. Might that not also apply to the hypermodern attachment to speed as an end in itself? If this is not so, then there are no alternatives to the speed culture of contemporary society, which would be surprising since society is, after all, what we, collectively, through our political and social actions, make it. The way in which corporate life is organized in the coming years will be central to determining the outcome of this collective process.

Note

1   This chapter is partly based on a previous version published in Chris Grey (2009) *A Very Short, Fairly Interesting and Reasonably Cheap Book About Studying Organizations.* London: Sage.

3

AESTHETICS AND AESTHETICIZATION

Philip Hancock

Introduction

As is the case with a number of the topics covered in this book, that of aesthetics and aestheticization might seem a curious one to be appearing in a discussion of corporate life. After all, isn't aesthetics something to do with art and somewhat ethereal questions about the nature of beauty? Okay, so companies of all varieties have long had an interest in collecting art, both as an investment and as a way of symbolizing corporate power or success, but surely isn't that as far as it goes? Well, maybe. It is the aim of this chapter, however, to encourage you to think about the aesthetic as a more 'everyday' aspect of both your working and non-working lives. In doing so, it is hoped that this will also lead you to question the nature and purpose of what I shall term here, *corporate aestheticization*; that is, the systematic conception and deployment of aesthetically rich systems of signification in the pursuit of corporate advantage. Now, such systems can take an array of forms which can range from the design of organizational buildings such as corporate headquarters, to the ways in which individual employees are expected to dress, walk and sound, and, in some instances, even smell. What unites them, however, is that in one way or another, they constitute ways of communicating the purported identities, values and aspirations of their corporate hosts to a range of stakeholders, be they customers, employees, shareholders or whoever.

In order to explore this proposition the chapter commences with albeit a brief introduction to the various ways of defining the aesthetic and how it has been used since its modern-day inception over 200 years ago. From there, it considers not only the impact that the aesthetic has had on how we might study corporate life, but equally, why it has only quite recently become an issue of some interest and what consequences this might have for the future trajectory of organization theory. Commencing with a discussion of the aesthetic as both a philosophical and socio-cultural discourse, the chapter then reviews some of the ways in which corporate management has increasingly come to engage with the organization of aesthetics. This theme is then developed in the following three sections which consider the ways in which corporations can be understood to be paying far closer attention, in relation to the expression of a desired image and identity, to the physical and aesthetic dimensions of their material resources and activities. Continuing this idea, the status of the human body is then considered in terms of its capacity to operate as an aesthetically rich corporate signifier, particularly in relation to the notion of what has come to be termed *aesthetic labour*. Finally, the chapter closes with a brief discussion of what might underpin some of these developments and how we might wish to think about them in the face of some of the more critical commentaries that have recently emerged.

The Aesthetic – Sensuality versus Reason

Beauty is truth, truth beauty, – that is all
Ye know on earth, and all ye need to know
(Keats, c.1884, lines 49–50, cited in Quiller-Couch, 1919)

As is so often the case with contemporary philosophical concepts, and indeed as the lines from Keats's poem, 'Ode on a Grecian Urn', (Quiller-Couch, 1919) suggest, it might be assumed that in order to establish the origins and meaning of the term 'aesthetic' we should consult the minds of European antiquity. Well, yes and no. Yes, in so much as what was said and written about such subjects as beauty, art and indeed truth during that period have an important bearing on the material we shall be considering; but no, in that the idea of the aesthetic we are predominantly dealing with here is in fact a relatively modern invention or, more specifically, an invention of the 1700s and that period known as the European Enlightenment.

As you may already be aware, the eighteenth century was a period of significant intellectual and political upheaval across Europe. The dominance of the Church and religious dogma, as well as the *ancien régime* of decaying feudal and aristocratic institutions were under increasing pressure as a new spirit of rational intellectualism sought to assert itself. Yet even as the predominance of rationality over superstition, and science over mythology seemed assured, there were certain aspects of human experience that continued to escape reason's totalizing claims. Prominent amongst these was the realm of sensual experience, or, as we shall know it, *the aesthetic*, described more recently by Eagleton (1990: 13) as:

'the business of affections and aversions, of how the world strikes the body on its sensory surfaces, of what takes root in the gaze and the guts and all that arises from our banal, biological insertion into the world'.

47

The aesthetic was, at first sight then, considered perhaps too messy and too irrational to be easily assimilated into the Enlightenment worldview. This was, however, until the work of Baumgarten, a German philosopher who, between 1750 and 1758, published his two volume work entitled *Aesthetica*, a word derived from the Ancient Greek term *aisthesis*, meaning 'sense perception' (Williams, 1983: 31).

Effectively inventing the field of modern aesthetics, what Baumgarten sought to do was construct a science of sensuality. It was an attempt, in effect, not simply to reconcile the intellectual and the sensual, but rather to bring the latter under the dominion of the former; in effect, to rationalize sensuality. Not that he was in fact the first to attempt such a thing. Hutcheson's (1725/1973) work, *An Inquiry Concerning Beauty, Order, Harmony, Design*, predated Baumgarten's own by around a quarter of a century and provided what is probably the first systematic account of the aesthetic as a particular mode of human cognition; a way of experiencing the world which was neither wholly sensual nor wholly intellectual.

Ultimately, however, both these works were overshadowed by what can perhaps be considered to be the most systematic philosophical statement on the nature of the aesthetic during this period, Kant's *Critique of Judgement*, which was published in 1790. While largely concerned with the experience of beauty and the appreciation of art, for Kant, underlying these preoccupations was the question of how we can justify claims to aesthetic 'knowledge'; that is, the fundamentally epistemic question of 'what is aesthetic judgement?'. Ultimately, Kant attempted to answer it through a fusing of the subjective nature of isolated sensual experience with the ability we have to share and evaluate such experiences and judgements in common. Central to the possibility of such intersubjective comparisons was the proposition that the faculty of taste is shared (though possibly differentially developed) in all rational human beings, and is expressed when they make what he termed a disinterested aesthetic judgement. In other words, then, while aesthetic judgement was in part sensual, in order to be communicable it also had to posses a shared rationality.

Aesthetic experience, while profoundly personal and particular, only became aesthetic judgement (and thus able to pass comment on the quality of that experience), therefore, when fused with the rationality, and relative universality, of taste. In true Enlightenment spirit then, reason was held to maintain the role of guardianship in such matters; providing the basis for a meaningful philosophical aesthetics that establishes a secure foundation for the rational consideration of questions of beauty and sensuous experience more generally.

Aesthetics, Art and Criticism

Now, as the aesthetic, or more properly aesthetic philosophy, developed during the twentieth century, the proposition that aesthetic experience consisted of a largely subordinated sensual and a dominating rational component generally held sway. This was particularly true as the perceived role of aesthetic philosophy became that of providing reasonable criteria by which 'art' might be evaluated and deemed to be of aesthetic value. A prime example of this tradition is to be found in the work of Bell (1915), for whom aesthetics pertained to the study of art – understood as the products of human creativity – in relation to its capacity to evoke what he termed an *aesthetic emotion*. For Bell, this meant that art only came into being if it demonstrated a capacity to generate this particular, though very weakly defined, emotional condition. Alternatively, institutional theory, which is represented in the work of say Danto (1964) and Dickie (1974), dismissed any attempt to reach a definition of what constitutes art as a quality of the object itself, but rather sought to define art in relation to its social or 'institutional' location or status. That is, rather than being defined by the possession of some largely metaphysical quality, art only becomes art when members of what Danto termed the *artworld* (see also Becker, 1982) – a particular milieu comprising of say artists, producers, patrons, critics, etc. – convey such a status upon it. Art, or more correctly the status of art, is thus, from this point of view at least, a social construction embedded within social relations of power and prestige.

Interestingly, while it might be inferred from this last comment that such an institutional theory of art is somehow critical of such power relations, this would not be a strictly accurate observation. Rather, such approaches have tended to be far more concerned with identifying such relations than subjecting them to some form of socio-political critique. Nonetheless, it is worth noting that there are a number of other traditions within contemporary philosophical aesthetics which are far more clearly allied not only with a more critical appraisal of art within society, but also with the political implications of aesthetic experience itself. Twentieth-century Marxist theorists from Plekhanov (1912/1947) through Lukács (1920/1978) to Brecht (1957), for instance, have all, in contrasting ways, sought to identify a radical aesthetic or style of art that could provide a catalyst for proletarian revolution. Equally, what is termed Critical Theory (see Adorno, 1970/1997; Marcuse, 1978) – a fusion of Marxism and Weberian concerns regarding the instrumental rationalization of contemporary culture – along with various strands of post-structuralist philosophy (see Carroll, 1987) have also engaged with art and aesthetic experience in an attempt to develop new critical resources for understanding contemporary societies. However, while we shall return to some of these issues in due course, it is now perhaps time that we considered some of the material that makes a rather more explicit link between corporate activity and the question of aesthetics.

The Corporatization of Art and Aesthetics – Management as Aesthetic Practice

While I have provided you with something of a taste of the historical development of the concept of the aesthetic, in order to make sense of the term here I intend to employ it in a fairly straightforward manner. Based on what in effect was Baumgarten's science of sensuality, I use the term aesthetic to refer to the realm of sensual experience. Additionally, I use the term aestheticization to describe the process by which our material environment is manipulated in order to enhance or stimulate such experience. Thus, while 'aesthetic' might refer to the experience of art it can just as easily refer to the ways in which we experience material commodities such as televisions or communicative practices such as advertisements. Similarly, aestheticization, in this context at least, describes the ways and processes by which such commodities are conceived, designed and constructed in order to maximize a desired aesthetic response from those who encounter them.

The aesthetic is, in this sense, therefore an integral part of our everyday lives. It is to be experienced in the high street, the supermarket, in the home and in the workplace. Yet, as these examples might suggest, it is also an increasingly corporatized dimension of our lives. From the designs of our mobile phones to the landscaping of our urban (and increasingly rural) environments, each and every day we engage with a material world that is sculpted and presented in line with the demands, expectations and promises of the corporation. What I hope to achieve over the rest of the course of this chapter, is to explore some of the ways we might be able to think about and understand this dimension of corporate life, and the ways in which aesthetic experience is itself an increasingly organized phenomenon.

First and foremost, the proposition that management is itself an aesthetic or artistic practice is one that has been around for a number of years, largely expressed in a predominantly metaphorical manner (eg. Dobson, 1999). More recently however, there appears to be evidence that such a relationship between management practice and artistic aspiration is becoming ever more closely entwined. In their research into the management of a UK call centre, for example, Alferoff and Knights (2003) observed how a deliberate attempt was made to manage employee practices and behaviour through the deployment of colourful signs, mobiles and other, largely ludic artefacts designed to promote competitive endeavour between colleagues. Similar practices have also been documented by Warren (2002), whose study of life in an IT company explored, in part, one departmental attempt to manage employees through the aestheticization of the spatial environment through decorative design, including the use of vibrant colour schemes, idiosyncratic decorations and works of art in an attempt to promote a sense and practice of 'creativity'.

Such empirical examples of a more aesthetic orientation to employee management strategies are reinforced by the fact that there is also a thriving academic and business sector emerging that is also attempting to bring such ideas and insights to the attention of the managerial classes more generally. Organizations and groups such as the self-styled 'Creative Alliance', part of the Learning Lab at the Danish University of Education, have, for instance, started to develop both research and publication projects aimed at informing business about what it can learn in terms of ethics, leadership skills and general self-organization from a study of 'the arts'. This is an approach perhaps best exemplified in de Monthoux's (2004) *The Art Firm: Aesthetic Management and Metaphysical Marketing*. Richly presented, this book celebrates the utility to be found by managers in studying art and how artists themselves create aesthetic value. Creativity, joy and anguish are all identified as the resources of tomorrow's business manager, derived as they are from the arts manager's experience of yesterday and today.

At the somewhat more mundane level of everyday management training and education, there has also been something of an explosion over the last 10 years or so of consultancies utilizing artistic or aesthetic techniques as technologies of corporate intervention in the service of executive training and motivation (Pollock, 2001). These range from actors freelancing as consultants offering self-presentation sessions for management executives (Crace, 2002), to what has been termed *corporate theatre* (see Clark and Mangham, 2004) whereby theatrical troupes enact plays designed to encourage employees to confront and explore organizational problems or to promote certain company products, changes, or programmes. In the field of Human Resource Development, Gibb (2004a, 2004b, 2006) has also contributed to such ways of thinking, arguing for the merits of not only learning from arts-based organizations, but equally promoting the introduction of arts-based training programmes, including elements such as those associated with theatrical techniques, as part of an overall human resource development strategy. Aesthetics then, particularly in relation to the practices and policies of the arts, have clearly started to make the shift from the domain of a limited number of creative industries to a valuable resource in the broader pursuit of corporate objectives.

Beautiful Corporations?

It is not simply art, and those management techniques that might be learned from how art is perceived and practised, that are increasingly having an impact on the corporate world, however. In their manifesto for the aestheticized organization, *Beautiful Corporations: Corporate Style in Action*, Dickinson and Svenson (2000: 3) argue that to be successful, companies will increasingly have to offer both their employees and clients 'style, beauty, a positive attitude and pleasing experiences'. While perhaps much of this claim can be put down to commercial hyperbole, there seems to be little reason to doubt that the more abstract qualities of style, beauty and experience have all become increasingly vital ingredients in the contemporary corporate mix. As Berg and Kreiner (1990: 41) observed some 17 years ago now, 'it is an indisputable fact that organizations increasingly care about their physical appearance'. Certainly today, vast sums of money are invested in the projection of corporate identity and image, including the commissioning of stylish corporate architecture, innovative internal office designs, landscape gardening, visual and aural logos, company uniforms and the like.

One significant reflection of this has been the relative explosion in design centres, corporate communications companies and internet-based creativity consultants which has taken place over the previous 20 years or so; each one exulting companies of all sizes and types to embrace the importance of aestheticization in the ongoing struggle for market supremacy. Take, for instance, the fact that the French automobile manufacturer Peugeot operates what they term a 'Perception and Human Factors Department'. It is here that scientists explore and refine the aesthetic qualities of their products; the ways in which their cars smell, sound and feel. All of which, according to Heptinstall (2004: 24), is achieved through:

'testing subjects' reactions to different seat fabrics, shapes of buttons or steering wheel materials. The gently-damped closing of an ashtray lid can imply an intrinsic aura of quality; the firm click of a glovebox can be as comforting as the mightiest engine roar'.

Indeed today, every activity from the management of internal organizational change strategies through the promotion of corporate responsibility programmes, to the launch of a new product or brand identity, increasingly appear to rely on the endeavours of the seemingly ubiquitous field of 'corporate communications'. In a world where it would appear that surface is the new depth, as *Cold Soba*, one of the myriad of new-wave aesthetic consultancies stress:

[m]arket-leading brands maintain a clear competitive stance and a dedication to aesthetics. Yes, aesthetics. Why? Because information-rich, time-poor clients value feeling more than information. Aesthetics can turn a generic service into a premium product. Any brand, backed with enough courage and imagination, can become a strong, charismatic brand. That means you! (http://www.coldsoba.com/on_paper/paper3.php)

Perhaps what we have here then is a reference to what Schultz et al. (2000) have referred to as the rise of the 'expressive organization' – companies for whom design and the material representation of identity through media as diverse as company logos, building design and even the ritualized behaviours of company employees has become increasingly central in the pursuit of corporate success. Of course, one might still ask just how is such an expressive organization created? What kinds of media are deployed to identify and maximize a company's aesthetic resources and how might we analyse them? It is to these questions that I now turn.

Landscapes of Corporate Aestheticization

Gagliardi (1990) in one of the earliest pieces of writing to focus specifically on the aesthetics of organizational life suggested that increasingly central to any corporate strategy of culture management or identity formation is the generation of an appropriately contrived organizational *pathos*; namely a way of perceiving and feeling the organizational values and practices. Such a desired pathos must therefore be achieved by management through a process of manipulation of particular organizational artefacts, ranging from furniture to lighting, spatial layout to colour schemes, a process he terms *landscaping*. It is through such landscaping that organizational actions, words, deeds and ultimately, espoused values and ideals are reified though their physical incorporation into the material environment.

Perhaps the most evident site of such landscaping is to be found in the design and architecture of corporate buildings such as factories and office complexes. Operating as media of meaning construction for employees and clients alike, effective corporate architecture is viewed as playing the role of anything from totemic symbol, uniting employees around a common goal, to the physical embodiment of the organization's history and espoused value. A good illustration of this, as Olins (1989) has observed, is to be found in the finance industry. Banks in particular have long been at pains to 'construct', through the physical design of branches, an aesthetic that conveys a sense of wealth and power, as well as one that would encourage the 'well off people to come in and the poorer to keep out' (Olins, 1989: 56). Where this was the case for local branches, it was multiplied tenfold for head offices, with Sir Edwin Lutyens's 1924 design for the headquarters of the now defunct Midland Bank in London a case in point. Today, even though neo-classical pomp and grandeur may seem somewhat staid; such institutions still lead the way in embracing the aesthetics of power and presence despite the turbulence of the financial markets. Think, for example, of the postmodern inversion of the Lloyds Building, or the phallic projection of 30 St Mary Axe – more commonly referred to as the Gherkin – both located in the financial heart of the City of London.

It is not only the outward or even structural design of such corporate buildings that should be of concern to us, however. Of equal, if not greater interest, are the ways in which internal building design has also emerged as a prominent preoccupation of commentators and designers within both the business and architectural professions. Of particular note here is the apparent identification of the needs of an increasingly knowledge driven economy with novel and innovative forms of office design which prioritize, as illustrated in Warren's aforementioned paper, the playful, innovative management of space and interior décor. Take, for example, Myerson and Ross's description of the offices of *Exposure*, a London creative communications agency:

> Standard workstations are off the agenda. Instead, each staff member was given an individual desk, albeit secondhand. The result is a richly eclectic interior designed to express the idea of a 'walk through the markets of the world'. Hybrid, invented styles such as 'Moroccan Techno' and Danish Punk coexist without really blending. Indian fabrics jostle with an old Japanese tea steamer on wheels; chain mail curtains demarcate areas; two red crosses from First World War hospital tents adorn Shah's [one of the managing directors] all-white private space. (2003: 148)

This particular office style is an example of what Myerson and Ross (2003) categorize as a 'neighbourly' design, in which social interaction and interplay is encouraged amongst all levels of employee. The landscaping of physical space need not, of course, be as dramatic as that suggested here. Indeed, it should be remembered that any such office space, or indeed industrial space, can be understood in aesthetic terms, even if it is the aesthetics of a regularized, bureaucratic layout; identical desks, identically laid out and spaced, and housed in a dull and uninspiring grey interior.

This observation notwithstanding, however, as argued in the previous section, attempts by corporate management to utilize aesthetics as a means of projecting a desired and highly stylized corporate identity, or motivating particular employees, is undoubtedly undergoing something of an upturn. Returning to the specific topic of art, for instance, this is evident in the recent explosion in the accumulation and display of corporate art collections and arts sponsorship (see Jacobson, 1993; Wu, 2002) which has brought art not only into the corporate boardroom, but also into the workstations and the canteens. Amongst the corporate players on the global art scene are, for instance, financial institutions such as Deutsche Bank who have, or so they claim, not only assembled the world's largest corporate art collection (around 50,000 works) but also have their own online magazine dedicated to their artistic activities, and are co-proprietors of the Deutsch Guggenheim art museum in central Berlin.

Nonetheless, despite such tales of grand art collections and other large scale, aesthetically driven corporate activities, it is the design and aesthetic qualities of more mundane items that are perhaps of most significance when it comes to understanding the patterns and contours of corporate aesthetics. Furthermore, the requirements increasingly placed upon corporate agency to constantly probe and penetrate the interior complexity of everyday organizational life in its endeavours to maximize identification, commitment and output suggests that the importance of such an aesthetics of the quotidian is only likely to grow in the foreseeable future despite even the most pessimistic of economic forecasts. It is perhaps not the obvious sources of aesthetic stimuli such as architecture, interior design or even art that we need to consider, therefore. Rather, in order to truly understand this particular dimension of corporate life, perhaps where we should look is towards that which is so often taken for granted; the realm of the everyday artefact that tends to pervade corporate life at every level.

Artefacts and Meaning

In his aforementioned essay, 'Artifacts as Pathways and Remains of Organizational Life', Gagliardi (1990) takes issue with the proposition – most commonly associated with Edgar Schein – that material artefacts merely represent the superficial flotsam and jetsam of organizational relations. Rather, he views such humanly engineered materiality as both representative and productive of a particular way of feeling about an organization, its activities and espoused values; that is, its 'pathos', as referred to earlier. He argues, therefore, that artefacts should be understood as primary cultural phenomena that influence corporate life from two distinct points of view. They, (a) make materially possible, help, hinder or even proscribe organizational *action*; (b) more generally influence our *perception* of reality, to the point of subtly shaping beliefs, norms and cultural values. By their very definition – namely, that of sensually efficacious products of human action – artefacts are, of course, difficult to define and perhaps delimit. In a certain sense, however, this is indicative of their significance to the corporate landscape. Artefacts are highly ubiquitous, experienced – although often seemingly overlooked – at every turn.

Perhaps one of the most notable attempts to subject an organizational artefact to detailed aesthetic scrutiny, however, is Strati's (1996) consideration of the humble chair; an artefact present in pretty much all corporations. As Strati observed, a chair can stimulate any if not all our senses. We can see its design and colour, feel its texture and shape, smell the materials it is constructed from (as well as the odours of those who have occupied it) and hear its movement. All of these potential stimuli tell us not only about the chair itself, however, but they can also tell us as much about the organization which it inhabits and the people who might or might not use it. The aesthetic qualities of a chair can suggest the status of its owner, the attitudes and values of the company as well as, possibly, its financial performance or its attitudes to clients, customers and suppliers.

In contrast, within what one might term the more practitioner oriented literature, such an interest in the aesthetic qualities of artifacts and their value to corporate achievement has tended to be directed more towards the successful construction of corporate brands and the manufacture of corporate identities, stylish outlets and the like. Schmitt and Simonson (1997) in *Marketing Aesthetics: The Strategic Management of Brands, Identity and Image*, for instance, identify corporations such as Cathay Pacific, IBM and particularly Starbucks as all having significantly improved their market position in part through a concerted effort to attend to the image they project by way of design, stylization and associated aesthetically-orientated technologies. Referring particularly to the material environment to be found in almost any *Starbucks* coffee outlet, Schmitt and Simonson note how:

> As they see, feel and experience soothing collections of things that seem to fit together, the customers are seduced by the aesthetic. Whether the customer appreciates art or not, the lure is in an aesthetic that delivers harmony on the one hand and planned contrasts on the other. First and foremost, these consistent systems of visual forms tantalise the eyes. The aim therefore is to tap into, or indeed create your own aesthetic niche through the cultivation of a corporate style(s). (1997: 82)

One study which attempts not only a more critical analysis, but also a widening of the definition of corporate space and aesthetics, is that by Carter and Jackson (2000) who consider the aesthetic experience engendered by the landscaping of cemetery space under the control of the Commonwealth War Graves Commission; an organization that provides for the 'care and maintenance of cemeteries and memorials for military war dead' (Carter and Jackson, 2000: 184). Using photography as a mode of illustrating the physical composition of such environments and the artefacts to be found within them – namely, orderly displays of kempt headstones or similar monuments set within a usually quiet and tranquil landscape – the authors argue that the symbolism and aesthetic qualities of the ways in which such spaces are materially produced engenders a largely instrumental effect – that is, one that generates an orderly and sanitized 'feeling of solace and peace and not of depression' (Gibson and Ward, cited in Carter and Jackson, 2000: 184), which, in doing so, denies the reality of such places as symbols of death, destruction and chaos.

Another example, of what is perhaps a more radical recombining of the symbolic, the instrumental and the aesthetic in the analysis of corporate or organizational artefacts is that found in Hancock (2005). Here the artefact in question is a single example of a corporate recruitment document, which is analysed in terms of both its symbolic and its aesthetic qualities. Ultimately, Hancock argues that what the document enacts, through a combination of text, photography, colour, texture and overall layout and composition, is not only a particular corporate identity but also a more general cultural mythology. That is, through the deployment of rural images, healthy young bodies and particular textual commentaries the document is configured in such a way as to construct and express what is in effect an ideological pathos that perpetuates the sense that corporate activity and aspiration is itself a natural and inevitable component of human expectation. The values, ambitions and rewards of capitalism in general, and of corporate activity in particular, are explicated from the contingent realm of historical development and sensually embedded within what is experienced as the timelessness of the natural environment and its association with growth and vitality.

To consider the aesthetic qualities of organizational and corporate artefacts only when and where they take the form of material objects and settings might be, however, to unnecessarily narrow our perspective on the issue. Artefacts can also take what might be considered to be more ethereal forms, including, for instance, human performances, rites, rituals and other activities. Cappetta and Gioia (2006), for example, observe how the seasonal shows of the global fashion industry are carefully constructed, aesthetically significant artefacts in their own right; ones that deploy a range of expressive elements in an attempt to construct a particular symbolic and aesthetic regime of meaning for the benefit of potential clients, sponsors and other stakeholders. In a similar vein, Strati (2006) has demonstrated the way in which the performance of a student's degree assessment suggests the polyvalent character of artefacts, and the ways in which performances within organizations – perhaps ranging from product launches to Annual General Meetings and disciplinary meetings to team building exercises – can provide a unified physical shape to what might otherwise appear as a disparate set of beliefs, values and aspirations.

One particular element that is common to the idea of performance as artefact, however, and one that requires further consideration, is the status of the human body within an increasingly aestheticized corporate world. For central to the idea of performance as artefact is that of body also as artefact; as something that might be sculpted, moulded and managed in such a way as to render it both instrumentally and aesthetically significant. Indeed, from what has been termed the idea of body as brand to the growth of aesthetic labour, the idea that the aesthetics of the human body represents a powerful source of market visibility and competitive advantage is one that has generated significant recognition.

Embodied Labour and Aesthetic Regulation

It is perhaps, you might argue, something of a self-evident truism that beautiful corporations require, in turn, beautiful people to work for them. Nonetheless, the realization that corporate organizations have increasingly developed a concern with the condition of their employees' bodies is one that has been arrived at relatively recently within organizational research. Not, of course, that bodies have ever truly been excluded from accounts of work. Even Taylor's (1911) concern with the development of a 'scientific' approach to industrial management emphasized the rational and systematic observation and regulation of the worker's body as key to an efficient productive process. Indeed, as one examines the history of modern working practices, from bureaucratic administration to industrial production and beyond, the need to control and manipulate the body of the employee through 'coercion, exploitation, discipline, control' (Rose, 1989: 55) can be viewed as an integral aspect of the managerial function.

What is of interest here, however, are those perhaps more recent interventions that have endeavoured to identify an increasing concern not so much with how employees' bodies function as instruments of production, but rather how they are cultivated as aesthetically significant carriers of a corporate pathos. Perhaps the most apparent example of such a concern with the body is that to be found in the field of organizational branding and dress. Harquail (2006), for instance, has commented on the extent to which it is increasingly common that, in an attempt to manage the internal branding activities of corporations, staff are expected to reproduce desired brand characteristics through physical self-presentation, potentially reducing them to the status of embodied corporate artefacts. She illustrates this claim with the example of American employees of *Land Rover* who were expected to wear clothes seen to be associated with a particularly English variety of rural life; an activity that became notably spontaneous as the employees increasingly identified with, and internalized, the mythological brand identity. More generally, Rafaeli and Pratt (1993) have highlighted how more traditional organizational dress codes can be understood to convey important symbolic and aesthetic messages such as the white of heath service workers which is deemed to be indicative of cleanliness and purity, or the dark blue of the police and other security organizations which projects a sense of power and tradition, while Tretheway (1999) has identified how female dress at work is often configured so as to disguise or suppress female embodiment, reining in the curves and spillages of the female shape in homage to the rationality of the projected male body.

Beneath the level of dress, however, there is, or so it would appear, an even greater concern amongst corporate management to encourage its employees not only to adorn their bodies in ways conducive to the company mission and image, but to take this to the next stage and train the body in line with idealized notions of fitness and physical development. McGillivray (2005a, 2005b) has, for example, explored the ways in which discourses of wellness and fitness have increasingly infiltrated managerial speak, and, while clearly contested, this has driven corporate initiatives in the service of creating healthier, better looking workers. Thus, the provision of subsidized leisure facilities, sporting away days and various similar activities can all be in part understood as contributing to what can perhaps best be described as an ongoing landscaping of corporate bodies.

While such observations can, however, be made about a range of working environments and industries, a significant driving force behind the increasing interest in the working body as an aesthetic artefact or extension of the corporate 'brand' has been the increasing rise to prominence within Western economies of the tertiary sector and, in particular, those industries concerned with providing various personal and leisure services. This has led to what has been termed, in particular quarters, the emergence of *aesthetic labour* (Dean, 2005; Hancock and Tyler, 2000; Pettinger, 2004; Witz et al., 2003). Such 'immaterial labor in the bodily mode', as Hardt and Negri (2000: 293) have described it, refers to the ways in which employees are increasingly required to present themselves as an aesthetically appropriate embodied presence within the workplace. Hancock and Tyler, for example, have observed with reference to the work of flight attendants how,

> the organizational bodies of these employees were required to embody the desired aesthetic of the company – to speak in the organizational 'tone of voice' and to adopt a flexible organizational 'personality', of which their embodiment became a material artifact. Furthermore, this aesthetic performance which was required of flight attendants in order to maintain the look, sound and sense of the airline, was clearly considered to be one of [their] primary roles. (2000: 117)

Furthermore, as Witz et al. (2003) have noted, this has led to what can be seen as an increased premium being placed on the aesthetic qualities of certain service sector workers; namely the 'appropriate' combination of build and figure, personal style, voice and accent. As leisure and other consumer outlets such as clothing stores (Pettinger, 2004) increasingly seek to identify with and exploit niche markets, so too are niche employees sought whose physical appearance, sound and even smell resonate aesthetically both with corporate identity and brand, as well as with potential customers. Employee corporeality thus itself becomes an object of corporate regulation whereby the human body is appropriated as yet another tradable commodity. And while various forms of aesthetic labour can also be identified in less surprising occupational arenas such as fashion modelling (Entwistle, 2002) and theatre and television (Dean, 2005), what the bulk of this work seems to suggest is that the extension of corporate interest into the management and manipulation of the aesthetic dimension of employees', customers' and clients' everyday aesthetic experiences is continuing well beyond the material environment they inhabit, and into the very physical make-up of the individuals themselves. As with the more general infusion of aesthetic themes into the day-to-day management of corporate life, the notion of aesthetic labour and its associated concerns perhaps challenges us to think about the relationship between work, organization and the role and nature of the aesthetic as an increasingly important resource in the service of corporate ambition.

Discussion

Hopefully by now, you will at least have a notion of some of the ways in which it can be said that the values and ideas associated with the term aesthetics have had an impact on both how corporate life is practised, and how, in turn, we might come to understand it. Yet this is, in organizational theory terms at least, an area of interest which is very much in its infancy. While organizations have for many years sought to express a sense of identity, purpose or value through a range of symbolic and aesthetically efficacious means, it is only relatively recently that a self-conscious language of corporate aestheticization has appeared at the forefront of managerial and academic thinking. What I want to consider in this closing section of the chapter, then, is why this might be the case and, more importantly, how we might respond to it?

While there continues to be much debate and disagreement over the nature and trajectory of Western industrialized societies, there is perhaps now some agreement around the basic proposition that, over the last 25 years or so, there has been a significant decline in (but by no means eradication of) the importance of traditional manufacturing industry in favour of a more service oriented tertiary sector. This has had at least two significant consequences in relation to the rise of an aesthetically sensitive corporate environment. On the one hand, the very real expansion of the tertiary sector has contributed to the need for, and emergence of, an increasingly educated and culturally literate populous; one that has both greater access to cultural and economic resources, and has become less willing to accept the Fordist standardization of consumer products. On the other hand, the growth of both financial and knowledge based services, as well as retail and leisure, has fuelled competition in an area of the economy within which the quality of service is gauged not simply by the quality of goods provided, but also by the quality of the overall service experience provided to the consumer (Leidner, 1993, 1999).

Both of these factors have, in turn, led to the expansion of what, in its most popularist form has been described by Florida (2002) as 'the creative class'. This emerging social formation includes, amongst many others, those who now achieve their income through creating the kinds of eye-catching logos, buildings and corporate identities I have discussed above. In equal part, these are also the people who not only create such an aestheticized corporate environment but also quite often run them and consume from them. And while it is undoubtedly dangerous to accept uncritically such sweeping claims about the economic and cultural power of any social grouping, there can be no doubt that we all live in an increasingly image and style conscious society; albeit one that has been slowly emerging since the post-war period. Cultural sociologists such as Lash and Featherstone have referred to this in terms of a postmodernization of the socio-economic environment, a prominent feature of which is a breakdown of the boundary between art and everyday life and the rise of what is a narcissistic culture of the self. A situation which for Featherstone is increasingly characterized by an environment that has,

> become aestheticized and enchanted through the architecture, billboards, shop displays, advertisements, packages, street signs etc. and through the embodied persons who move through these spaces: the individuals who wear, to varying degrees, fashionable clothing, hair-styles, make-up, or who move or hold their bodies in particular stylised ways. (1992: 280)

It is the coalescence of such factors that has led Böhme (2003) to refer to what he describes as the rise of the *aesthetic economy*. Working within a broadly Marxian framework, Böhme argues that while the economy was previously dominated by values grounded in use, exchange or symbolism these have now been joined by a quintessentially new mode of value, that of *staging value*. This refers to the value a commodity generates neither through its relation to utility, nor to its position within an exchange economy, but rather to its capacity to 'stage, costume and intensify life' (Böhme, 2003: 72). The aesthetic economy, therefore, refers to the valuation and exchange of commodities in direct relation to their ability to act as aesthetic resources, directed at the generation and temporary supplication of desire for experience and sensual gratification. Böhme is not alone in such an evaluation of the current contours and trajectory of economic and socio-cultural life, however. In a far more celebratory tone, the American libertarian commentator Postrel (2003) has also identified such an aestheticizing trend within the contemporary economy; a world in which she claims beauty and design are the driving forces not only of production and consumption, but equally, human self-actualization. It is not only art as a product then, but the aesthetic principle of a unique, transcendent experience which itself provides, if not a defining, then at the very least a configurational logic, for contemporary corporate activity.

Having located the rise of the corporate aesthetic within the context of a very real shift in the dominant mode of economic and potentially socio-cultural production and reproduction, how then might we wish to respond to it? For instance, is the aestheticization of corporate life and the economic and cultural arrangements that both sustain and emerge from it to be celebrated or met with perhaps a more wary caution? Clearly opinions are divided on this. As I acknowledged earlier in the chapter, there are those who perceive a great opportunity in a stronger relationship between business and the arts for the emergence of a more creative, more dynamic and ultimately, perhaps, a more humane corporate form. From organizations such as the Arts and Business Fellowship in the UK, who endeavour to connect 'creativity and commerce', to a range of increasingly cited individuals who seek to create both an intellectual as well as a practical space within which aesthetics more generally can inform successful business practice, there is a tangible move towards a more meaningful rapprochement between the aesthetic and the corporate beyond that of the company art collection.

Nonetheless, as I indicated earlier, there also exists a substantial sense of unease at such developments. The idea that art and, more generally, aesthetic experience has become identical with corporate interest has in a number of instances become more closely identified with a process of colonization than one of mutual enablement or sensual liberation. As I was at pains to identify in the opening sections of this chapter, the aesthetic has, almost since its conception, been involved in a struggle with forces of rationality that have sought to subsume it under a predominantly performative logic. Today this unease centres, therefore, on what is viewed as an ongoing assault on art's ability to act as a critical resource in society (Carr, 2003); one that by virtue not only of its seemingly inherent lack of practical utility but also its ability to represent the taken for grantedness of the everyday world in novel and uncompromising ways, defines, for many, the nature of truly great art. For the likes of say Hancock (2003) or Pelzer (2006), this collapse of art, and the aesthetic qualities that define it, into the commercial and largely instrumental realm of big business represents an 'implosion' (Pelzer, 2006: 75) whereby art loses its critical distance from the reproduction of mundane social and economic relations, rendering it impotent and meaningless both as a critical commentator and an avenue for spontaneous creativity.

Welsch (1997) has also warned against the possibility that constant aesthetic stimulation can, ultimately, only serve to diminish and disable our capacity for aesthetic judgement and appreciation, a process he refers to as 'anaesthetization' (see also Dale and Burrell 2003). As Welsch (1997: 25) expresses it: 'Our perception needs not only invigoration and stimulation, but delays, quiet areas and interruptions too ... Total aestheticization results in its open opposite. Where everything becomes beautiful, nothing is beautiful any more; continued excitement leads to indifference; aestheticization breaks into anaesthetization'. It is this threat of anaesthetization – that of a denigration of the capacity for aesthetic pleasure and judgement that gradually renders one insensitive to a sensually rich environment – that perhaps represents the most disturbing aspect of any corporate drive to aesthetically embellish its products, buildings, livery and even employees.

Conclusions

In line with the theme of the book more generally, what I have attempted to do in this chapter is provide an albeit concise and short introduction to how one might wish to think about the relationship between the aesthetic and the ways in which corporate life is increasingly practised and reproduced. In doing so, however, there is much that has had to be omitted. For instance, there can be no doubt that this is a largely occularcentric account of corporate aestheticization, omitting any meaningful discussion of the organization of smell or sound. Furthermore, little or no mention has been made of the impact aesthetics has had on the techniques by which organizations and other corporate bodies might be studied; that is, the aesthetic as an epistemological and methodological resource (see Strati, 1996). Rather, I have sought to focus on the ways in which the aesthetics of various aspects of the corporate environment are themselves becoming increasingly organized in a predominantly instrumental fashion.

Now, while undoubtedly multi-faceted and open to multiple interpretations, what such an organization of aesthetics as has unfolded here seems to suggest is a continuation of an historical struggle, that between the aesthetic as a predominantly sensual and non-conformist way of experiencing and knowing the world, and the demands of a largely systematized and formalized rationality that seeks to divide the world into knowable and, ultimately, operationalized chunks. To what extent such a movement is itself legitimate is, of course, open to continuous debate. Art, beauty and the very quality of sensuality are resources that undoubtedly could offer greater enjoyment and indeed greater opportunities for creativity within the workplace, and after all, despite the mythology of the starving artist, hasn't art always, in one form or another, been about business? Furthermore, even if the relationship with corporate life should prove to be less than beneficial for the quality of contemporary aesthetic experience do we need to be concerned? After all, the aesthetic has, over the centuries, proved remarkably resilient in the face of various assaults on its integrity, while art itself has continued to provide a radical and iconoclastic voice in society despite its continued institutionalization.

However we might choose to answer these questions, one thing appears reasonably certain, nonetheless – namely, that aesthetic experience, both in our everyday and working lives is likely to increasingly bear the mark of corporate interest and intervention. And whatever the form this mark might take in the future, for this, if for no other reason, it is worth recognizing the importance of aesthetics in our endevours to understand corporate life.

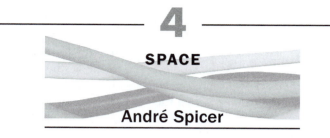

4

SPACE

André Spicer

Introduction

Imagine that you meet someone at party. After some initial niceties, your partner in conversation will inevitably begin to ask what you do for a living. They might even ask you *where* you work. To get a sense of your work-life, they want you to describe the actual space in which you work. Is it an office? A factory? An airport? The door of a night club? Where in your workplace do you spend most of the days? Do you have a corner office with a wonderful view over the city? Are you isolated in a pig-pen arrangement with hundreds of their co-workers surrounding you? What is on your desk? Is it covered with pictures of sports cars? Family photos? A picture of the English football star Wayne Rooney? After your new friend has asked these questions they might have a better sense of your work-a-day world. They would get a sense of whether you are powerful in the organization, whether you are a potential victim of the next wave of corporate downsizing, or whether you are a carefree creative. The insights we can glean from asking someone about where they work reminds us that space is an important dimension of corporate life. It shapes who we are, who we can relate to, and what others think about us.

When we begin looking at organizational space, we usually think about the concrete and physical workplace. However physical workplaces like offices, factories and shops are only the most obvious aspects of organizational space. There are a whole range of different levels, or 'scales', of organizational space. The most immediate level is the 'workstation' where we actually do our work. Our workstation might be a desk, a check-out, or a position on a production line. At this most immediate level, we have a whole range of objects, tools and furniture which are close at hand. For instance a bartender's workstation might include glasses, the taps for pouring beer, and the cash register – all within easy reach. The next level of organizational space is the workspace. This includes the immediate room in which we work. A bartender would work in a bar which might include a number of workstations, as well as seating for customers, and a place where thirsty punters can line up. The workspace is usually included in a bigger building. Our bartender might work in a larger establishment which also houses a restaurant, some toilets and a kitchen. Each of these spaces are clearly separate zones, but they are also held together by the same building which has a certain style of decor and architecture. The building is in turn located in a neighbourhood where there a mixture of different buildings that house a variety of organizations. Our bar may be located in a neighbourhood filled with other bars which are popular among office workers after work. Finally, that neighbourhood is contained within larger spaces such as the city, the region, the nation and ultimately the globe. The point is that organizations are embedded in multiple spaces. Each of the spaces that they are embedded in will have some effect on the organization.

In this chapter I seek to identify why it is that workspace is so important to us. I do this by drawing on studies of the role of space and place in organizations. I begin by investigating some of the main reasons we have become so attached to our workspaces. I then consider three dimensions of space, and then show how managers try to manipulate these. I conclude by noting some of the major changes in organizational space that have occurred recently.

Why is Space Important to Us?

Space is an important, but often unrecognized aspect of corporate lives. Just how important space can be is seen in the concern sparked by minor changes in workspace. Imagine if we tried shifting someone from one office to another. When the victim of our experiment finds out that they have to move, they will almost certainly think 'how can they do this to me!' After some shock, they may invent a whole series of reasons why they simply must stay where they are. They might suggest that they need to be close to their immediate neighbours or they might claim they need the sun that streams in a large window to battle seasonal affective disorder. We know for sure they will share the injustice of the attack on 'their' workspace with any colleague who is willing to listen. Why is it that we grow to love our insignificant patch of turf in the corporate jungle?

Perhaps one of the most fundamental reasons that we become so attached to 'our' space is that we build up social relationships there. The human relations movement found that employees who interacted with one another in the workplace would tend to be happier and more productive. In contrast, employees who were isolated and did not engage in social interaction would be more troublesome and less productive (Trist and Bamforth, 1951).

It was realized that people working together like to be co-located together. When their co-workers are close at hand they can work more efficiently and effectively. When they are spatially isolated from their workmates they become unhappy and less productive. The importance of co-location of social groups explains why it is that an employee isolated from their group often becomes so upset. It is simply because it becomes difficult to access, talk with, and feel a degree of intimacy with, their friends.

Co-location also shapes one's position in the political structures of a firm. If your desk is in a prominent location in the office were people frequently pass by, then you are far more likely to have the opportunity to have informal discussions with a whole range of people (Pfeffer, 1992). Similarly, if you are co-located with powerful people, then you are likely to have an advantage over colleagues who are not. When people get shifted around in organizations, many of these informal power networks get shaken up. People find that they are now separated from their allies. Sometimes people even find that they are made invisible. The upshot is that they will fight long and hard to keep their space.

In addition to social networks, we often feel a degree of territoriality over our workspace. We all know that we feel edgy when someone we don't like comes too close and intrudes into our 'personal space'. We also know that we would be troubled if a guest in our house began sifting through all our drawers and undertook a close inspection of the nooks and crannies of our bedroom. It is not too hard to work out that we also become very defensive when someone begins interfering in our workspace. Imagine the consternation if a cleaner took it upon themselves to reorder the messy piles of books, papers and forgotten student essays they seem to clutter up every professor's office. Our disorderly professor would probably reprimand the cleaner for disturbing their carefully contrived 'filing system'. Underlying these rather irrational reprimands is a more subtle reason. The professor has a feeling of territoriality. This involves an attachment to a certain space and an associated attempt to defend that space (Brown et al., 2005). This sense of territory arises out of a sense of psychological ownership. That is because even though a worker does not economically own a space they work in, they nonetheless feel a degree of intense attachment to that space. They feel as if it is theirs. Any attempt to deprive them of their space would make them feel like someone has stolen a precious possession. Obviously we expect that if someone stole something that we really valued, we would be angry. The same is true for territory. When someone 'steals' a space we 'psychologically own', we become distressed and angry.

To avoid unpleasant feelings, we often go to great lengths to defend our territory. Sometimes we show that we psychologically own a space through marking it out as our own. This might involve very obvious signs that a space is ours such as a nameplate on an office door or scattering our possessions over a desk. We may also use subtle means, such as throwing our coat over a chair or playing our music in the room. Once we have marked out our territory, we need to defend it from potential intruders. If we are forward thinking, we may develop 'anticipatory defences'. These are aimed to stop people coming into our territory before they do. For instance, most large corporations employ security guards in the lobbies and senior executives employ secretaries to defend them from marauding visitors. But what happens if the intruder actually gets into our space? This is when people begin using 'reactionary defences' to beat back the intruder. The most extreme case would involve physical violence. Organizational members might use more subtle forms of defence, including asking someone to leave, glaring at the intruder or making an ironic remark.

In addition to social networks and territoriality, we often value our workspaces because they are so closely connected with our identities. The size of our office says something about how important we are. Consider the difference between someone who has a large corner office overlooking a river and someone who occupies a tiny desk in a windowless office they share with many others. The decorations around our desk say something about our interests. If someone's desk is covered with pictures of their children, we can surmise that family is important to them. In contrast, if someone places their awards and qualifications in a prominent space, then they might be saying they see themselves as an 'achiever'. The position of our workplace in the city also says something. Consider the difference between a lawyer who works in a large glass tower in the City of London and a lawyer working in an old house in a small rural town. In each of these cases, we notice that the actual space that people work in says a lot about who they are. This is because we often use 'physical identity markers' ranging from where we work and our building, to how we decorate our desk to express something about our identity (Elsbach, 2004b).

Another implication of change in workplace identity is that changes in our workspace are often experienced as significant threats to our identity. For instance, in a study of a Californian hi-tech firm, Kimberly Elsbach (2004b) examined the effects of a move from individuals having separate desks to a 'hotelling' arrangement where they occupied a desk temporarily. She found that employees found this arrangement was a serious threat to their identities. By the removing all signs of their individuality such as postcards and decoration, their sense of being a unique individual was threatened. By breaking up defined social groups who were often co-located, employees' sense of belonging to a distinctive social group was threatened. By removing opportunities to show how important one is through status symbols like a large office, an individual's sense of personal status was called into question. The result was that employees felt very frustrated about their ability to express their own sense of who they are. In order to deal with this, employees began making heavy use of portable artefacts such as business cards to display their identities. They also began to use prohibited permanent artefacts such as introducing personal posters in certain parts of the workplace. Finally, they began expressing their identities through behaviours such as incessant self-promotion. The result was that employees were able to re-craft a sense of self even in this apparently damaged and damaging situation. Ultimately this shows that changes in organizational space represent such a threat to people that they need to engage in defensive action to preserve their space.

What is Space?

Now that we have established why space is important, we can now turn to a more fundamental question – what do we mean by space? The idea of space is a strange one. If we look in the *Oxford English Dictionary*, we find that space can refer to a gap of time between two points, a delay, a place, room, the unimaginable depths, and so on. The word 'space' can be used to describe anything from a bedroom, to a newspaper column to an interplanetary voyage. Well developed theories about space can be found in philosophy, physics, geography and architecture to name just a few disciplines. Indeed there is a long history of thought in relation to the concept of space (see Casey, 1999). In this rich body of thought, we can identify at least three basic ways of defining space. In what follows we shall look at each of these definitions in turn, and draw out what they mean for how we study organizational space.

Probably the most common definition of space is as a physical phenomenon. Space is the distance between two or more points. For instance, a space is the distance between myself and my colleague, a consultant and their computer, a company and their customer, a chef's hand and the fish he intends to fry. The distance between these points can be measured. If we wanted, we could measure how far away in centimetres a chef is from his ingredients, or how far in kilometres a salesperson is from her clients. We could also measure how much time it takes to get there. For instance, how long does it take the chef to reach for the Dover sole? How long does it take for the salesperson to negotiate the busy city centre to see her client? The crucial point here is that if we assume space to be the distance between two points, then in order to understand it, we must measure the physical manifestations of the gap.

By measuring the distance between points, we can begin to surmise a lot about an organization. For instance, the early scientific management researchers realized that the way a workstation is 'traditionally' set up is often very inefficient. The things which should be close together are far apart. This means that the worker has to spend too much time reaching, bending or walking to get the parts they need to make something. Prophets of scientific management like Fredrick Taylor (1947) repeatedly showed through their time and motion studies that if only workspace could be engineered in the right way, then huge efficiencies can be introduced. For instance, a 'scientifically designed' coffee shop would ensure that all the necessary items for an employee to make a cup of coffee are within easy reach. This would save them moving around the workstation and wasting time (Becker, 1981). Similarly, architects and office designers have tried to design particularly appealing offices by manipulating the distance and layout of various aspects of the office furniture and where people sit. The office landscaping movement tried to ensure people were clustered into little cells and separated by pleasant greenery that created an appealing office environment (Augé, 1995).

Architects manipulate entire buildings to increase efficiency and effectiveness. For instance, designs of early modern factories were largely driven by the practical intention to ensure that work flowed through the building in the most efficient way possible and that people were co-located in the right places (Darley, 2003). Similarly, airports are designed to ensure a smooth flow of passengers from the car park through the departure halls, the various duty-free shops and onto the plane (Pascoe, 2001). The point here is that the very building itself is a central part of ensuring that people are positioned close to each other and that they are able to interact in an appropriate fashion. Finally, organizations are situated in certain neighbourhoods, cities and regions so they are close to key resources and customers. For instance, steel mills sprang up around coalfields because coal was one of their key inputs. Similarly, biotech industries have often sprung up around well known universities to exploit the knowledge and reputation of 'star scientists' (Zucker et al., 1998). The major point we find in these studies is that distance makes a difference in organization. Indeed, a long history of research shows that everything from the distance from a hand to a knife to the distance between scientists and a corporate research lab has a major impact on the daily functioning of an organization.

These studies remind us of the importance of space in determining how efficiently we work, with whom we interact at work, and what resources we have access to. Most of all, by approaching space as a physical phenomenon, we are reminded that organizations have not totally disappeared into the 'thin air' of the virtual environment (Leadbeater, 2000). Rather, organizations continue to be located in the brute physical world of distance. Despite these major insights, it is important to recognize that thinking about space as a largely physical phenomenon has some important limitations. Only focusing on the physical aspects of space leads us to ignore the role that interpretation and meaning play in shaping our understandings of space. This is important because space is not just the brute physical distance between two points. It is also our perception of that distance. For instance, a farmer in the Australian outback might feel their neighbour is close-by even though they are 40 kilometres away. Whereas an urbanite living in the middle of London may feel significant distance from their neighbour – even thought they may dwell a matter of centimetres from their front door. This reminds us that our perceptions play a vital role in shaping the space we live in. By only paying attention to measurable physical distance, we miss the importance of perceptual or psychological distance between people. There is also a second major shortcoming of physical interpretations of space. By only focusing on distance, we are often unable to answer the question of why these patterns of distance and proximity arose rather than others. It is difficult to pinpoint exactly why it is that some people in an office building are closer to the beautiful views, have access to all areas of the building, are allowed to roam around, and sit within close proximity to powerful people like the chief executive officer. In order to explain why someone has all these spatial advantages, it is necessary to dig below the surface a little. This would involve identifying the power relations which allow some actors more spatial advantages than others.

In order to account for the role that interpretation and perception play in shaping our understanding of space, a second major approach to space was mooted by a school of philosophy called 'phenomenology' (Bachelard, 1958; Merleau-Ponty, 1946; Tuan, 1977). They argued that space is not only a physical thing made up of distances that can be carefully calculated and fed into a computer, for them, space was first and foremost about our experience of it. For them, space is completely shaped by the way that we feel in that space, the way we interpret it, and the meaning we attribute to that space. Consider two houses. One house is the place you grew up. Undoubtedly you remember most nooks and crannies of that house. You will remember where you hid, where you ate, where you slept, where you cried. Now consider a house you may have stayed in for a few nights. Perhaps it is a friend's or relative's house. You might remember some furniture, a few rooms, perhaps a particularly garish picture on the wall. What you probably cannot remember is the same kind of overwhelming memories and experiences which colour your experience of your own home. This little thought experiment reminds us that space is far more than just a collection of walls and distances. A space is given its special character by the meaning, experiences and understanding which we give it. A space is somewhere which is full of memories, thick with interpretation, covered with signs and symbols. It follows that in order to adequately understand space, it is vital to track how we interpret that space. It is vital to uncover the meanings that crowd in a space. It is important to give voice to the many signs and memories which make up the spaces we dwell in. By doing this we can begin to uncover how we interpret and experience a space.

If we begin to look for the layers of meaning that colour our experiences of organizational space, it is easy to become quickly overwhelmed. There are so many ways which people invest their workplace with significance. Just look at a workstation in an average office. You will see a thick layer of meaning there. You will find that people attempt to invest their rather anonomized workstations with items of personal significance and meaning. You might find pictures of friends and family, certificates of achievement, pictures of their favourite band or movie. All this paraphernalia gives the occupier a sense of meaning and connection. Similarly, the whole work-space swarms with symbols. For instance, an office will usually contain a whole range of signs such as corporate propaganda of the 'you don't have to be crazy to work here, but it helps' kind. The style of how a workspace is laid out can say a lot. Is it open plan? Are employees allowed to decorate their workstations? Do they have any private space at all? Is it light and clean? Is it dirty and noisy? All these things say something. For instance, modern car factories are fastidiously clean spaces, well lit, and rationally laid out. This communicates the hypermodern, technically advanced and above all efficient nature of the production process.

The entire building is also a major source of meaning in an organization. The style of the architecture, the location of the building, the hallways, the condition of the building, the ease of accessing the building, all say some-thing about the organization. For instance, large professional services firms often choose to be located downtown in prestigious glass towers. These glass palaces communicate the status of those working inside as well as the mod-ern and technologically advanced nature their jobs. In contrast, small media firms are often located in converted lofts which reflect the supposedly bohemian lifestyle associated with the 'no collar' workforce (Ross, 2004).

The neighbourhood that a business is located in tells us a lot about it. For instance, tourist regions are usually associated with certain kinds of experi-ences. Think for instance of the difference between a 'cultured' destination like Florence and a 'fun and sun' destination like Ibiza. Some regions conjure up different meanings and associations. Think for instance of the meaning attrib-uted to working in 'the City of London' (the centre of finance and banking in Europe) or 'on Brick Lane' (an immigrant enclave in central London with many small traders). Each location is only a few hundred meters from the other. However working in the City signifies wealth, suits and international financial deals. In contrast if you worked on Brick Lane, we might imagine that you worked in one of the Lane's many curry houses or perhaps in one of the ultra-hip boutiques that have recently sprung up. Each of these examples remind us that a space is not just a physical manifestation. It is also shaped and created by a whole range of experiences and patterns of understandings.

By understanding space as a pattern of meaning and interpretation, we are able to open up a whole new dimension. This way of looking at it shows how space is the creation of not just walls but is also our memories and experiences. Following this approach, measuring the distance between people is not enough. We must also uncover the patterns of interpretations and significance which people use to understand spaces. This would involve 'reading' space like we might read a novel. Although this might yield some extremely important insights about the meaning of a space, it may also blind us to some other things. One of the most interesting aspects of organizational space is that it has a clearly non-symbolic dimension. That is, spaces are not just the memories and stories we carry around with us. Rather, space is also made up of very physical things such as doors, walls and barriers. The result is that space is something which has an irreducible physical aspect to it. It is something which is fixed and located. This means to properly understand space, we must take into account its physical manifestations. The second, and perhaps more important, limitation of approaching space as meaning is that it makes it hard to discern why some interpretations are more dominant that others.

In order explain this neglected dimension, it is vital to consider space as a materialization of forms of control. This perspective was largely suggested by researchers influenced by Marxist thought (e.g. Harvey, 1974; Lefebvre, 1991). They argued that spaces are purposefully designed and manipulated to ensure those who use the space do some things rather than others. For instance, lecture halls are designed to ensure students face the front and pay attention to their boring lecturer. Factories are designed to ensure that managers and supervisors can literally oversee what is happening on the factory floor. Finally, large office buildings are designed to regulate and restrict the flow of 'unauthorized' people into the building. In each of these cases we see that power relations are literally materialized through built space. The power relation between the teacher and student is embodied in the lecture hall. The power relation between worker and manager is embodied in the factory. The power relation between the public and the large corporation is embodied in the glass office tower. The crucial point is that everyday things such as the design of a seat in a lecture theatre embody attempts to control people in organizations.

If we look closely at the spaces we work, consume and live in, we begin to notice how relations of power and domination are materialized in so many different ways. Consider a supermarket check-out. There are a whole range of spatial features that control how the check-out attendant does their job. These include the conveyor belt which brings groceries to them, the scanning machine which gets rid of the need for the check-out operator to add prices up, and the space where the customer packs their bags. The supermarket check-out is designed very carefully to ensure the job can only be done in a very particular way. If a check-out operator tried to intro-duce their own way of processing our items they would probably snarl up the system. Relations of power and domination are also embodied in the broader layout of organizational space. In an office, the status of different people is often indicated by the size of their office, the quality of their fur-niture and the comfort of the surroundings (Baldry, 1999). If someone has a particularly large office, we would assume that they have high status in the organization. This large office may allow its occupant some degree of privacy and security which their colleagues lower down the pecking-order do not enjoy. The entire design of buildings is also often an embodiment of patterns of control and domination. For instance, many workplaces are specifically designed to increase surveillance of employees (Sewell and Wilkinson, 1992a). Factories often have large open spaces to allow managers to watch the production process and spot workers who are not performing. Large 'open plan' offices are also designed to facilitate surveillance and minimize space where employees can hide and shirk their tasks. Finally, the very neighbourhoods and regions where organizations are positioned are also embodiments of relations of power and control. Consider how cities are carefully planned to ensure a sectioning off of different types of businesses, how they concentrate workers around their factories and create spaces for the managerial and professional classes in leafy suburbs. Indeed, many large modern cities are specifically designed to ensure effective policing if a riot or strike should break out. They are also designed to keep 'undesirables' from loitering in certain parts of the city by ensuring there are few places to sit and 'hang out'.

Studies of space as a form of control provide some significant insights. They show us how many of the spaces which we encounter are engineered to shape what people can and cannot do at work. By attending to how space controls us, we begin to recognize that one of the central ways that people exercise power in organizations is by developing and designing advantageous spaces. In many ways, if a well designed space embodies certain relations of power and domination, then there is no need for these to be exercised by actual people. While spaces may control and dominate use, they are also the locus of a lot of contention and struggle. Many studies of workplace life show that employees are able to take advantage of the various opportunities and gaps that are afforded by organizational spaces to 'slack off'. For instance, in a study of a factory Mahmood Ezzamel and colleagues (2001) found that workers would often use hidden corners of the factory to sleep, play card games, or 'shoot the breeze' during work time. In many ways, their workspace provided them with an opportunity for freedom from monotony. Thus, to properly understand organizational space it is necessary to pay attention to the consistent struggle between those forms of power that seek to build domination into organizational space, and resistance that carve out opportunities for freedom and escape.

How is Space Organized?

Having established some of the reasons that space is so important to people, let us now turn to how people try to manipulate workspace. Perhaps one of the most useful ways of thinking about the various aspects of organizational space can be found in the work of Henri Lefebvre (1991). Lefebvre largely built on the control approach to space. For him, space was an embodiment of relations of consistent struggle between those who sought to control space and those who sought to take advantage of the freedoms which might be found in a space. In order to understand this constant struggle, he argues that we need to take into account three dimensions. These are our everyday spatial practices, the way in which space is planned, and the way that we imagine space. He argues that organizational space comprises an ongoing interaction amongst these three facets. In what follows, we shall look at each of them in turn.

The first way that space is made and re-made in organizations is through the daily practices of using space. This involves all the everyday ways we negotiate a space. For instance it would include the way we sit on a chair, the idiosyncratic route which we take through the city when we walk to our favourite park, and the way we lay out our desk. The point is that all these ways of using space only involve the most fleeting and temporary modifications to it. For example a worker may occupy a 'hot desk' workstation by scattering their belongings and personal items across the desk. This workstation would not be 'theirs' as such. Rather they would only temporarily occupy it. By occupying this workstation, they are able to momentarily change the space. There are different ways people occupy spaces momentarily. One way involves how people move about in a space. For instance, people in one workplace might tend to walk very quickly down the corridor to show how busy they are. In another workplace, they may take things at a slower and more leisurely pace. As well as movement, people occupy spaces through their skills and abilities. For instance, a particularly skilled office worker might learn many tricks such as leaving their coat over their chair to show that they are at work when in fact they are taking a break in a nearby coffee shop. Another classic way people use spaces is through occupying them. This might involve anything from leaving personal items on a desk to actually physically 'taking over' a space with their body, their voice, or even their commanding gaze. People also seek to make more permanent 'modifications' to space to make them inhabitable. This might include shifting office furniture around into a more agreeable arrangement, removing offending walls, or even building new walls. A famous example of this is an office worker who had bored a hole through the cubicle wall dividing her and a co-worker. This allowed them to chat without having to go to the trouble of standing up.

A second way that space is actively organized is through spatial planning. This involves attempts to rationally map out and modify spaces 'from the top down'. Examples of this include office layout, assigning people to certain desks, the architecture of a whole building, ergonomics where the most efficient layout of a workplace is sketched out, and even city planning which seeks to rationally reorganize the city. Each of these forms of spatial planning involves an attempt to impose order from the top down through strict grids. In an organization, spatial planning takes on a variety of forms. A classic example of efficiency oriented spatial planning is the ergonomic practitioners who seek to make production more efficient through the careful ordering and planning of the work process. Space might also be planned through changing the rules and regulations that determine what can and cannot be done within organizations. An example of this is changing the rules around how one should dress in the workplace, the hours during which people should occupy the workplace, and the kinds of behaviour which are permissible. Finally, organizational space might be regulated through deeply embedded and unrecorded norms that shape what can and cannot be done in organizations. In some firms, taking over a workspace may be formally ruled out, but it is informally permissible. This means managers turn a blind eye to attempts to take over certain workspaces.

The final way that people manipulate and organize space is through how they imagine space. Imagination of space includes a whole range of complex symbolism and signs. It is the image that people have in their mind of what the organization is or indeed might be. Perhaps most prominently, signs are images and metaphors that people use to describe the space they exist in. For instance, one office worker might describe their workplace as being a prison. Another might describe their workplace as a playground. The point here is that the image each office worker uses will colour and shape exactly how they experience the space they exist in.

As well as images, our imaginaries of space are also embodied in spatial narratives. These are stories about what has taken place within a certain organizational space. For instance, a story about the bawdy hi-jinks at an office party might haunt the office space. Stories about what happened in 'the good old days' at a department store that is past its prime might also shape how people imagine a space. Alongside these narratives is a set of specific discourses that shape and condition how people think about organizational spaces. These are the linguistic building-blocks that actors use to understand the space they exist within. Some examples of discourses used by employees include 'humanization' and the need to develop 'people-sized' spaces, or the 'information age' and associated calls to develop fluid 'knowledge spaces'.

The final way that imagined space is shaped is through the development and articulation of cosmologies. These give order to nature and identify the position that man should take up in that natural scheme. These cosmologies are often deeply rooted patterns that hark back to religious schemes. Some examples include the notion that the higher you are, the closer you are to the power of the heavens. This means corporate executives take the highest floors in the building. We should add that these imaginares often provide a space where alternative worlds and spaces can be explored and small-scale insurrections mounted. Indeed, the imagined dimension of organizational space often proves to be more pliable and open to contestation and struggle than the planned or practised dimension.

How has Organizational Space Changed?

Now that we have identified how organizational space is constructed, we can turn to our final question of how organizational space has changed in organizations over the last two centuries or so. I shall argue that each point in this history has involved a quite unique configuration of organizational space. By this we mean that there have been quite different ways of using the workspace (practices), ways of ordering the workspace (planning), and ways that people have thought about the workspace (planning). In what follows we shall trace through the various transformations in the ways that organizational space has been practised, planned and imagined in the last two centuries.

Let's imagine we are in a workshop before the industrial age. It could be an ironsmith, a weaver, a jeweller. We would be struck by many things about this workshop. First, it is probably very small. There are probably only a handful of people working here. There might be a master, some journeymen, perhaps an apprentice or two. The workshop would also be attached to the master's house. There would be no separation between home and work – home was work and visa versa. The workshop would probably be located in a rural area or perhaps in the heart of a merchant city. It probably would also be poorly lit and ventilated. The work would be harsh and physical, and the workers bodies would be pressed together in a small dark room. There would be little or no systematic design of this space – the set-up of the workshop would largely be prescribed by tradition. A workbench would be designed as it was because that is the way that it has always been designed. The kinds of image and language that haunted these workplaces were largely associated with family, kinship and tradition. The workspace was a space of tradition, a space held together by strict bonds of hierarchical order between master and servant, husband and wife, father and son. This was a space tied together by a God-given cosmological order.

These small workshops were largely swept away by the great industrial revolution of the nineteenth century. This involved the massive expansion and concentration of production activity. The work of hundreds of small workshops scattered across the countryside was concentrated into a few large factories. Instead of having a handful of people under one roof, there was suddenly hundreds if not thousands of people in a factory. The size of these buildings was so vast and unimaginable that many of the early factories became tourist attractions. For instance, people would travel to the Peak District in England to marvel at Arkwright's mill. While there were some exceptions, these factories were often quite chaotic and disorderly places.

They had poor ventilation, little light, and there was a high risk of fire and accidents. These were the poet William Blake's 'dark Satanic mills' which Karl Marx described with such rancour. If we looked at how factory workers used these spaces, we would notice that they were not the kind of hyper-efficient machines we usually think about working in such places. Yes, the workers would often be engaged in highly repetitive work. They would be fixed into one space. But because the factories were such complex and labrythian spaces, there were many places to hide, retreat to, and generally skive off in. Indeed there are many stories of factory workers who invented minor labour saving innovations that allowed them to leave their workstation (often unnoticed) and pursue more enjoyable tasks elsewhere in the factory. The way these factories were planned was often haphazard and highly inefficient. There was rarely a clear line of production connecting all parts of the factory. There were many rooms which were poorly connected. Little thought was given to flow of production through the factory. These hot, loud, fiery spaces were often equated with the infernos of hell. For instance, J.W.M. Turner's painting of the industrial town of Dudley in the West Midlands of the UK picked out some glowing furnaces that look like gateways to the underworld in the middle of the countryside.

These dark Satanic mills began to change during the early twentieth century. This was the result of the rise of scientific management and attempts to forge a rational order out of unheavenly chaos. Fredrick Taylor's attempts to create a rational process of production and organization were coupled with schemes by modern architects to design rationally ordered buildings (Guillén 2006). These buildings would provide a slick flow of production through great manufactories. Everything and everyone would be in its correct place. The application of modern architecture and modern scientific management techniques led to the construction of some of the great icons of early twentieth-century architecture including Ford's River Rouge plant, and the even more massive 'red star' tractor factory in St Petersberg. These new factories would be built using steel beams and suspended roofs that had been initially developed for the shopping arcades of Paris. They would let light in, and create huge empty spaces where production could be rationally laid out. This ushered in a golden age of spatial planning where the design of workspaces would be specified to the most exacting detail. Whole suburbs, cities and transport systems could be planned to efficiently serve massive factories. The same techniques were increasingly applied to offices and retail spaces. These were concentrated and the light of reason was cast on every little detail of the production process. The result was that these spaces gave rise to fantasies and images of perfect order, hyper-rationalization, and in some cases accusations of inhumanity, and the creation of 'non-spaces' (Augé, 1995) which are utterly devoid of meaning.

The image of a rational grid clearly continues to dominate many of the hypermodern offices, service spaces and factories that we inhabit. However in some organizational spaces there has been a fundamental move away from the aesthetic of the hyper-rational hypermodern space. This is indicated in the appearance of what some call 'the new office' (Duffy, 1997). This is a work-space that emphasizes knowledge sharing, media images, communication technology, virtuality, fluidity and flux. Instead of trying to fix everything into a strict grid of organization and rationality, the new office blurs the lines between home and work and disturbs the idea that people have a single space in which they should sit. The new office is made up of pods and cafes where mobile knowledge workers can temporarily log in before rushing off again. These are spaces where images of leisure come into the workplace and work activities go out into the world of consumption. They are spaces where work is ever present and never present. These kind of 'new offices' give rise to the images and imaginations of free flow of work and ever present communica-tion which we so frequently find in mobile phone advertising.

Conclusion

In this chapter I have explored perhaps one of the most important, yet less frequently recognized aspects of organizational life. I have tried to argue that corporate life is not lived on the head of a pin. Rather, it is something which people do every day in very specific and sometimes unusual spaces. To properly understand corporate life we therefore need to understand the spaces that we live it in. Here I have argued that these spaces are inevitably multiple and would include everything from the work desk to the nation. Indeed, understanding organizational space is perhaps so urgent because it seems to matter so much. We have seen that any threats to our space are often the spark that ignites vicious reprisals. This is because our workspace is inti-mately bound up with our identity, our social networks and our sense of territoriality. To get a proper sense of how organizational space works, I have argued that we need to keep in mind three different definitions of organizational space – physical distance, patterns of understanding and materialization of control. By bearing these different definitions in mind we are able to begin to tease out the different aspects which go into making organizational space. These are the planned, practiced and imagined dimen-sions of organizational life. These concepts allow us to understand how organizational space is ordered and the history of how it came to be. The importance of practices and imagination in making and remaking organiza-tional space might also provide us with some promising spaces where we can find freedom and autonomy within the corporation.

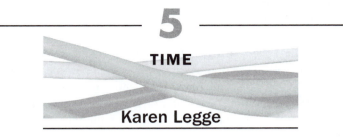

5

TIME

Karen Legge

Introduction

What is 'time' and what is its relevance to organization theory? Is time 'real', 'concrete' and 'objective' (*chronos*) or is it a network of subjective meanings (*kairos*)? Is time homogeneous, with time units sharing equivalency (*abstract*), or is it heterogeneous, with time units experienced differentially (*contextually embedded*)? Should time be regarded as a 'unified, quantitative commodity' – 'time is money' (*economic resource*) or as a 'manifold qualitative experience' (*embodied consciousness*)? (see Heath, 1956, cited in Hassard, 1996: 581–2). Further, is women's time different from men's time, as writers from a feminist perspective (e.g., Adam, 1995, 2002; Kristeva, 1981) would assert?

'Time' and the writing of organization theory are inseparable. For example, organization theory is written in time and reflects the fashions of the time and location of writing (Abrahamson, 1996). Two pivotal concepts in organization theory, 'structure' (defined as relationships which persist through time) and 'agency' (temporally embedded action), can only be understood with reference to time. Much of the research on which organization theory is based makes explicit assumptions about the relationship between time and the phenomenon of interest, most obviously when attempting attributions of causation.

Our experience of time is multilayered, in that we simultaneously live through and experience many different 'times'. As I write this, I am subject to an internalized time discipline that reflects a linear 'clock time' that I first learnt at school, and I anticipate that at the very least I will be at my desk for the '9–5' 'standard' working hours of industrial society. At the same time, I know that I will probably stop writing when diurnal rhythms suggest that it is time to eat or go to sleep. I am working at home as the cyclical rhythm of the academic year tells me that it is vacation time and that the 'clock time' discipline of term time may be relaxed. At home, work and social activity become intermingled in a 'task/social time', reminiscent of the pre-modern world evoked in Thompson's (1967) classic paper. I am aware that the shortest day of the year is approaching and that the season of darkness and midwinter is upon us, to be mediated by the feasts of Diwali/Chanukah/Christmas, when 'light' symbolically enters the world. If I venture into my formal workplace, this 'festival time' may tempt me to break away from my desk to indulge in some leisure time ('the Christmas lunch') in 'work hours' with colleagues. I know that time 'will go fast' if the writing flows and I become immersed in my argument. In this case 'task' time may prevail and I will ignore 'clock time' and work on into my 'leisure time' and 'night time'. If the writing does not go well, time will 'drag' and I may find myself 'clock watching' (if a Protestant work ethic prevails) or, guiltily, I may convert task time into social time. A phone call from a friend with the surprise news that a mutual colleague, at a university where I worked previously, is unexpectedly taking 'early' retirement, sends me reminiscing back to past times in a Proustian/Bergsonian stream of consciousness or *durée*. In contrast, the very notion of 'early retirement' suggests that different activities have different 'appropriate' durations and that career is a sequence of events rather than a flux. Although all that I experience is in the present, the present lacks meaning without the mediation of the past and the anticipation of the future (Mead, 1932/1980). Thus, as Adam (1990, 1995, 2004) has powerfully argued, there are a multiplicity of 'times' past, present and future that may be experienced simultaneously – 'my' experienced time, 'our' collective time and 'other' times of other societies weave together in a mutually implicated web (2004: chap. 1).

In this chapter, I wish to explore how our beliefs about the nature of 'objective' time (cyclical, event, task/social and linear time) and people's 'subjective' experience of time have been mutually implicated with corporate organization and organizing. In particular, I wish to examine how notions about time are implicit in our ideas about identity, control and resistance, through ideas about what time does to us and of what we do to time. I will base this discussion, first, on Adam's useful framework of the 'five Cs': the *creation* of time to human design, its *commodification, compression, control* and *colonization* (Adam et al., 2002; Adam, 2004). Second Foucault's image of a carceral society, where 'doing' time is common to careers in all institutions, will be employed to explore the role of time in identity creation and agency. In conclusion, the relevance of Adam's (1995) notion of a 'timescape' and Filipcove and Filipec's (1986) of 'spiral time' will be considered and methodological conclusions drawn for the study of organization.

Conceptualizing 'Objective' Time

In a sense, to speak of 'objective' time is a misnomer as all forms of categorization are social constructions. By 'objective' time it is generally meant those forms of time that are observable and measurable collectively, rather than being our personal constructions and individual experience of time. As such, four types of objective time may be identified: cyclical, task/social, event and linear 'clock' time.

Cyclical Time

All people are grounded in two major cycles, those of the natural seasons and their own life (Adam, 2004; Hassard, 1996). While the first is *experienced* as a repetitive cycle of seasonality, including diurnal rhythms of sleeping and waking and of menstruation, the second can only be *observed* as a repetitive cycle of birth, maturation, decay and death. For each individual it is necessarily experienced as a *linear* passage of time, except possibly in the notion of the 'second childhood'.

In pre-modern times, these cycles were even more evident than today, given dependency on agriculture, very limited artificial lighting and shorter human life cycles. Nevertheless, a form of seasonality still exists in modern organizations. First, the 'normal' working period, if under pressure from the 24/7 post-industrial society, is still seen as 'daytime', as any commuter will attest. Secondly, we still follow annual cycles of activity, some of which had their origins in the agricultural and religious event year: the tax and auditing year, the academic year, the annual pay increase and promotion round. Seasonality is linked too with the predictable, cyclical events of religious festivals and now secular holiday/leisure time: 'Sunday' – now the weekend – leisure time, Christmas, Easter, summer and half-term holidays.

The relationship between employment and the human life cycle is evidenced in conventional views about the appropriate time to gain promotion (particularly in bureaucracies) and when to retire. Witness the concept of 'early' retirement and the present uproar in the UK at the prospect of people's working lives being extended due to increased life expectancy and pension shortfalls. The idea of life cycle also surfaces in population ecologists' ideas about the 'survival of the fittest' in a population of firms, and in ideas about the obsolescence of product and organizational forms. Note, for example, claims about the 'death of bureaucracy', from the 1960s onwards, despite its remarkable resilience (e.g. Bennis, 1966; cf. Du Gay, 2000). The cycle is very evident too in our conception of flows of money ('the circuit of capital') and patterns of work (repetitive job and work cycle times).

Task/Social Time

The embedding of time in natural seasons was mirrored, in pre-modern times, according to Thompson (1967) and Ingold (1995), by its embeddedness in activities involving social relationships in which 'work' and social life were not clearly distinguished either temporally or spatially. Social activity was intertwined with cycles of the non-human environment, such as seasons, winds, tides, night and day, needs of animals and so on. This meant a lack of a standard working day or week. Work was marked by its irregularity, where the working day varied according to daylight hours and the season of the year. Intense activity (as at harvest time) might be followed by periods of relative inactivity with days of the week, such as 'St Monday', taken as leisure unless work was required. 'Work' comprised 'tasks' of use value (i.e., the production of useful objects/services) rather than exchange value (i.e., for exchange with other commodities, such as money). As such, work involved human skills and relationships that defined someone's personal and social identity and were part of the activity of the community. Sorokin and Merton (1937) label this as 'social' time, qualitative and heterogeneous, as compared to the homogeneous, abstract time of the modern period.

Although task/social time is conventionally identified with pre-modern times, it is by no means non-existent today. Members of traditional professional groups (medicine, law, academia) may perceive their work in terms of its use value just as much as its exchange value and their personal identities may be grounded in their occupation, its culture and status. Further, for many professionals, their work and social lives may be highly intertwined. This is particularly so where working hours are long due to a culture of task completion against deadlines and where there are high levels of interaction between colleagues. Freelance, self-employed workers (such as independent consultants), particularly when their office is home-based, may experience an intertwining of work and social life combined with an irregular/flexible pattern of working hours. Moreover, the pattern of women's work (part-time, job-sharing, flexible hours) is often the result of a need to combine employment with familial roles.

Event Time

Apart from predictable, cyclical events, time is perceived and evaluated by reference to traumatic, unpredictable events. At a societal level, the event may be a natural disaster (in the recent past, the 'Boxing Day tsunami', the Kashmiri earthquake, the flooding of New Orleans) or a war that impacted directly on people's daily lives or an event, such as '9/11', that called into question US taken-for-granted assumptions about 'the end of history' (Fukuyama, 1992). At organizational level, the event might be a major strike (e.g. the 1984 UK miners' strike), a takeover (e.g. Rupert Murdoch's takeover of the *Wall Street Journal*) or the advent of a new CEO (e.g. Iaccoca at Chrysler, Jack Welch at GEC or Archie Norman at Asda). While such events may be depicted as objective markers or standard reference points in the flow of time (pre-war, post-war, post-9/11), they are also constituted as dividing lines in the human experience and evaluation of ongoing life in a way that is contextually embedded. For example, while 'pre- (Second World) war' times might have been looked upon by the British aristocracy with nostalgia, my father's experience was one of unemployment, insecurity and poverty, greatly alleviated 'post-war' by Keynesianism and the welfare state.

Linear Time

This 'clock time' is the dominant conceptualization of time in the modern world – so dominant that to ask any adult in the industrialized world 'what is the time?' will provoke an automatic glance at a clock or watch. Whereas cyclical time is often presented as 'natural' or 'God-given', variable, context-dependent, encoded in being and becoming, linear, 'clock time', in contrast, is seen as artificial, abstract, invariable, external to and independent of the processes it measures (Adam et al., 2002: 12). As such, because it permeates organization, capitalism and globalization, it will be discussed in detail below. Suffice to say here that the linear imagery associated with clock time surfaced well before the Protestant ethic of modernity. The Christian myth is one of the mediation of finitude and death through God embracing human form and temporality and thereby providing a path to eternal life. In place of the 'archaic' 'myth of the eternal return', the *linear* progression of redemption and salvation is offered (Eliade, 1959). In this process, time is not to be wasted. In Dante's *Inferno*, Virgil reminds Dante that souls find themselves in Purgatory, not just on account of past sins of commission, but from sins of omission arising from the deadly sin of sloth, of not using 'your allotted time to best advantage' (Adam, 2004: 14). Well before the discipline of the factory, as Weber (1904–5/1989) points out, the Rule of St Benedict promoted a time-based, routinized ordering of monastic life aimed at freeing monks from natural impulses and keeping the Devil from making work for idle hands (Zerubavel, 1981: 33–4). Indeed, it was the fourteenth-century Benedictine, Richard of Wallingford who, as 'God's Clockmaker', is attributed with the invention of the first mechanical clock in the Western world (North, 2005). The mechanical clock overcame the limitations of sundials and water clocks (due to diurnality and climate) and, through allowing miniturization, portability and personal use, enabled an internalization of time discipline in Western Europe well before the industrial revolution (Adam, 2004: 113; Glennie and Thrift, 1996; cf. Thompson, 1967).

'Subjective' Time

'Subjective' time is our individual experience of time, our personal mental constructions of time. As such, in contrast to the homogeneity and equivalency of linear 'clock time', it is highly heterogeneous, discontinuous and nonequivalent. For example, time can be experienced both as static ('time stood still') and as flux ('an ever-rolling stream'), as long or short, fast or slow, as full of activity or as 'empty'.

From a social psychologist's perspective, time may be seen in terms of individuals' perceptions of the duration (long or short), pace (quick or slow) and intensity of activity (fullness or emptiness) (Starkey, 1989). In contrast to the concept of biological cycles as a measure of the perception of duration, Ornstein (1969) suggests that perceptions of duration are related to the size of the memory store used in processing information. All stimuli contain information, but new information takes more memory space to store. As a consequence, whereas familiar routines generate unreflective responses, novel experiences require more information processing and expand time relative to other times. Hence, a 'normal working week' is generally experienced as one where 'time flies' and one week rapidly merges into another. In contrast, a 'weekend break abroad', packed with new experiences, in its immediate aftermath, is experienced as longer than its chronological time. Yet, a week after the weekend break, the holiday no longer seems so long, as in memory the holiday experience becomes 'chunked' in more broad-brush terms. Similarly, time passes more quickly for the old than the young as most stimuli that older people process are no longer novel, whereas youth is a time of discovery. Also, the experience of duration, pace and intensity are interactive. Thus, time that is filled with activity passes quickly, unless experienced as qualitative underload and lacking true fullness, and empty time drags, unless perceived as a time of rest and relaxation (and hence having optimal fullness). Time that passes quickly appears shorter in duration than time that drags. Time may also appear longer or shorter if its duration is longer or shorter than we would ideally like.

Time may be experienced as constraining when individuals lack discretion and control over it. Although managers and professionals in the Western world often work longer hours than manual and white-collar staff, if they *freely choose* a workaholic lifestyle in a job that allows much discretion, they tend to exhibit less stress than subordinate grades who may not have the choice, nor the same control over their use of time. Individuals appear to experience stress when, with the time compression of clock time, the pace and fullness of time (speed and task overload) seem to be excessive and superimposed. This is particularly evident when a quantitative overload is combined with a qualitative underload as in the Fordist assembly lines. Nevertheless, time 'dragging' is perceived as equally undesirable. Classic ethnographic studies identify workers' preference for time 'to go fast' and their identification of different days of the working week as either 'fast' or 'slow' (Burawoy, 1979; Roy, 1960). As a result, game playing strategies and social activities are employed to speed up experiential time. Roy (1960) memorably recounts how a group of machine operators broke up the tedium of an objectively long working day (12 hours) and week (six days). This was achieved by regularly translating working time into social time through the enactment of social rituals ('banana time', 'peach time', window time', 'pick up time', 'fish time', 'coke time') in which identities outside the confines of the task could be constructed.

Conversely, there is much evidence that people find long periods of unstructured time to be debilitating, particularly if it is unlooked for and unwelcome. Jahoda's (1972, 1982) classic studies of long-term unemployment, where people had 'surplus' empty time, reveal psychological deterioration and anomie. Starkey, in analysing Jahoda's findings, puts this succinctly:

> The loss of work, and the rhythmic quality work gives to social life, impairs the time sense. Amongst the unemployed the watch loses its function as an organizing device, unpunctuality [sic] becomes the rule, plans for the future become more and more difficult to make, the individual becomes trapped in an endless present. (1989: 53)

This is also reported as the experience of long-term prisoners, where time 'is no longer a resource to be used, but rather an object to be contemplated – an undifferentiated landscape which has to be marked out and traversed' (Cohen and Taylor, 1992). Similarly, Roth (1963) shows how TB patients, faced with uncertainty about the length and course of their treatments and the need to manage indeterminate time, create their own timetables, based on the experience of other TB patients. Dissonance arises when such timetables, that invariably construct an optimistic scenario about the speed of recovery, clash with the doctors' more cautious medical timetables. The need to structure time by creating benchmarks or reference points appears to be part of the human condition.

As will be discussed below, where the purposefulness of a future orientation is eroded, identity itself is undermined.

The 'Five Cs' of Clock Time

The ascendancy of linear clock time in the developed world and particularly in employment relationships and the workings of capitalism is evident from personal experience quite apart from scholarship. In major contributions, Barbara Adam (1990, 1995, 2002, 2004; also Adam et al., 2002) has critically analysed how this came about and its implications for organizations and society in terms of '5 Cs': the *creation* of time to human design, its *commodification*, *compression*, *control* and *colonization*. In this section I will briefly summarize her arguments.

Time and Capitalism

The creation of linear 'clock time', discussed above, was a necessary condition for the development of capitalism, the factory system and globalization and, hence, is central to our understanding of Western economic and cultural organization.

The recognition of linearity through Christian notions of redemption carried with it some unfortunate baggage from the point of view of the development of capitalism – that time was a gift of God to the natural order, a collective good that could not be owned by individuals (Goff, 1980). Hence, time could not be commodified and usury was denounced as a sin.

For time to be commodified, as Adam (2002: 17) points out, two preconditions had to be fulfilled. First, usury had to be transformed from a sin into a virtuous act, in service of God, just as avoiding time-wasting needed to be converted to the more positive act of using time as productively as possible. Ironically, as a result of the pervasiveness of the Church, by the fourteenth century, the Benedictine time discipline had permeated countryside and markets, stimulating a rethinking on usury which was underwritten by Renaissance perspectivism and the Protestant Reformation. While perspectivism placed man at the centre of the universe, the Calvinist doctrine of justification by faith made it incumbent on the righteous to self-monitor their state of grace, lacking the fresh start afforded by confession in the Roman Catholic Church. A state of grace (via God's gift of faith) could be demonstrated by suppressing physical desires and enjoyment and exhibiting a life of 'rationally calculable action' (Adam, 2004: 43). This resulted in prioritizing the virtues of hard work and the accounting of every minute spent (to the glory of God). The Enlightenment and the associated rise of secularism allowed the disassociation of 'rationally calculable action' from its religiously inspired roots and fostered its embedding in the secular capitalism of modernity.

The second precondition for the commodification of time is that production had to shift from task-centred, context and situation specific use value to abstract exchange value. This shift underpinned three of the major institutions of modernity: capitalism, industrialism and surveillance (Giddens, 1990) and is implicated not only in the commodification of time, but in its control and compression.

Thus, capitalism's foundations of free markets and valorization of the process of accumulation assume that exchange value is represented by money. The exchange of something for money requires a third, context-independent, mediating value. 'Empty' clock time, abstracted from content and context, fulfils this function. Hence, Benjamin Franklin's much quoted observation that 'time is money' – that is, a valued *commodity*.

If 'time is money', profit is generated by using as little of it as possible to produce and sell products and services, thereby reducing the costs of labour, warehousing, machine running, interest payments, and so on. Because capitalism is about accumulation, the control of time becomes imperative and is achieved, first, through the factory system and the tightening of worker surveillance in the interests of labour intensification (Marglin, 1974). Thus, by separating 'work' time from 'home/leisure' time, time becomes a boundary condition that assists labour intensification through the elimination of the work irregularity associated with seasonality and the 'social time' of labour as use value (Thompson, 1967). Mumford's (1934: 14) famous comment that 'the clock, not the steam engine [was] the key machine of the industrial age' is apposite.

Second, using as little time as possible to complete any given work activity, may be seen as control through compression or the speeding up of activities within time in such a way that time itself seems to be speeded up (see section on 'Subjective Time'). This may be seen in the introduction of machinery of greater capacity and speed (e.g. the assembly line and mechanized handling in general), or in the redesign of work to optimize time saving (e.g. Taylorism and Fordism), or in using peaks and troughs more effectively (flexibalization) or by eliminating all 'wasted' time from the work process (just-in-time production and consumption and business process re-engineering), or a combination of these strategies (Adam, 2004: 128). Further, the clock's ability to synchronize disparate activity over time and space enabled the production planning, scheduling and coordination of the functional specialization that characterized the factory system and large scale industrial organization (Hassard, 1996). As Castells (1996: 439) put it, time is not just compressed, but *processed* in the interests of control.

It is not surprising then that time as a commodity became central to battles on the frontiers of control of the labour process, whether about the length and structure of the working day, week, year or working life, pace of work, break times, overtime, holiday entitlement and so forth. 'Not a minute on the day, not a penny off the pay' was *the* rallying cry of early trades unionism. Resistance to the discipline of clock time may also be seen in absenteeism, whether bodily or in the mental form of day-dreaming escapism (Cohen and Taylor, 1992).

Post-Industrialism

If modernity is characterized by the institutions of capitalism, industrialism and surveillance (among others), post-industrialism is generally considered to be moulded by intensified globalization enabled by information and communication technologies (ICTs) (Giddens, 1999). Globalization embodies some interrelated ideas such as 'accelerating interdependence' (Ohmae, 1989), 'action at a distance' (Giddens, 1990) and, importantly here, 'time–space compression' (Harvey, 1989) on a global scale. 'Accelerating interdependence' is understood to be the growing intensity of international enmeshment among national economies and societies, such that developments in one country impact directly on others. 'Action at a distance' refers to the way in which actions of social agents in one locale can come to have significant and unintended consequences for the behaviour of 'distant others'. 'Time–space compression' refers to the manner in which globalization appears to shrink geographical distance and time. In a world of near instantaneous communication, distance and time no longer seem to be major constraints on patterns of human organization and interaction.

Thus, following Adam et al. (2002) and Adam (2004), globalization has been enabled and stimulates colonization *with* time. That is, that 'clock time', along with industrialization, has become the 'normal' time of the urbanized, globalized world. Transport and trade lay at the heart of this development. When travel was slow, minor local variations in time were unimportant. When railways massively speeded up transport, standard times and time zones became necessary for co-ordinating national and international railway networks. In 1880 Britain adopted Greenwich Mean Time as the standard time across the UK. In 1883 North America instituted Standard Railway Time and in 1884 the International Meridian Conference agreed to standardize time across the world. Similarly, the development of marine chronometers in the eighteenth century, by enabling sailors to establish longitude and therefore safe navigation at sea, directly stimulated trade and empire building and, ultimately, global markets and the forerunners of our present-day multinationals. In 1913, when the Eiffel Tower transmitted the first wireless signal across the globe, world time was instituted. This world time, that underpins the global network of communication, whether of planes, wireless telegraph, telephones and ICTs, is central to the organization of world trade in goods and services, the media and government. 'Normal' time, worldwide, is now the abstract, uniform, time-zoned, 24-hour clock.

But late twentieth- and early twenty-first-century developments in electronic ICTs, Adam argues, have allowed an instantaneity and simultaneity that transcends this framework of world time. As Virilio (1991) puts it, 'real time' electronic communication is no longer part of chronological time, but is part of 'chronoscopic' time, where real space is making room for decontextualized 'real time' processes. This transition from sequence and duration, characteristic of linear time, requires the rethinking of taken-for-granted assumptions about clock time. For mechanical clock time to exist, it has to be measurable, as continuity is tracked through discontinuous oscillations, a duration between two points in time. Our speed of communication is now both instant, representing 'compression down to point zero' and simultaneous in that it offers the possibility for 'the supernatural power to be everywhere at once and nowhere in particular' (Adam et al., 2002: 19). This might be compatible with quantum physics, but is incompatible with the Newtonian world of duration and causality that we subjectively experience. But, in theory, people located anywhere with internet contact can communicate in real time with others similarly networked, blurring cause and effect relations and rendering obsolete control systems associated with clock time (e.g. office hours), even if potentially enabling the new controls implicit in 'ever-accessibility' (Bell and Tuckman, 2002). Indeed, both Poster (1990: 3) and Bauman (1998: 58) have argued that this intense level of interconnectivity makes social networks more fragile and less amenable to control. The world becomes more unpredictable and volatile in the light of the paradox of unintended consequences and as time for reflection between cause and effect is lost.

Virilio (1991), for example, has recognized this paradox of consequences in his so-called 'dromological law' [dromosphere = sphere of beings in motion]. That is, that increases in transport speed increase the potential for gridlock. 'Real-time' communication, in practice, loses instantaneity and simultaneity as people become overloaded and bogged down in a superfluity of information that their human sequential information processing mode cannot cope with. In other words, chronoscopic time jars against not only chronological time, but importantly against the embodied and contextualized cyclical rhythms that real people experience in their daily lives.

Further, in theory at least, the established strategies of modern management may lose their potency. Thus, when communication is almost instantaneous and distance 'shrunk', acceleration is no longer the source of competitive advantage that it once was, if all competitors are able to effect the same economies. This is the route of 'competing to the bottom', and fails to secure the margins that the accumulation process seeks (Adam et al., 2002: 22).

Additionally, there is colonization and control *of* time, whereby the 'natural' cycles of day and night, of cold and hot seasons are colonized by 'artificial' power sources, to lighten darkness, heat the cold and air-condition the heat. In the industrialized and, even more so, in the post-industrialized world, we now live in a '24/7' environment where all work and consumption, instead of following the rhythms of the natural world, are never ceasing and speeded up. Las Vegas is iconic in all these respects. The temporal divisions of day and night can be overridden in the interests of capitalism and consumer preference. But if this reverts to a mechanical, indeed, Newtonian, conception of time and space, capitalism, combined with science, has allowed the colonization of the future (Adam, 2004).

The argument is this. Capitalism is future-oriented and rests on the belief that the future can be regulated, exploited and designed in and for the present. It focuses on systems of credit, on share prices rising or falling on projections of future profits, on investment with the expectation of future returns and so forth. The trade in stock market futures, which was estimated at $18 trillion in 1999, equalled the entire stock of fixed capital in the world at that time (Adam et al., 2002: 21). This adds to the subjective experience of a 'runaway world' (Giddens, 1999) as futures trading – bets on future stock market and currency prices, interest rates, etc. – is trading in time that creates wealth on the basis of volatility. But, as Adam points out, the future is understood with reference to the threats or benefits it offers for the *present* – it makes 'parasitic' use of the future. It borrows from the future to finance the present or protects against future disasters through savings and insurance. Novotny (1989/1994) characterizes this as an 'extended present', as the future is thought about, protected and organized in terms of the present. The failure of the industrializing and post-industrialized world to sacrifice present consumption and development in return for protecting future generations' ecosphere, against global warming on the one hand and nuclear power on the other, are obvious examples of the future being sacrificed to the present. The same might be said of the inherent short-termism of liberal market economies wedded to globalized capitalism.

An extreme expression of the colonization of time is the idea that humans may develop into cyborgs via protheses provided by xenotransplantation and nanotechnology. While these ideas are speculative, as Adam suggests, we can already see how change in nature can be massively speeded up through genetic modification of plants and animals and, potentially, through cloning experimentation. Further, genetic material that has existed from the beginning of time, in its modified state, is now the material that will exist into the future, with unknown and uncontrollable effects. While this colonization of the future is achieved on the basis of objective, abstract time, its unintended consequences will be experienced in people's embodied and subjective time.

The '6th' C: Career In and Out of Organization

Foucault (1979) famously observed that we live in a carceral world where 'prisons resemble factories, schools, barracks, hospitals' (1979: 83). Just as in prisons, so in our carceral world we 'do time' in the embrace of organizations with which we are enmeshed (e.g. Roth, 1963; Sennett, 1998). 'Doing time' is central to establishing our identity or identities in the eyes of others and ourselves and disciplinary practices, from parental socialization through guilt-making, to the self-examination induced by failing to consume as the media defines as appropriate, mould our subjectivity. The work of 'doing time' in formal and informal, socially sanctioned or deviant organizations normally involves enacting a 'career' over time. The concept of a 'career' may enable individuals to reinterpret the exercise of disciplinary practices (and associated labour intensification) as 'benevolent aids to career development', as support to the project of establishing a successful work identity (Grey, 1994: 494).

Throughout people's lives, rooted in physiology, there is the notion of time-related growth and development, before the inevitability of decay and death. Calendars and timetables are used to categorize and locate what counts as 'normal' development, indeed, a 'normal' life or career. In the developed world, children are measured for physical, intellectual and social skills growth on a regular basis, even before entering school. Schools themselves are regulated by calendars and timetables on a daily, termly, and annual basis, teaching students from an early age not only an understanding of linear clock time, but to recognize that certain hurdles have to be negotiated sequentially at times deemed appropriate by those in authority. There is the graduation from junior to senior school, examinations, transition to further/higher education or to employment, at fixed points in time. Implicit in this time-sequenced array of activities is the notion of progression dependent on norms of achievement for different age groups and within age groups. Within a cohort, above average students in terms of attributed 'leadership' or intellectual ability may be promoted to 'prefect' (or even 'Head Girl' or 'Head Boy') or win scholarships to prestigious universities at the appropriate time. This mirrors the hierarchical and performativity oriented world of employment that they will encounter as adults. Success or failure (as evaluated by hierarchical observation and normalizing judgement) are likely to result in self-fulfilling attributions, through the process of examination.

Just as with 'time', 'career' may be viewed from an objective or subjective perspective. In the world of legitimate employment, from an objective perspective, 'career' traditionally meant a sequence of jobs, arising from bureaucratic structure and organizational strategic choices in the light of perceived market opportunities and constraints. It contained assumptions about progression up a hierarchy, a lifetime's employment within one organization/profession/industry with concomitant enhanced pay and responsibility. As such, it resonated with modernist imagery associated with speed, movement and a linear progression up the hierarchy through the survival of the fittest: 'fast track', 'high flyer', 'career ladder', the 'tournament' model/'sink or swim' (Newell, 2000). The very word 'career' came from the Latin for chariot racing and as a verb in English means to move swiftly or wildly. The connotations of such imagery are that success is defined as winning and getting to the top as quickly as possible. Even today, this is the conventional use of the term, although, with moves towards decentralized flexible organization, delayering, downsizing and greater job insecurity, the idea of 'portfolio careers', of frequent movement between employers, with spells alternating between employment, self-employment (freelancing) and non-employment (sabbatical as househusband or wife, or in order to travel, or engage in self-development) is gaining currency (Handy, 1995). The concept of 'portfolio careers' links well with Arthur et al.'s (1989) subjectivist definition of career as 'the evolving sequence of a person's experiences over time'. The imagery here is more associated with task/social time, with an emphasis on 'career anchors' (that are not necessarily about climbing the hierarchy, but may be about technical/professional competence, security and stability, autonomy and independence, innovation and creativity), 'work–life balance', developing a 'life-narrative' (Schein, 1978; Sennett, 1998).

Different concepts of time are embedded in current issues about careers. Edwards and Wajcman (2005) report that many people are said to subjectively experience 'time squeeze' or 'time poverty' as a result of the effects of objective time compression occurring in work organizations and its mismatch with the timescapes of leisure and family life, eroding 'work–life balance'. Further, it is evident that women's life-cycle patterns of childbearing are at odds with the time trajectories of developing a conventional managerial career that are geared to a man's life-cycle.

Although, in aggregate, hours at work in the developed world have not increased over the last 30 years (and, indeed declined over the last century), their distribution has changed. With the rise of the service sector economy, neo-liberal market deregulation, and the intensification of competition over the last three decades, several trends have emerged. First, there is a polarization of working time between those working very long hours and those who work few or no hours (Edwards and Wajcman, 2005: 47). Second, the number of people on part-time, casual or fixed-term contracts has increased (Cully et al., 1999). Third, many people working 'full-time' feel pressurised to work very long hours (often on unpaid overtime or 'time off in lieu') to show commitment in a world of perceived greater job insecurity ('presenteeism') (Vielba, 1995). Fourth, while women overall are contributing more hours to employment, men overall are contributing less (due to sectoral changes in employment) (Edwards and Wajcman, 2005: 47). Partly for these reasons and partly due to women's liberation and demands for self-fulfilment in work outside the home, combined with rising aspirations concerning consumption, dual earner households are now the norm. It is such *households* that are now contributing more hours to employers than ever before, especially if each partner works full-time (Edwards and Wajcman, 2005: 47). However, given the 24/7 economy, many of these hours are at unsocial times (evenings and weekends) and this is particularly true of women in the service sector (and especially single parents), juggling their day around child care provision.

How these enhanced and mismatched hours are experienced depends on the identities individuals seek and prioritize (Collinson and Collinson, 1997). If the identity of 'sharing partner' and 'caring parent' is important, the present length and pattern of employment hours can be seriously inhibiting, as the greedy organization eats into family and leisure time. Although both male and female parents now devote more time to childcare than three decades ago, the proportional rise in the time men spend in housework reflects the reduction of women's time as a result of their increased participation in the labour force, rather than any great increase in male activity on non-childcare tasks (Edwards and Wajcman, 2005: 53). Thus, the desire to be a 'super mother and wife', while simultaneously pursuing a conventional professional career in a long hours culture, ironically, can reflect and reinforce the globalization of linear time. This is because Third World women and migrant labour are encouraged to enter the globalized economy of substitute domestic labour and fast food production (Edwards and Wajcman, 2005: 59). Ironically, too, while such professional career women may be able to negotiate more flexible hours (if at the cost of slower organizational career advancement), women without recognized employment skills, generally speaking, are only able to achieve the flexibility offered by unsocial hours and part-time employment. There is the further irony that one coping strategy for 'time squeeze' is the adoption of Taylorist techniques of linear clock time to organize home life: 'even "quality time" with children is compartmentalized and rationalized, lived in a quasi-industrial way' (Edwards and Wajcman, 2005: 52). Further, time compression also enters the home in the form of labour/time saving devices, including convenience foods.

Nevertheless, the traffic is not all one way. Working hours may be a time when individuals can develop a sense of identity and achievement through the exercise of competence in challenging, interesting and highly rewarded work with close, congenial colleagues providing emotional satisfactions to boot. In such circumstances, some people (mainly men?) may *choose* to spend long hours at work rather than engage in potentially stressful, time pressured family life (Hochschild, 1997).

In Conclusion: Timescapes and Spiral Time

This chapter has focused on the different ways in which we might think about time in relation to organization and has focused on the creation of time to human design, its commodification, compression, control and colonization. It has also explored the role of time in identity creation.

That time is a concept central to organization theory there can be no doubt. The two concepts that underpin organization theory and that surface repeatedly in this book – structure and agency or action – are embedded in assumptions about the role of time. Structure, by definition, persists through time and constitutes the constraining and enabling conditions of action. Action, embedded in structure, is informed by the past, situated in the present and oriented towards the future. Action, over time, changes structure through the iterative processes of 'structuration' (Giddens, 1979). Without memory of the past or the capacity to envision a future, identity is eroded and, with it, the meaning of present time and the stimulus to action.

One problem encountered in the discussion of time in organization theory is the tendency, consistent with a positivistic epistemology, to analyse it in simplistic Cartesian dualistic terms (Adam, 1995: chap. 7). This takes two forms. First, we dichotomize (quite apart from the objective/subjective distinction) and then categorize simplistically. Thus, linear time is often contrasted with cyclical time, clock time with task time, decontextualized time with embedded time, the former term in the binary pair then being associated with modernizing and the latter with traditional societies. (Note, too, in Derridean terms that the former term is invariably privileged.) Yet we know from our own experience, as outlined in the introduction, that different 'times' can be experienced co-terminously and almost simultaneously. Equally, in analysing research on 'modern' organizations, many concepts of time are relevant. Although modern time may rest on the linear associations of material accumulation, the cyclical image of time is not lost. Accumulation also implies the repetitive *circuit* of capital. Workers subject to 'objective' time control and compression have strategies of resistance to 'beat the clock', to 'make time' or 'save time' in order to engage in activities associated with 'social' time and/or to shorten experiential 'subjective' time. What is evident in Roy's (1960) famous account of 'banana time' is the repetitive, cyclical enactment of rituals designed to obliterate the monotony of intensified work in linear time, through the construction of 'social' time, in which identities outside the confines of the task could be constructed.

Second when analysing conceptions of time held by societies different from our own, there is a tendency to use Western conceptions of time as the non-problematized benchmark against which such 'other' times might be conceptualized (Adam, 1995: 31–4). The nature of time in such societies is configured in terms of how it *differs* from Western linear time, without the necessary reflexivity about the nature of the researchers' own Western taken-for-granted assumptions around the nature of time. In a comparably imperialistic/chauvinist manner, work that is not easy to fit into a clock time structure (e.g. 'caring' activities) or which does not conventionally feature in countries' economic accounting structure (Third World subsistence farming, unpaid housework and child rearing), that is, work that is usually performed by women, is rendered invisible and non-valuable (Adam, 2002).

One way to avoid these pitfalls is explicitly to recognize and deconstruct the multifaceted nature of time and the mutual interrelatedness of our own subjective time, our collectively shared time and, in a globalized and gendered world, to seek some reflexive understanding of 'other' time. Adam (2004: 144) suggests that a useful analytical tool is the notion of a 'timescape' – comprising temporal features of life that are contextually embedded, inseparable from space or matter. A timescape includes ideas about *time frames* (days, years, eras); *temporality* (process, irreversibility, impermanence); *tempo* (pace, intensity of activity); *timing* (synchronization, *kairos*); *time point* (moment, juncture); *time patterns* (rhythmicity, periodicity, cyclicality); *time sequence* (series, cause and effect, simultaneity); *time extensions* (duration, continuity); and *time past, present and future* (horizons, memory, anticipation). All are mutually implicated.

Filipcove and Filipec (1986) have likened time to a spiral, represented as a coiled snake. The snake biting its tail represents the mutual dependence but antagonism between the two dominant concepts of cyclicality and linearity. It also represents the tension between change and continuity. In Burrell's (1992) adoption of this image there is recognition that movement along the spiral involves progression, continuity and reversal, such that organizational forms of the past, which may appear anachronistic at one turn of the spiral, may be resurrected at a future twist. Blyton and Turnbull (1994: 298), reflecting on the continuities and changes in employment relations in the 1980s and early 1990s, make a similar point: 'Nothing changes yet everything is different: as we twist round the spiral of capitalist economic development we experience progression and return, never a return to exactly the same point but always to a place that is familiar'.

'Time', apparently the most widely used noun in the English language (Adam, 1995: 19), lends itself to metaphor and perhaps it is through metaphor and deconstruction that this concept's relevance to organization is best explored – certainly from the perspective of a postmodern 'linguistic turn'. But time and tide dictate that such an exploration is for a future essay and a different text.

6

GLOBALIZATION

Glenn Morgan

Introduction

The concept of 'globalization' conjures up images of large-scale macro-changes that emerge from forces that seem beyond human control. 'Globalization' can be seen as something from outside that forces societies, organizations, localities and individuals to change their traditional patterns of action. To examine globalization as an everyday phenomenon of organizations is therefore something of a challenge. It suggests shifting from macro-discussions of trade flows, economic competition, multinational firms towards a focus on how we experience globalization, how we interpret that experience, how that affects our behaviour and how we organize under these new conditions. From this perspective, globalization is not a state of 'being' but rather a process of 'becoming' which is uneven, diverse and multi-faceted, affecting many aspects of our everyday life.

This chapter is divided into three sections that reflect this concern with the impact of globalization on everyday life. In the first section, I provide a conceptual framework in which the distinctive processes of globalization in the current period are defined in terms of an increased interdependency between social actors over a global scale. The rest of the chapter is devoted to an analysis of how this interdependency is revealed in the everyday experience of work and life. Two particular aspects are examined. First, the chapter examines how the current form of global economic processes constitute and shape the everyday experience of social actors inside and outside work, as both employees and consumers, through the restructuring of firms, processes and consumption. The second part examines the way in which social actors themselves develop what has been described as 'globalization from below'. This refers to new forms of interdependency that arise from the movement of peoples across national boundaries.

Globalization and the New Interdependencies

It is a common truism that globalization is nothing new. Internationalization has occurred before and this is simply an intensification of internationalization processes following their decline in the period between the two world wars. Hirst and Thompson (1999), for example, argued that finance was more international at the end of the nineteenth century than it was in the 1990s. There had long been patterns of trade across the large Eurasian land mass (the silk route that took Marco Polo from Venice to China) and across the seas (round the Cape of Good Hope to India and the Spice Islands as well as across the Atlantic to the New World) (Chanda, 2007). In the nineteenth century, India (with tea, cotton and opium) and China (with tea and porcelain) (see Hobson, 2004; Morgan, 1985) were already integrated into the international economy. It is estimated that in the eighteenth-century slave trade between Africa and the Americas six million people were forcibly transported across the Atlantic. International 'voluntary' migration peaked in the late nineteenth century when Europeans migrated in their millions to the Americas, Australasia and parts of Africa, whilst in the immediate aftermath of World War II large numbers of displaced persons and refugees moved across newly formed international boundaries (Therborn, 2000). The transfer of legal and educational systems that occurred within the European empires of the nineteenth century and led to imitation and copying elsewhere, such as Japan, was probably the largest international diffusion of such systems ever to take place. Consumers and artists discovered the styles of Africa, China, Japan and India in the nineteenth century, transferring them into architecture, opera, painting, sculpture and furniture (Bayley, 2004). The nineteenth and early twentieth centuries also saw the rise of the first multinationals, companies such as Tate and Lyle (with its sugar plantations around the world) and Anglo-American Mining (with its gold, silver, copper and platinum mines spread across southern and eastern Africa), oil companies such as Shell, BP and Standard Oil, Unilever (with its dominant position in the manufacture and sale of tea), and the United Fruit Company that dominated the importing of fruit into the USA from Central and Latin America for many years.

These arguments are important reminders that it is necessary to be specific about what is different in the current era. There are two aspects to this. The first and most obvious aspect is that of scale. When the concept of 'globalization' is used, the scale which is being invoked as relevant to social action is the world itself. Obviously there are scales which continue to exist and are folded into the 'global', e.g. regional, national, local, etc., however, a global scale points to interconnections that are planetary in scope (see Scholte, 2005). Globalization relates therefore to the process of both temporal and spatial compression in which action can be instantaneous across geographical space, thus enabling 'global' geography to be meaningful to actors. This has also been described in terms of the social horizon which has relevance for actors. The transformation of this horizon from the local, the regional, the national, the continental, through to the global implies that social actors see themselves in a new light as participants in this global order (see also the discussions in Ong and Collier (2005) on what they term 'global assemblages'). Beck identifies globalization as a process in which 'the world horizon opens up' (Beck, 2000: chap. 1).

This process is easier to identify in some organizational arenas than others. In financial markets, for example, actors in different parts of the world can interact through the medium of the screen that displays buy and sell prices and enables the settlement of deals electronically, in theory at any time, between actors located in any geographical space (Knorr Cetina and Bruegger, 2002; Knorr Cetina and Preda, 2005). Many multinationals have real-time information systems which enable the monitoring of activities in any part of the world; such systems also communicate with suppliers, altering quantities and specifications of orders on a real-time basis. Information and communication technologies sustain linkages across global space enabling the coordination and diffusion of new forms of production and consumption (Castells, 1996).

The scale of social action is reinforced by the second feature of globalization which concerns the idea of interdependency. The credit crunch of summer 2007 began because of fears about the ability of borrowers in the US sub-prime housing market to pay off their loans. Banks which had bought securitized assets consisting of bundles of such loans found that they were worth much less than previously believed. They therefore started to refuse to roll over these bonds, i.e. renew them after their expiry date (often 6 months from issue), leaving institutions which depended on such a roll-over technically bankrupt as they now had to pay back the total sum. One of the many consequences of this was the first run on a British financial institution (the Northern Rock building society) for over 100 years. It also brought an end to a period of easy borrowing for companies and speculative investors such as those dealing in hedge funds and private equity. This in turn resulted in the collapse of a range of major financial deals across the US, the UK and Asia. The global financial system is linked together such that events in one part will invariably impact on all the other parts even if the nature of the impact is different depending on domestic circumstances.

Interdependency is not confined to financial markets. This is most obviously the case in terms of raw material products like oil where the impact of the destruction of Kuwait in the first Gulf War and the more long-term subsequent closure of Iraq as a source has both pushed up prices and raised issues about the security of access to oil. The rise of China has pushed up energy and metal prices across the world as it has stoked up demand for these basic necessities. China has also become a central node in manufacturing trade, exporting vast amounts of goods to the USA and Europe. The extended period of relatively low inflation in these countries has derived significantly from falling prices of basic manufacturing goods that are increasingly produced in China. The advanced industrial economies are increasingly dependent on China for the momentum in their own economies, whilst China's growth is dependent on the continued openness of these markets. Closure on either side for political or economic reasons would have drastic impacts. One of the clearest demonstrations which we now acknowledge of global interdependency is climate change. The impact of global warming affects not just those countries which produce greenhouse gases but all other countries as well. All social actors are affected by this; no society, group or individual can escape the effects of global warming. Similarly, a solution to the problem cannot be achieved by one or more countries acting alone. A transplanetary solution that recognizes interdependence between societies is the only possible option.

The interdependency which is created has two sides to it. One is a negative side, the other is positive. In negative terms, interdependency creates risk that often cannot be understood or predicted in advance, for example where the effect of global warming is going to be at its most acute at particular times. Similarly, the risks which have emerged are at such a global level that only global action offers a chance of resolving them, a situation in which the individual feels powerless. Thus, the global society is a 'risk society' (Beck, 2000; Giddens, 1999). In our everyday lives we are living with these risks and their potential impact on our health, our employment, our way of life. But interdependence also has positive sides. In economic and consumption terms, it means that there is a global division of labour which in principle if not in practice enables people to benefit from the comparative advantages of specialization. Consumption expands as specialized production cheapens the price of particular goods and services. In broader terms, interdependence reduces the homogeneity of societies and increases diversity that contributes to cultural change and processes of hybridity, allowing new social and cultural forms to emerge (see Hannerz, 1996 for an anthropological discussion of hybridity). Such processes undermine traditional social relations and have led to powerful counter-movements, particularly in the Islamic world and the broader 'clash of civilizations' (Huntingdon, 1996). They can also be interpreted as diffusing a particularly American version of modernity, one that does not just undermine tradition but seeks to negate other models of modernity in favour of the McDonaldization of the world, a shift from what Ritzer labels 'something' to 'nothing', from diversity to homogeneity and sameness (Ritzer, 2004).

Globalization and Economic Interdependency

Economic interdependency can be viewed from two interrelated perspectives. First, it refers to the creation of global value chains whereby components and processes are produced and processes organized in different parts of the world based on calculations regarding cost, quality, regulations, market access and government support. Second, economic interdependency is reflected in processes of consumption and their basis in a global division of labour and the unequal rewards derived from it.

Global Value Chains

This idea incorporates first the disaggregation of the value chain, second its dispersion geographically and third its coordination in new ways (see Dicken, 2006 for an extended discussion of different forms of global value chains; also Gereffi, 1996, 2001, 2005; Gereffi and Korzeniewicz, 1994; Kenney with Florida, 2004).

Disaggregation of the value chain refers to the way in which a production process is split up into its component parts, each of which is analysed in detail in order to identify the most appropriate way in which it can be organized and the most appropriate location. Locational possibilities have multiplied as transport costs have cheapened, tariff barriers have declined and regulatory barriers have been dismantled. The dialectical relationship between the large-scale organizers of these processes, mostly multinationals from the developed economies, and the potential suppliers in low-wage areas (which in turn may be small family-based firms or increasingly large-scale companies in their own right) creates a dynamic of relocation, built on reorganizing the production process into modules, segments and different value added activities. China has become one of the most important sub-contractors for all standardized manufacturing because of its low wage costs (Hamilton, 2006). India has become the site of contractors specializing in call centre services for the US and the UK and software services for the world, primarily because of the English language skills of employees, their education, their technical skills in certain areas and the not unimportant fact that these skilled employees are much cheaper to employ than their counterparts in Europe, the US and Japan. Other economies compete to attract international capital and multinationals into their locations. Furthermore, this flow of activities is not simply from developed countries to developing ones. It can also be between developed countries, as Multinational Corporations (MNCs) move part of their operations to regions that have strong positive agglomeration effects, for example research and development facilities into Silicon Valley in the US or Silicon Fen in Cambridge, UK, or into the Boston-MIT biotech system (Kenney, 2000). More recently Research and Development (R&D) investment has also started to flow out of developed countries to developing ones, for example the decision of Novartis, the Swiss pharmaceutical company, to make Shanghai in China its third major R&D hub along with Basle (its home base) and Cambridge, Massachusetts.

In his book *The World is Flat* (2005), the US journalist, Tom Friedman illustrates these processes through examining the production of his own Dell computer. He describes the various 'modules' of his computer – the microprocessor, the memory, the cooling fan, the motherboard, the keyboard, the LCD display, the wireless card, the modem, the battery, the hard disk drive, the CD/DVD drive, the notebook carrying bag, the power adaptor, the power cord and the removeable memory stick – as well as all the elements required to facilitate action and transaction (the phone ordering, the construction of the single ordered computer with its specific and potentially unique configuration, the loading of the software, the packaging and labelling of the item for transportation). Friedman describes this as 'the supply chain symphony' and argues that it is 'one of the wonders of the flat world' (Friedman, 2005: 417). He reports that, 'The total supply chain for my computer, including suppliers of suppliers, involved around four hundred companies in North America, Europe, and primarily Asia, but with thirty key players' (Friedman, 2005: 419).

An obvious question which emerges from this process of disaggregation is how is it coordinated and managed? In traditional terms, what has emerged is partly market-based, partly firm-based and partly network-based (Powell, 2001). In market terms, many of the contracts are based on a price set and agreed between the companies. Some of the contracts may be purely internal between subsidiaries where price is determined through processes of internal accounting. Some of the contracts may be network based in the sense of consisting of durable and flexible relationships between firms that are not simply market and price based – what is known as 'relational contracting'. What becomes crucial here is the effectiveness of these relationships which in turn is measured through a variety of benchmarks, for example profitability, performance, etc. Benchmarks become the means whereby senior managers judge whether a particular site or a particular mode of coordination is worth sustaining. This in turn becomes a means of engaging in 'coercive comparisons' (Mueller, 1996; Mueller and Purcell, 1992) whereby employees are warned that their performance is below the benchmark and unless they work faster/harder/cheaper, production will be moved elsewhere.

A different question, however, from the point of view of the experience of globalization is what does it mean to work in one of these global value chains? A number of aspects can be considered. First is the question of time – what may be called the contrast between local time and global time. In global financial markets, for example, over a 24-hour period, Tokyo opens first, followed by London and then New York and then for the next day back to Tokyo, etc. Dealers in the market live in a form of global time (Knorr Cetina and Bruegger,

2002). They arrive well before the market opens in order to find out what has gone on in the market that is just closing and to take tips from their colleagues in other locations about what is emerging. They stay well after their own market closes in order to inform their colleagues in the opening market about what they have learnt and to tie up any loose ends in their dealing. Call centre operators in India are similarly on global time. Their shifts reflect the regions with which they are working. In Indian terms, they start late and finish late in order to be present during UK or US working hours and immediately after. This shift pattern undermines family and friendship commitments, making it more difficult to maintain contact due to work pressures. A similar disengagement from the local culture also occurs as call centre operators are shown TV programmes from the US and the UK in order to enable them to recognize and understand cultural references that may come up in the course of a conversation with a customer (Mirchandani, 2004; Taylor and Bain, 2004).

Another aspect of coordinating global value chains is the amount of travelling that senior managers have to do in order to keep abreast of what is going on in various parts of their business. Although it is possible for information to be electronically and instantaneously transferred, this does not substitute for or undermine the necessity of face-to-face dealings. The more complex the issue, the more necessary such face-to-face contact becomes in order to create common and shared understandings of problems and possible solutions. A recent study of a merger within the relatively narrow confines of Scandinavia found that one of the most obvious impacts was the increased length of the day for managers arising from the fact that they had to spend a lot of time outside their home office coordinating with new colleagues in other countries (Soderberg and Vaara, 2003). A related consequence of this was pressure on family life and a disillusionment amongst women managers in particular who felt that what was happening was making it difficult for them to sustain their work–life balance which had traditionally been an important consideration in the Scandinavian context.

As well as the managers of manufacturing multinationals, this creates a globally mobile workforce in areas where service is customized and complex, for example law, consultancy, some aspects of auditing and accounting, architecture, engineering, etc. Often these travellers touch down in what have been termed 'global cities', which consist of an agglomeration of businesses, capital markets, professional services, regulators and political actors, often networked more intensely with other global cities in other countries than with other cities inside the country, for example in the area of financial markets (Sassen, 2006; Taylor, 2004). These global cities attract and generate wealth in the context of a form of hybridized cosmopolitanism; they are underpinned by shared values of conspicuous consumption reflected in architecture, the arts, fashion, culture, the media and entertainment (Massey, 2007).

Finally, it can be suggested that what this creates is a high level of uncertainty and risk for individuals as firms undergo frequent and rapid restructuring of their global value chains in response to market conditions. In the introduction to his book *The Corrosion of Character* (1999), Richard Sennett describes how he met on a plane the son of one the people who had participated in his earlier study (with Cobb) *'The Hidden Injuries of Class'* (1993). The 'Hidden Injuries' was concerned with people trapped in jobs that were unfulfilling, tedious, hard and boring. Resistance in so far as it was expressed emerged through minor acts of industrial sabotage and joining trade unions. Outside work, people lived in stable and fixed communities, which were often traditional and conservative with an undertone of frustrated violence, in the family and on the streets. However, community life outside work also offered some people the chance to develop personal dignity that was denied them in work by participating in family life and voluntary activities, in politics, sports, religion, etc. The son whom Sennett meets, is an executive, better educated than his father, with much higher earnings and a job in which responsibility and authority is exercised. But the son has had a number of different employers and jobs as his companies have downsized or restructured. In order to stay in the managerial labour market, the son has had to move his family to a number of different parts of the US and has never put down any roots in one locality. Community ties and community activities are limited, leading to what Putnam has described as the 'Bowling Alone' culture where instead of playing in teams with workmates, or friends from local churches and sports teams, people play alone as part of the only strong social grouping remaining – the nuclear family (Putnam, 2000), though even this is increasingly under strain as divorce rates rise – often due to the pressures of this style of life. The son of Sennett's original interviewee lives his life in a continual state of uncertainty, never knowing how global competition and the response of his company is going to affect his employment prospects. In these conditions of globalization, the 'glittering prizes' of large, even huge, income and wealth beckons to the many in a way in which it never previously has done. To engage with this, however, is to sacrifice stability, to place personal and family life as a lesser priority, and to commit to long hours and frequent travel – without ever gaining any certainty that everything will not be snatched away by the forces of global competition.

Consumption and Economic Interdependency

The economic interdependency of work relations is mirrored by interdependence in the domain of consumption. Three themes need to be explored; the first relates to how consumption is stimulated by the production of ever cheaper commodities and services generated by the process of globalization. The second relates to the centrality of global brands in this process and the effects and risks which emerge from these. The third theme relates back to the issues of individualism and social context discussed in the previous section.

Globalization in the current period has had a fundamental impact on consumption through the creation of economies of scale and the resulting cheapening of prices. Across a wide range of standardized consumer products – clothes, TVs, videos, DVD players and recorders, computers, mobile phones, toys, cars, furniture – the disappearance of regulatory barriers has led to the potential for large economies of scale and subsequent price stability, if not price reductions in some sectors of the market. For example, the price of video recorders dropped from around £300 in the early 1980s to around £40 in the mid 2000s whilst the quality of the picture and the addition of functions has upgraded the machine. Location of production has moved from Japan, the USA and Western Europe into parts of Eastern and Central Europe and China. The price of low-value clothes has also fallen dramatically as production has shifted to China and other countries in Asia, such as Bangladesh, Vietnam, Laos, Cambodia and Indonesia (Rivoli, 2005). These price movements in standardized products enable an expansion of consumption either into more of the same, for example more clothes per person, more TVs and videos per householder, or into new areas, for example into new personal service areas such as health club membership, more visits to restaurants and cinemas, private healthcare, etc. Moreover this expansion of consumption can occur with only modest increases in wages and salaries.

This process is also associated with the establishment of global brands that become key in adding value to products and enable firms to extract higher value from the production process. Brands that are recognizable in a global context, for example Coke, Microsoft, Sony, Nike, maintain this through continual advertising and marketing in diverse national markets. The brand itself, however, becomes interdependent with the firm, its activities and its customers over a wide range of contexts (Goldman and Papson, 1998; Klein, 2000). It becomes vulnerable to negative publicity such as that which has been directed at Nike on a number of occasions when its suppliers have been discovered using unauthorized child labour or factories without adequately implemented safety regulations (Carty, 1997). Nike can produce shoes through its sub-contractors and its global value chain at a very low cost whilst selling them high by transfixing consumers with the value of the brand.

Finally, and related to this, is the way in which consumption inserts itself in the massification of society discussed earlier. The idea of individualism is reinforced and reproduced by the act of consumption in which individuals are encouraged to create their own selves through purchasing particular objects and styles of objects. Of course, this all takes place within the proliferation of lifestyle, class and age segmentation categories that have been created and formalized by marketing departments and consultancies. So ultimately there is no individualism *per se* achieved through the act of consumption, rather a making up (the creation of a bricolage) of a self within categories pre-defined by others as the basis for personal identity. Marxist critics would argue that consumption is the cloak with which individuals cover the emptiness of their lives at work and outside. What Marx termed 'commodity fetishism' is rampant under globalization as people attach themselves, however provisionally or tangentially, to brands and things, as a way of giving meaning to their lives and identity to themselves. In a globalized environment, a proliferation of identity markers from different societies becomes available, sometimes as commercial products and entrepreneurial opportunities, sometimes as informal lifestyle imitation and adaptation processes. This hybridization creates new products and lifestyles that are transnational in form, for example the creation of 'balti' as an 'Anglo-curry' dish by Indian people living in the UK or the development of 'bangra' music, or the way in which McDonald's is reshaped and hybridized by its location within specific social contexts (see Watson, 1997); also, De Grazia (2005) on the way in which US models of consumption are more generally transferred and adapted in different countries.

An interesting perspective on this process is developed by Rivoli who describes the waste that is generated by this process (Rivoli, 2005: Chaps 10 and 11). Focusing on clothes, she describes how the rapid turnover of fashion leads individuals to throw out perfectly wearable clothes. This has led to a whole new economy of recycling. The clothes often find their way into charity shops in rich countries. Charities in turn sell the bulk of them off in packs measured by weight which are transported to Africa. In Africa, blocks of clothes are sold off to merchants by weight. Merchants then unpack them and sell them in street markets. These clothes are known as *mitumbi* and the purchasers are as keen to find bargains and to find style and brands as any consumer in the developed economies. Recycling has other global dimensions, with developing countries using cheap labour to retrieve all sorts of electrical and other items from the rubbish of the West, creating new forms of interdependency.

In conclusion, it is clear that globalization has created new forms of interdependency that are based on global scales of interaction. Firms are restructuring their supply chains and in doing so they link together different parts of the world in a precarious and time-limited coordination process, mixing market, hierarchy and network forms of control. These processes create new forms of interdependencies for employees, some of whom get locked into 'global' time and correspondingly locked out of 'local time and culture'. The result is a massive increase in uncertainty for the individual as firms race towards structural adjustments. Individualism of a sort flourishes as one way to protect against uncertainty is to limit it as narrowly as possible by only taking responsibility for the self and close family. The consumption process reinforces the tendency towards individualism allowing people greater options for constructing their identity within certain prescribed categories of sociality by making use of global and local vocabularies of the meaning of products. But again this creates uncertainty, primarily because of the uncertainties of employment. The economic interdependency of globalization has contradictory effects. On the one hand, it enhances the consumption possibilities of many people, allowing them to build new and hybrid identities that transcend the constraints of national and traditional contexts. On the other hand, this is only possible because of a growing interdependence of economic, social and political life that creates new risks and gives everyday life a quality of instability and uncertainty.

Movements of People in the Period of Globalization

The economic interdependency described in the previous section could be considered as deriving from a top-down process of change, driven by firms and capital, as they seek production locations and markets. In this section, I focus more on 'globalization from below', in particular, the way in which individual and community actors respond to the possibilities opened up by globalization and in doing so create new processes.

The central issue here is that of the movement of people under conditions of globalization. As discussed earlier, there have been many previous occasions of massive migration across long and short distances. The current era is different in a number of respects. First, migration can no longer be analysed as a one-off step that separates communities, families and societies. Migration is now part of a broader movement of people across borders in the search for employment, education, leisure and lifestyle. In this respect, legal and illegal movements shade into one another rather than being entirely separate categories. Second, connections are retained and identities reconstructed in 'transnational communities' originating in a particular location but now taking on a diasporic form, spread across different locations across the world. Third these connections have evolved into a specific pattern of economic interdependence in which part of the wealth generated in the advanced economies of the world is recycled to other less developed societies through the mechanism of remittances. This creates an interdependence between the sending and the receiving society and encourages migrants in the sending society to take an interest in the politics of their home society not just for reasons of vestigial feelings of nostalgia but also in order to protect their own investments there. Fourth and associated with this, migration of low and high skilled employees particularly impacts on the economic structure of both sending and host societies. Fifth, migration in the current period is also part of the restructuring of domestic life that is occurring under the pressures of globalization. I deal with these processes in the following sections.

Migration, Transnational Communities and Remittances

'Transnational communities' can be identified as forms of collective organization amongst social actors based on the identification and maintenance of affiliation identities associated usually with particular 'home' contexts, even if a significant proportion of the group now live outside the specific place as a result of migration and diaspora processes. For example, Melbourne is now the third largest Greek city outside of Athens and Thessalonika, while 1.2 million people claiming Greek descent live in the USA, 350,000 in Germany and a similar number in Australia as a whole. Over 50 million people of Chinese descent live outside mainland China, the biggest group in Asia, but substantial numbers in the US and in Europe. Transnational communities constitute relay mechanisms for both labour and capital. In terms of labour, they act as sources for the collection of information about job opportunities, conditions of work, and the social position of migrants. They also frequently work as sources of first jobs for entering migrants and for social support in terms of housing, language, education and knowledge of the system which is being entered, thus creating a class of intermediaries and entrepreneurs, making money out of these processes (Portes et al., 2002). These linkages pass over national borders, creating a paradoxical combination of strong identification with a local region from a population often scattered outside that location. It is the broader transnational community that becomes the frame within which new definitions of identity are formed through processes of cultural experimentation and political organization. These identities may be highly politicized where the idea of the home state is problematic in some way, for example anti-Castro Cubans in the US. Transnational communities can be mobilized to support particular parties and candidates in elections (Guarnizo et al., 2003). Wealth earned outside the home society or reputation and education gained on the international stage may be used to build a political base inside, even where an individual has spent most of their life outside the home country. The age and gender structure of transnational communities can vary with effects on the nature of cultural and political organization. For example, some transnational communities are predominantly female and young, for example the dispersion of young Filipino women to act as household servants, particularly in China and south east Asia. The influx of Indians and Pakistanis into the UK in the 1960s was mainly young males, working in various low-paid industries. Over time, wives joined and families developed with their base in the UK. Recent influxes to the UK from new EU entrants in Eastern and Central Europe seem to consist of both men and women of varying ages, sometimes with skills to sell, at other times simply selling their labour in unskilled occupations.

In economic terms, transnational communities are also centrally involved in flows of money around the global economy. These are generally described as remittances indicating their status as funds 'remitted' back from one location to the perceived home base. As a proportion of the overseas investment received by a number of societies, remittances are highly significant, outstripping development assistance from developed governments by a large amount. A recent UK government report stated that in 2001 'remittances represented 42% of total FDI flows and 260% of Overseas Development Assistance … Regionally, Latin America and the Caribbean received the lion [sic] share of remittances in nominal terms with $25 billion followed by South Asia with $16 billion' (Sander, 2003: 4). The report goes on to state that

> the single biggest contribution of remittances is to the welfare and improved livelihood of the receiving household – be it in terms of basic necessities, such as food or clothing, of bettter health and education, or to a smaller extent in terms of savings or business investments. (Sander, 2003: 4)

Remittances often go to support the young and the elderly who are unable to undertake migration but who are also weak in earning power in their home location. Predominantly young men and women engage in the migration and in sustaining the linkages across the transnational community and its representatives in the home society.

It is also clear that remittances sustain a black economy of money traders and criminals. Immediately after 9/11, the US government identified remittance networks amongst Middle Eastern communities as a potentially significant source in the funding of Al-Qaeda terrorism. Whilst it was relatively easy for it to stop this occurring through formal channels, by, for example, tightening up money laundering laws and enforcement, it soon became obvious that this was only a small part of the remittance process. What is known as *hawala* (or hundi) is a system working in the Middle East and South Asia to transfer funds without actually moving them across borders. In effect a transfer of money occurs between two parties in the host location and the person transferring the funds trusts that the other party will ensure that a matching transaction will take place in the other location. In fact, for most migrants, these systems are easier and quicker than bank systems where clearing processes can be quite expensive and can take days especially where foreign exchange is involved. In the *hawala* system, the intermediary charges for the transaction and usually makes money on the exchange rates but the whole process remains informal and is based on trust. Similar systems exist in China and other parts of the world.

Such processes potentially involve a lock-in effect, binding individuals and groups into a dependence on the wider transnational community. Barriers and boundaries may be difficult to cross in these circumstances, creating a dual process whereby the transnational community becomes the way in which globalization is organized and experienced by many of those inside the community but also potentially becomes a constraint and dependency that may constrict and restrict certain processes. Nevertheless these sorts of social relationships are an essential part of the everyday life of many people in the era of globalization.

Migration and the Structure of Economies

The dynamics of growing economies have specific impacts on the labour force in terms of both low skilled and high skilled migrants. The most common feature that is identified is the role of low skilled migrants in filling vacancies in the low paid part of the labour market. From an economic perspective, as jobs open up in more preferred occupations, those that are able will move themselves up the system. The consequence of this is to leave vacancies in the low end of the labour market. Increasingly, these vacancies are filled by the entry of migrants from low-wage economies (Dicken, 2006; Faist, 2000; Martin, 1999). Sometimes this happens informally and illegally to such an extent that even rigorous border controls such as those exercised in the US to prevent entry from Mexico fail to stem the tide of people willing to work illegally in sweatshops or as domestic servants (given that there are people willing to employ them without papers). At other times, this can happen legally, most obviously recently in the European Union where recent phases of extension have opened up labour markets for people previously kept outside, allowing them to fill a variety of jobs from skilled manual tasks (such as plumbing) through to others where the nature of the work requires long hours often in unpleasant conditions, for example in the building trades, in agriculture (crop-picking), in personal social services (working in care homes for the elderly) and in the 24-hour retail economy (serving in shops, fast food outlets, cleaning, security, etc.).

Alongside this, there is also increased circulation of professional and trained employees. One aspect of this concerns situations where developing countries invest in the production of these highly skilled workers only to find them moving to developed countries where salaries are much better. The most obvious cases of this are African doctors and nurses who have begun and in some cases finished their training in societies where opportunities are few or poorly rewarded and who then move to Europe or North America to complete their training and practice their skills. A recent article in the *British Medical Journal* reported that:

> Currently there are thought to be more than a million African healthcare professionals working in the West; a figure close to the number of professionals that the Commission for Africa said should be trained in Africa by 2015. Doctors who have trained in Africa make up a large minority of doctors in the NHS. Michael Pelly, the associate director for global health at the Royal College of Physicians, said that a third of the doctors in the United Kingdom (and over 40% of senior house officers) had trained overseas, and that figure did not include European Union graduates. (*British Medical Journal*, 1 April 2006)

The British NHS has depended on this transfer of resources from Africa in order to work. Africa in the meanwhile loses what it has invested. The South African government, in particular, has voiced its concern about this process and in 2004 reached an agreement with the British that their doctors would not be poached. Ironically, South Africa itself has become a popular destination for doctors from other parts of Africa.

These issues are rather more complex in relation to science-based industries such as computers and biotechnology. What has happened here has been a strong trend for the best and brightest potential PhD candidates to look for places in US universities. In Silicon Valley, the attraction of Stanford and Berkeley, particularly to Chinese and Indian students has created a magnet effect, bringing into the locality the elite of these countries' educational systems. Given the close connection between Stanford and other universities with the businesses of Silicon Valley, many PhDs will go on to take positions in these companies. In effect, the best of the world's talent comes to the US to work for the US economy and US firms, a process which was slowed by the restrictions in the aftermath of 9/11, much to the chagrin of US universities and employers in Silicon Valley. These processes can create a strong remittance effect with well paid migrants supporting families at home and often facilitating them in following in their footsteps by providing advice and help about how to negotiate entry into the US higher education system. It has also proved to be useful in terms of creating a generation of successful migrant business people in the US who are willing to go home and start businesses there. Saxenian terms these migrants who have travelled and succeeded in US business and education whilst sending remittances and investments home 'the new argonauts'. She argues that what could once have been described as a 'brain drain' should now be considered 'brain circulation' (Saxenian, 2006). Thus, the Silicon Valley model gets transferred by these entrepreneurs and new cross-regional connections, which circulate people, ideas and investments, are created, such as the links which the Taiwanese government and Taiwanese businesses have tried to develop between Hsinchu Science Park and Silicon Valley.

Migration and the Domestic Division of Labour

These processes have a powerful impact on domestic divisions of labour. The first point is that much migration is about restructuring the domestic division of labour as it focuses around the provision of relatively cheap childcare and servant arrangements (Anderson, 2002, 2006). For example, there are approximately 140,000 Filipino maids in Hong Kong providing domestic services and child care arrangements. In all, it is estimated that there are milllions of Filipino women working as domestic servants in places like Hong Kong, Singapore and the Middle East. In some of these places, this facilitates the women in the family employing them to go out to work or become a 'lady that lunches'. Some of these maids will have children of their own but the terms of their contract will prohibit them from bringing their children with them. The incentive to work overseas is great when wages for low skilled work are as poor as in the Philippines. Women often also leave their husbands behind to look after the children, which in societies that remain strongly male-centred creates problems of generational reproduction and socialization. Children may be brought up by combinations of grandparents and relatives, leaving the sending society with the problem of the absence of young women and mothers, the impact of this on fertility and the pressures of this on men and elderly generations left behind (a pressure which is partly reduced by remittances).

In some advanced economies, domestic servants have become common again amongst wealthy families where both partners are working. Sometimes this is achieved illegally leading to a new underclass of domestic workers dependent entirely on their employers. Such processes are also linked to the increasing trade in sex workers across national boundaries. Thus, there is a growing and unequal interdependency of the global division of domestic labour arising from these processes.

Conclusions

This chapter has sought to provide an overview of globalization processes with a particular focus on how they impact on everyday life. The basic argument is that our economy and much of our social life could not continue to exist if it was unable to call on resources on a global scale. In the first part of the chapter, the centre of attention was how firms organize production through global value chains. There are certain counter-movements that aim to restrict these processes. The idea of food miles, for example, which is a way of counting the environmental cost of supply chains that are geographically diverse, or the idea of counting the carbon footprint of aircraft miles, both in their way oppose the unproblematic expansion of globalization in global value chains. However, the process of interdependency has become deeply embedded in current models of production and consumption. Furthermore, in terms of our everyday experience, it is an essential part of cheapening costs and putting many products within reach of the mass of the population. At the same time, the economic dynamism of globalization and its compititve processes undermines stability of employment and pressurizes employees in many industries to find new more efficient ways of working, otherwise they will lose their jobs. This turnover in employment is a cause of geographical mobility and unsettles and strips away collective forms of organization based on locality and work relations, creating a void into which religion, nationalism and other ideologies can move, creating further uncertainties and antagonisms. The experience of globalization as pushed from the top, from the MNCs, from the advertisers, from the trade organizations, is one of uncertainty as well as increased consumption.

Interdependency also arises from 'globalization from below'. As barriers fall and labour markets open up, it is scarcely surprising that people seek to move across borders in order to better their lives. Primarily they move with the help of the institutions of transnational communities. Transnational communities and their flows of people, information and money are central to the experience of the mobile worker in the era of globalization. A key aspect of this is the flow of remitttances around the system. Remittances play a role in overcoming the social gaps created by migration but they do not fill these gaps entirely. Interdependency arises between the provision of jobs to migrants and the sustaining of their home connections, especially the maintenance of family relationships and the bringing up of children, the next generation of migrants. Interdependency also arises between economies as flows of people enable processes of upgrading for insiders and allow low skilled posts to be filled by the migrants. In high skilled areas, this interdependency has two sides. The first is the exploitation of developing countries' investment processes by developed countries – most obviously in the way in which doctors and nurses move out of Africa, Asia and Eastern Europe to work in the health services of Western Europe and North America. The second is a more complex process of 'brain circulation' where highly skilled students come to the US to learn and work in high-tech industries. Eventually some of these may become entrepreneurs in their own right and establish businesses in their home countries, where the business often depends on the pre-existing link to Silicon Valley or one of the other high-tech regions in the US and Europe. Finally these flows are part of a reshaping of the domestic division of labour across the globe. In developing countries where women are often valuable exports, child care is left to fathers and grandparents. In other countries it is the men who leave and the women who wait. The uncertainties which this creates mirror the broader uncertainties in a globalized economy described earlier. Meanwhile this migration, particularly into areas of personal service, is part of a renewal of domestic service and has the danger of giving personal, unregulated power to the employer over the employee. For families being serviced in this way, the dual career model becomes more possible.

In conclusion, the argument here is that our everyday experience of work, consumption, family and community is being restructured under the impact of globalization. More or less everything that we do, everything that we are is being remade in the light of growing global interdependency. If we turn the spotlight on our own lives, we can soon recognize that. The clothes we wear, the organizations in which we work, the food we buy, the brands with which we identify, the doctors and nurses who treat us, the domestic servants and the employees in low paid service tasks which we see, the identities which we form that connect us transnationally – are all becoming more clearly embedded in globalization processes. The maintenance of our way of life is dependent on the stable reproduction of these relationships. But to say this is to immediately identify the underlying contradiction which is that globalization itself with its restless processes of competition and change is always undermining that stability. If Marx had not coined that wonderful phrase 'All that is solid melts into the air' so many years ago, it would need to be coined now to describe globalization. On the other hand, the fact that he did coin it so long ago is perhaps a reminder that we should not get too carried away with the historic uniqueness of the current period.

7

COMMUNITY

Chris Land

Community can be the warmly persuasive word to describe an existing set of relationships, or the warmly persuasive word to describe an alternative set of relationships. What is most important, perhaps, is that unlike all other terms of social organization (*state, nation, society,* etc.) it seems never to be used unfavourably, and never to be given any positive opposing or distinguishing term. (Williams, 1983: 76, italics in original)

Introduction

At first glance the idea of 'community' seems to have little relevance for contemporary corporate life. The word, and derivatives such as 'commune', sound like throwbacks to the 1960s, redolent of tie-dye t-shirts, free love and alpaca knitwear, or perhaps to the now apparently defunct 'working-class communities' found amongst Northern mining towns before the strikes of the 1980s. In a more contemporary vein the term community perhaps conjures up the 'Muslim community', regularly called on by the government to decry terrorism and extremism, or the 'gay community', in short any marginalized group who are in some way perceived as having distinct sets of interests and concerns from the political mainstream (Rose, 1996). At best the discourse of 'community' seems marginal. At worst it just sounds 'fluffy' and ill suited to the hard-nosed corporate world of early twenty-first-century capitalist work and organization.

As the editors of this book recognize in their introduction, however, 'organization' is about more than work and employment, and corporate life extends well beyond the confines of the workplace. Organizing is a general process through which the social world is ordered, associations are formed and regulated, and the material world is rendered predictable and useful. The same might be said of 'corporate life'. 'Corporate', in one of its definitions in the *Oxford English Dictionary*, means 'united into one body' and so refers to a variety of forms of human coexistence within social entities, only one of which is captured by its more limited definition as 'business'. Understood in these broader senses 'community' has long been a sociological concept used to analyse traditional, pre-modern modes of social organization (Delanty, 2003; Tönnies, 1887/1963) or to explore the patterns of geographically localized forms of association (Vidich et al., 1964). Association in a community is ordered within and through a homogeneous social whole – *the* community – often positioned in contrast to the more geographically distributed, rationally administered, public sphere of 'society' (Tönnies, 1887/1963). Communities are characterized by a shared consciousness of collective identity, ritual and tradition, and a sense of moral responsibility on the part of members, both for other members and for the community as a whole (Muniz and O'Guinn, 2001). In this sense 'community' is the 'other' of the rationally administered state bureau on which Weber based his writings on bureaucracy and which provided an important precursor for administrative science and organization theory (Weber, 1991).

Community then can be related to organization in at least two ways. On the one hand, it is a historically specific form of organization. On the other hand, it provides a model for comparison against which our present forms of organization can be measured and evaluated. But there is also a third way in which community bears upon contemporary corporate life. The dysfunctions of modern, rationalized forms of organization are now well documented and understood. Indeed, a critique of Taylorism and bureaucracy is a staple starting point for undergraduate courses in Organizational Behaviour. It is unsurprising, therefore, that both managers and academics are looking for alternatives and that, in the topsy-turvy, postmodern world of globalized networked organizations, these alternatives are often found in the pre-modern (Hancock, 1997). Today the idea of community is held out as both a salve to ease the ontological insecurity of our postmodern, fragmented selves, and as a management tool to increase motivation, commitment and knowledge sharing in a time of high job mobility and precarity. In so doing community cuts across the full range of corporate life, from the synthetic communities forged by managers in search of strong 'corporate cultures' and 'communities of practice' to bolster weak social relations in the sphere of production, to both autonomous and synthetic communities formed around brands and consumption activities. In such accounts the pre-modern world of community has been thoroughly rationalized and brought within the sphere of circulation of contemporary capitalism.

There is also, however, a fourth and final intersection between community and corporate life. A red thread, connecting 'community' with 'communism', posits an oppositional relationship between community and capitalism, suggesting community as a radically democratic and anti-capitalist model for social organization and incorporation, entirely at odds with the dominant logic of capitalist work organizations. This chapter works through these four versions of the relationship between community and corporate life in turn.

Community and Society

In classical sociology 'community' stands against 'society' and is most closely associated with the work of Ferdinand Tönnies (1887/1963) who characterized the two as *Gemeinschaft* and *Gesellschaft* respectively. In this tradition, society or *Gesellschaft* is seen as a modern development, based upon the dissolution of traditional forms of community, or *Gemeinschaft*, and their replacement with more rationalized forms of association. For Tönnies, *Gemeinschaft* is governed by 'natural will' and characterized by family-based forms of association grounded in a specific locale. *Gesellschaft*, on the other hand, is governed by the 'rational will' of society and characterized by contract and exchange (Tönnies, 1887/1963). The distinction is often conceived as one between town and country and relates to wider social changes associated with industrialization. In this light Tönnies can be read as a romantic, highly critical of modern forms of rationalized social life and seeking a return to the more natural values of the community.

Tönnies' ideas have not been without their critics. Emile Durkheim turned Tönnies on his head in *The Division of Labour in Society* (Durkheim, 1893/1984; see also Delanty, 2003: 36). Here Durkheim argues that it is not modern society that is 'mechanical' but rather traditional forms of community as they are reproduced with each member the same. This form of social reproduction means that social units can split off without a major change, therefore social solidarity is limited. For Durkheim, modern industrial society, with its complex division of labour, generated a diversity of experiential viewpoints within society but bound the whole together more tightly because of the increasing interdependencies thereby produced. This form of cohesion he referred to as 'organic' because, like an organism, organic societies are comprised of a range of functionally specialized parts, all dependent upon one another for their continued existence. Such societies could not simply split off to form separate social groups, as they could before the division of labour. From Durkheim's perspective, the industrial division of labour does not negate community but produces its own distinctive forms of association that enhance social cohesion through interdependency.

Whatever evaluation is put upon these changes, both Tönnies's and Durkheim's analyses represent the dominant form of association changing from traditional forms of community to something else. The massification of social life in industrial cities and the decline of traditional, more agriculturally based, communities went hand in hand with changes in both the organization of production and of governmental administration. In the sphere of production, industrialization brought a new set of problems relating to the coordination and management of work, shaping the contours of employment relations. In the public sphere, the bureaucratic rationalization of administration led to developments in the structuring of organization that still dominate the contemporary organizational landscape (Höpfl, 2006; Weber, 1991). In this sense the problems addressed by most contemporary organizational theory arose as a result of the movement that Tönnies identified as the shift from *Gemeinschaft* to *Gesellschaft*.

Despite his critics then, Tönnies' ideas provide one of the dominant legitimating meta-narratives of mainstream organization theory: a linear progression of rationalization as modernism, capitalism, bureaucratization, Taylorism, Fordism, and even McDonaldization, come to rationalize the organization of production and consumption in accordance with modernist conceptions of science and technology (e.g. Ritzer, 1996; cf. Burrell, 1997). Whether this 'rationalization' is seen as the inexorable march of progress, efficiency and economic health or interpreted as the bleak, disenchantment and instrumentalization of life, the narrative inherited from Tönnies of a move from irrational tradition to rational modernity remains. Behind either evaluation is the spectre of community, so whilst community rarely features in conventional textbooks on organizational behaviour or management, without it the history and development of management practice over the last 200 years makes little sense. Indeed, many of the problems facing modern management are arguably the result of rationalization and the disembedding of work from traditional communities (Bauman, 2001; Veblen, 1964).

The Loss of Community and the Problem of Labour

Pre-industrial labour was geographically located, rooted in the land and the seasons. Most importantly, work was enmeshed within a tight social system of meaning and significance: the community. Materially and symbolically located within the networks of kinship, descent, association and meaning that make up a community, work had no need of external motivation. It was an integrated part of life. This all changed with the enclosures of the commons, the uprooting of communities, the relocation of a previously rural population to the new industrial cities like Manchester, and the disembedding of tradition that we have come to know as modernity. Due to these events, work itself was uprooted and emptied of any inherent social significance.

According to textbooks, management pretty much begins with Frederick Taylor around the start of the twentieth century. The problem of labour, as Taylor conceived it, was twofold. First, the workers often had a greater knowledge of their work than did their managers, so they were able to control the rate of work without management voicing effective opposition. Second, the workers were either inherently shiftless or instrumentally limited their rate of work so as to maximize their earnings and minimize their efforts, the process Taylor referred to as 'systematic soldiering' (Taylor, 1911). Taylor solved both of these by seeking to wrest control over the rate and the content of the labour process from the worker. Without going into the details of his approach, the key problem that Taylor faced was one of motivation and control. In the absence of any inherent or socially embedded meaning to their labours, industrial workers took an instrumental attitude to these activities. For Taylor the solution was to control the minutiae of the labour process itself and to appeal to workers' economic rationality by offering higher wages for compliance with his system. The key point here is that this instrumental attitude, and the whole 'problem of labour', was the result of the separation of work from its traditional location in the community. Industrial capitalism forced a rupture with tradition and community. Devoid of either inherent or social significance, work became drudgery, a burden to be avoided, and the inclination to minimize effort appears as a 'natural' laziness (Bauman, 2001; Veblen, 1964). From this perspective we can see that the suppositions concerning human nature informing Douglas McGregor's (1987) well known 'theory x' are not, as is usually assumed, the product of an ignorant managerial class or poor theory. Workers' instrumental attitudes to work were not managerial misperception, but the product of social changes wrought by the destruction of community. In the absence of any socially grounded meaning to work, a shiftless attitude becomes natural as the foundations of traditional meaning and community are replaced with an abstract and universal instrumentalism.

If the key lines of control and resistance in the nineteenth-century workplace were being drawn up around meaning and community, so were many of the wider social struggles relating to work. Sabotage can be explained, at least partly, with reference to the decline of community. As several historical studies of the Luddites have suggested, the spate of 'machine breaking' that swept England in the early nineteenth century were not simply irrational, knee-jerk rejections of progress, science and technology. They were responses to the ways in which the emergent, laissez-faire form of capitalism was disrupting traditional systems of meaning and authority (Hobsbawm, 1998; Jermier, 1988; Noble, 1993; Webster and Robins, 1986; cf. Grint and Woolgar, 1997). The introduction of new machinery into the workplace stood as a symbol for more widespread disruptions to traditional, community-based forms of social organization and reproduction, in particular the decline of parental authority and changes to the organization of the labour process that included an erosion of the status and significance of specific trades within the wider community (Webster and Robins, 1986).

This perspective raises two important lines of continuity between work and community. On the one hand, changes in the workplace have an often dramatic effect on the reproduction of the wider community and its patterns of authority and meaning. On the other, changes in the workplace are dependent upon changes in the wider community and society. In the case of the Luddites the introduction of machinery to deskill the cropping of cloth, a previously well paid and highly skilled activity, was possible only with massive state intervention and the repression of what was, at the time, a popular uprising. To put the response of the state into context, at the peak of the Luddite rebellion some 12,000 troops were sent to the North of England to quell the rioters and bring the ringleaders to court: more than were in the army Wellington took to fight Napoleon in 1808 (Hobsbawm, 1998: 8).

The sequestration of 'work' into factories during the industrial revolution did not herald the start of work-related resistance of course. Contestations over the products of peasant labour had long been a feature of pre-industrial labour, as highlighted in Marc Bloch's (1967) study of the organization of agricultural labour in medieval Europe. Nor does it imply that power relations were absent from earlier organizations of the labour process, as Cynthia Cockburn's (1983) analysis of the early guild-organization of printing labour clearly demonstrates. What changes with the industrial revolution, however, is that 'work' is separated off from the more general life of the community. A guild organized work and life as a whole. It did not separate out a private sphere of 'life' and public sphere of 'work' (Cockburn, 1983). The two were articulated together as a whole. Similarly, whilst landowners might seek increased control over the products of peasant labour, for example by controlling access to milling technologies (Bloch, 1967), they were less inclined to involve themselves in the actual organization of that labour, a process that was left to the local and grounded knowledge of the peasantry. It was only with the development of the factory system proper that control over the labour process itself became contested and subordinated to external control by the owners and agents of capital (Marglin, 1974). This has important implications for the development of management and the 'problem' of labour. The factory system saw both the separation of work from other spheres of life, and its spatial and temporal confinement within the factory. In conjunction with the enclosures acts passed by the British parliament between 1760 to 1830 (Linebaugh, 2005) the development of the factory system forced the relocation of large sections of the rural population to the rapidly growing industrial towns and cities in search of wage-labour, uprooting rural communities in the process. The dissolution of community lies at the very heart of industrial organization.

Creating Meaning in the Absence of Community

The analysis outlined in the last section suggests that one of the dominant problems facing modern management – the recalcitrant and lazy employee in need of motivation – is itself the product of modern forms of social organization that separate work from any intrinsic and communally grounded system of meaning. This absence of meaning in contemporary, rationalized, work organizations has been well recognized by managers and organizational theorists following in the wake of the Human Relations school (Carey, 1967; Grey, 2005). According to the conventional historical narrative of organization theory, the bad old days of dehumanized, alienated and Taylorized work were relatively short lived and by the 1940s academic researchers had come to the rescue. The key break with Scientific Management came with the discovery that management was not all rational design and ergonomics. Even as human resources, people are inherently irrational and must have their emotional and social needs carefully tended.

As the story goes, it was Elton Mayo who made this discovery during a study of the effects of lighting levels on productivity in the bank wiring room of General Electric's Hawthorne plant near Chicago (Grey, 2005). Extrapolating from the 'Hawthorne Effect', whereby the activities of researchers can change the behaviour of the subjects they are studying, the Human Relations school encouraged managers to attend to the subjective as well as the objective, taking an interest in employees as individuals, offering counselling and guidance to troubled workers and ensuring that their activities were located within a human system of meaning through job redesign.

One of the key insights attributed to the Hawthorne experiments was the importance of informal social groups. The 'bank wiring room' study focused on peer pressure within work groups to limit output and prevent 'rate busting' (producing faster than the average rate): the same process of systematic soldiering that Taylor had sought to contain through rationalization and functional control. Where Taylor sought to eradicate these last vestiges of 'irrational', community-based control over the labour process, however, the Hawthorne researchers saw the informal group as an inevitable feature of industrial organization and one that could potentially be harnessed in the interests of the organization. For Mayo the objective was to balance and complement scientific management's focus on the technical aspects of work with the effective alignment of the social dimensions of work into the functional unity of the organization. Management needed to develop a set of social skills that would facilitate cooperation and commitment and replace the traditional forms of socialization, found in the craft-guilds or in rural peasant societies, with a synthetic form of community produced and managed in the service of the industrial organization. As Thompson and McHugh (2002: 49) put it: 'The task was to recreate a sense of community inside the workplace'.

Synthesizing Community at Work

This emphasis on the meaning of work has been developed most notably through the organization-wide meaning systems of corporate cultures (Casey, 1995; Kunda, 1992; Peters and Waterman, 1982; Smircich and Morgan,

1982; Willmott, 1993). Corporate cultures can be seen as an attempt to address the lack of meaning associated with rationalized work and to locate workers within a semiotic system – the corporate culture – that gives their activities meaning and situates them within a socially grounded value system. The archetypal exemplar of this meaningfulness is given by Peters and Waterman (1982: 37) when discussing a worker employed on the Honda production line who, 'on his way home each evening, straightens up windshield wiper blades on all the Hondas he passes. He just can't stand to see a flaw in a Honda!' This model worker is, according to Peters and Waterman's analysis, so committed to Honda and so identified with its corporate culture that an imperfection on a Honda, however slight, is a sleight upon his own identity.

Meaning for the ideal worker represented in the corporate culture literature is entirely determined by the interests of the company. The corporation itself comes to replace the traditional community, taking on its function of providing a meaning system for employees and a totalizing identity through which workers can simultaneously self-actualize and realize the goals of the company (Du Gay, 1996: 41). This alignment of identity with the interests of the organization is implicitly connected to pre-modern forms of association by the culture guru William Ouchi when he refers to a form of 'clan control' (Ouchi, 1981). Following Durkheim's critique of Tönnies, Ouchi recognizes that 'the process of modernization ... suggests that societies will eventually dissolve as individuals lose their sense of community and of mutual obligation' but claims that the work organization will come to replace the community in the provision of 'primary relations' (Ouchi and Johnson, 1978: 297). As employees' sense of identity, meaning and community is aligned with the organization, Ouchi and Johnson (1978: 310) suggest, the dehumanized, contractual world of *Gesellschaft* will give way to a resurgence of *Gemeinschaft*, albeit now at the level of the work organization rather than the rural village community (Hancock, 1997; cf. Parker, 1997).

Corporations cannot, however, offer the same kinds of stable bases for identity work that traditional communities are supposed to have offered. In times of economic difficulty or restructuring the employee may be unwillingly forced from the synthetic community of the corporation. The psychological contract that identification presupposes is necessarily broken if the more formal employment contract is no longer financially viable. At best a corporate culture can provide only a precarious locus for identification (Hecksher, 1995; Sennett, 1998). There is also a wealth of empirical research suggesting that culture is not amenable to managerial control and cannot be aligned with strategic objectives (Ackroyd and Crowdy, 1990; Fleming, 2005b; Fleming and Spicer, 2003; Ogbonna and Harris, 1998). Regional, class, occupational and gender identities precede, and can present a more stable source of meaning and identity than, synthetic corporate cultures (Ackroyd and Crowdy, 1990;

Collinson, 1992). Even within a corporate culture there is no guarantee that *the* culture is actually homogeneous (Meyerson and Martin, 1987). Rather it is likely to be comprised of a number of sub- and counter-cultures that will resist the imposition of a unified corporate culture, even using their antagonism and resistance to such as resources for collective identity work and the construction of shared meaning and community (Collinson, 1992). What these empirical studies of corporate culture management programmes suggest is that, despite efforts to manage meaning from the top down, culture remains a socially and geographically located phenomenon connected to wider communities and following relatively autonomous lines of association beyond the control of any one individual or organizational group. Despite this recognition, managerial attempts to control meaning through culture have not abated in recent years and have even been joined by an innovation in the management of meaning whereby 'community' has been directly mobilized in the service of the corporation. It is to this development that we now turn.

Management, Knowledge Work and Discourses of 'Community'

Just as 'culture' has been subject to managerial intervention in recent decades, so too has 'community' become a tool of management through the discourse of 'communities of practice'. The idea of a community of practice was first developed and popularized through Lave and Wenger's (1991) theory of 'situated learning'. Lave and Wenger's key idea was that learning is socially situated and takes place within specific 'communities'. Using a range of examples from Yucatan midwives to recovering alcoholics in the USA, Lave and Wenger developed the idea of 'legitimate peripheral participation' to explain how learning is an embedded process of socialization through which individuals develop a particular identity and come to embody the social competencies associated with a specific form of expertise. As they put it, 'learning involves the whole person; it implies not only a relation to specific activities, but a relation to social communities – it implies becoming a full participant, a member, a kind of person' (Lave and Wenger, 1991: 53). Through legitimate peripheral participation a subject enters into a community of practice and can lay claim to the forms of knowledge and expertise that membership entails. From this perspective learning is as much about developing a particular social identity and learning the behaviours and discourses associated with that identity as it is about the mastery of a set of technical accomplishments or knowledges.

Although in this original formulation the idea of a community of practice is 'left largely as an intuitive notion' the authors call particular attention to the need to analyse 'unequal relations of power' and the control of resources, particularly resources related to the production of collective identity (Lave and Wenger, 1991: 37, 42). As a theory of subjectivization, the original 'communities of practice' approach was influenced by Marxism and critical theory (Lave and Wenger, 1991: 50–1) and is commensurate with the critical social theoretical approaches to learning and change found in actor-network theory and Foucauldian research (Fox, 2000). As it has been developed and popularized, however, primarily through the subsequent work of Etienne Wenger (Wenger, 1998; Wenger and Snyder, 2000; Wenger et al., 2002), the idea of a community of practice has lost this critical edge. Power relations have disappeared from the analysis to be replaced with a more managerial model that can be used and applied to 'cultivate', if not directly manage, communities of practice within organizations (Contu and Willmott, 2000, 2003).

As Wenger and his colleagues define them, communities of practice are: 'Groups of people who share a concern, a set of problems, or a passion about a topic, and who deepen their knowledge and expertise in this area by interacting on an ongoing basis' (Wenger et al., 2002: 4). Although these people may not work together all of the time they nevertheless 'develop a common sense of identity' as a result of their ongoing interactions (Wenger et al., 2002: 5). These interactions are not instrumental in a narrow sense as informal status and collective identity remain a key concern of community members. What does disappear, however, is the focus on contestation and power relations. The community of practice becomes a social space where apparent equals come together around a shared interest. Divested of power relations, a community of practice becomes an organizational tool for managing knowledge:

> Many companies are discovering that communities of practice are the ideal social structure for 'stewarding' knowledge. By assigning responsibility to the practitioners themselves to generate and share the knowledge they need, these communities provide a social forum that supports the living nature of knowledge. (Wenger et al., 2002: 12)

Connecting to broader discourses of knowledge management (Davenport and Prusak, 1998; Newell et al., 2002), Wenger et al. make the argument that managing knowledge is the most important challenge for organizations today. As much knowledge is tacit, competitive advantage in a knowledge based economy depends upon an organization's ability to leverage its members' idiosyncratic knowledges and expertise and to encourage them to share this knowledge. The assumption is that if managers follow the principles of community of practice (or CoP) they will be able to 'cultivate' the ideal conditions for communities to develop in a way that follows the interests of the organization. The framework of understanding is a unitarist one in which an alignment of interests across the organization is not only possible, but is the way to achieve sustained competitive advantage in the knowledge economy.

By cultivating communities, the subjectivities of workers can be managed so that self-actualization is harmonized with the interests of capital and profit (or 'the organization').

This community-based approach to the management of knowledge workers is an extension of the normative-ideological or concertive control associated with corporate cultures and teamworking (Barker, 1993; Willmott, 1993). It extends the logic underlying human relations and corporate cultures – the synthetic production of community within a corporation – so as to align meaning and identity with extrinsic goals such as profitability. Where there is an intimation of potential conflict, it is limited to warning senior management that they must listen to communities of practice when formulating strategies, as community members will be closest to the knowledge upon which sustainable competitive advantage is based. There is no underlying conflict in the social ontology of communities of practice. Employees' identities can be reconciled with corporate objectives and, in their desire to self-actualize within their own communities of practice, knowledge workers will communicate and share their knowledge in such a way as to further the interests of the organization.

Customer Relationship Marketing and Brand Communities

So far this chapter has considered the relationship between community and work, focusing first on the disembedding of work from traditional, community-based systems of meaning and then on the various attempts to create a synthetic form of community within the workplace. The connections between community and corporate life go beyond the sphere of production however. In recent years there has been a growing interest in the relationship between community and consumption. Whilst the centrality of consumption activities in the maintenance of communities has long been recognized (Kanter, 1972), more recently the idea of community has come to prominence both as an analytical lens for students of consumer behaviour (Muniz and O'Guinn, 2001) and as a potential tool for marketers to increase brand loyalty (Kozinets, 1999; McAlexander et al., 2002). Referring to 'consumption communities', or 'brand communities', analysts have sought to move customer relationship marketing beyond a dyadic customer–brand model to incorporate the socially situated, often communal, context of consumption and relationships between customers, products, brands, other consumers and marketers (McAlexander et al., 2002). Proponents of the brand community perspective argue that the modernist narrative of consumerism individualizing and isolating subjects is a myth. Consumption is a profoundly social and symbolically saturated activity and acts of consumption cannot be understood independently of the social contexts within which they occur. In many cases, acts of consumption, particularly of publicly consumed, branded products, will generate a sense of shared identity with other consumers that develops into community proper, with traditions, rituals and a shared sense of moral responsibility both for the brand and for each other (Muniz and O'Guinn, 2001). Whilst this sense of community may arise spontaneously, it can also be manufactured and added to the marketer's toolkit. By creating face-to-face encounters based on communal acts of consumption (McAlexander et al., 2002) or by facilitating online, virtual communities, or 'e-tribes' (Kozinets, 1999), marketers can create authentic, meaningful communities that proponents claim can enhance the well-being of consumers and even serve to democratize consumption.

The idea of a 'brand community' goes beyond the simple recognition that consumption is often communal and carries a weight of social meaning. Proponents claim that 'brands' can generate systems of social meaning that are equivalent to more traditionally conceived communities (Muniz and O'Guinn, 2001). As with communities of practice, writers on brand communities see no particular reason why authentic community cannot arise, and even thrive, within the circuits of late capitalism. Giving examples such as communities of Harley-Davidson and Jeep enthusiasts (McAlexander et al., 2002; Schouten and McAlexander, 1995), X-Files fans (Kozinets, 1999) or Mac users and Saab drivers (Muniz and O'Guinn, 2001) these writers explicitly reject the notion that these communities are inauthentic. Following a postmodern line of argument (Elliot, 1998), they reject meta-narratives of modernist, capitalist alienation from pre-modern social cohesion, suggesting that all forms of community are imagined (Anderson, 1991) and produced through acts of symbolic communication. If this is the case then Tönnies' idea of a fall from the natural cohesion of communal relations is an error. The shared sense of identity that characterizes community is forged through processes of representation and subjectivization that are never free of power relations (Foucault, 1982). If all forms of community are mediated and managed, commercially oriented brand communities (or communities of practice for that matter) are not inauthentic, but merely the community form of association that appears in late capitalist societies. Indeed, rather than being impoverished, the freedom to join or to leave a brand community, and the relatively low cost associated with doing so, may even be liberatory when compared to more traditional, ascriptive communities (Kozinets, 1999).

Against this apparently democratic and liberatory potential of brand communities it must be borne in mind that these are *commercial* communities: 'Brand community rituals and traditions exist in a hypertexual media environment, where the commercial canon is pervasive, proximal, and perhaps primary ... brand communities represent a historical moment and circumstance that is defined by the commercial. It is, however, still indicative of community' (Muniz and O'Guinn, 2001: 424). Community and subjectivity in brand communities necessarily flow through the commodity form. Of course, this does not mean that either the subjectivities cultivated within brand communities, or the interpretations of brands they develop and promote, are in any simple sense functional for capital. Indeed, the opposite may well be the case. As Muniz and O'Guinn (2001: 419) note, for some brand communities the maintenance of a marginal and exclusive status can serve the interests of community members whilst working against the interests of the company producing the commodities to which the community has attached itself. What it does mean, however, is that the psychic and cultural ecology within which community forms of association are reproduced, and subjectivities are worked, is thoroughly imbued with the logic of the commodity and its circulation; they are absorbed within the (always contested) circuits of the reproduction of capital and capitalism itself (Dyer-Witheford, 1999). Regardless of how successful these practices are in harnessing *Gemeinschaft* to the interests of capital, the current wave of interest in managerial discourses of 'communities of practice' and prescriptive customer relationship marketing discourses of 'brand communities' both suggest that this is a clear objective in the governance of contemporary corporate life.

Contesting Community: Counter-Communities, Communes and Anti-Capitalism

From this discussion it would appear that 'community', once associated with communism and anti-capitalist forms of organization, has been thoroughly subsumed by capitalism. This is not the case, however, and we would perhaps be better characterizing community as a contested terrain within late capitalism. In both form and content, communities are sites of struggle. Brand communities work against the commercial interests of brands. Communities of practice orient their activities towards resisting management and work intensification. Anti-capitalist communities develop autonomous forms of organization, engaging in direct action and rejecting overtly commodified forms of consumption as bases for collection identification.

Warwick Business School's Innovation, Knowledge and Organisation Networks (IKON) research unit conducted research with a mobile phone company that was introducing communities of practice as part of a global knowledge management strategy. Evidence of resistance was found at both the global and national levels. In some cases this resistance was a simple refusal to communicate. Respondents justified this refusal by explaining that they didn't have the time to engage in formalized community communications and saw no advantage, either for themselves or for the company, in doing so. By passively refusing to engage with a community of practice, these employees maintained their exclusive expertise, and therefore their informal power-base within the organization and simultaneously refused the whole grid of meaning, identity and integration that communities of practice promise.

In another example of resistance, the same company had sought to use a community of practice model for organizing their internal quality auditors. These auditors were a nominally voluntary group, though if an employee's supervisor suggested they should join they did not always feel that this request could be refused. As the quality audit was a very formalized process, auditors found little use for the official communities of practice but instead formed an informal community, meeting face-to-face, for example over a meal, or phoning each other to share work-arounds and shortcuts that would make the lives of the auditors easier. In this example we can see the resurfacing of contestations over the purpose of community. Such informal communities are little different from the informal work groups attacked by Taylor, rediscovered in the Hawthorne studies, and found in a significant number of sociological studies of work organization since (Burawoy, 1979; Thompson, 1989). These examples of resistance to, and resistance within, community forms of organization fit well within the established traditions of industrial sociology, which has long recognized that the exercise of power at work invariably generates some form of resistance. The focus on the workplace however, even if extended to incorporate brands and markets, limits the scope for identifying a second, equally significant locus of resistance to corporate control over community.

'Community' and the associated ideas of 'commune' and 'communism' have traditionally belonged to the political left and, despite increasing interest from other sections of the political spectrum, this strand of radicalism has not entirely died out. It is possible, therefore, to trace a second, more radical, thread through history, one which runs counter to the narrative of dissolution and commodification outlined earlier. This second thread connects contemporary forms of anti-capitalist organization and politically ideological communes to a heritage that stretches back through the 1960s and 1970s counterculture (Kanter, 1972), the Israeli Kibbutz (Warhurst, 1996), and the pirates of the early eighteenth century (Land, 2007; Rediker, 2004), at least as far as the Diggers and other non-conformist utopians who sprang from the soil of the English civil war (Hill, 1975). Despite there being a large number of such communities from around the globe and throughout the history of modern society, they have received little attention from organizational scholars (for notable exceptions see Fournier, 2002, 2005; Parker et al., 2007; Wilson, 2004). One reason for this might be that many alternative communities and communes are short-lived, but then the same can be said of business organizations (de Geus, 1997), very few of which live as long as the three generations that has been used as a guide for successful communes (Friesen and Friesen, 2004; Kanter, 1972). A more simple explanation might be the institutional location of most organizational research in business schools, leading to a tendency to equate organization with business (Grey, 2005). Whatever the reason, the neglect of this area is palpable and has effectively bypassed an entire tradition of small, countercultural, *Gemeinschaft*-like organizations that have contested capitalism since its early days.

As studies of communes and pirates have demonstrated, such organizations are not primarily oriented toward external or instrumental goals, such as accumulation, but rather to the preservation of the community itself and its particular way of life (Land, 2007). This logic of organization is perhaps the crucial distinction between commercial and anti-capitalist communities. Regardless of how authentic the subjectivities produced in a postmodern brand community, or a community of practice are, as soon as they are subject to management and functional control these communities are no longer primarily concerned with the maintenance of the community itself or with the 'common' interests of the community members. As Rosabeth Moss Kanter has characterized them, utopian communities, on the other hand, are precisely concerned with the 'common' as it is determined by the members:

> Because members choose to join and choose to remain, conformity is based on commitment – on the individual's own desire to obey its rules – rather than force or coercion. Members are controlled by the entire membership or by individuals they respect within the community rather than by outside agents or political forces. (Kanter, 1972: 2)

Voluntary association is a part of the rhetoric, if not always the reality, of communities of practice and is clearly a feature of brand communities, but both of these commercial communities are consciously designed and guided by 'outside agents': knowledge managers, consultants and marketers.

Some religious utopian communities are also externally oriented, organizing their lives around an interpretation of religious texts or prophets, but even in these cases the interpretation of scripture is often idiosyncratic and vested in a member, or several members, of the community (Kanter, 1972). With more politically oriented communities the goal of consensus and democracy in decision-making and organization is often the main concern of the collective. As Valerie Fournier (2005) has noted, this can lead to the organization of production on communes becoming inefficient, but then efficiency is not their main goal. To quote Kanter (1972: 3) again, 'Maintaining the sense of group solidarity is as important as meeting specific goals.' If maintaining solidarity and meeting the needs of all of the community's members comes at a cost to efficiency, perhaps this is a price worth paying? Our current model for organizing agricultural production, for example, may be market-efficient but it is far from efficient in human terms and often means poverty, long hours and poor working conditions for farm-labourers, small-scale farmers and other agricultural workers (Fournier, 2005: 202). Organizing less efficiently and in line with principles and goals determined immanently by the community, rather than with those that are externally imposed as a transcendent goal, may offer a more humanized form of social organization than mainstream capitalist corporations are currently capable of.

Conclusion

This chapter has traced a line of argument that suggests a 'fall' from an original state of community or *Gemeinschaft* and into a rationalized, modern, industrial world of *Gesellschaft*. Aligned against this linear narrative are two distinct movements. On the one hand, is the commercial or capitalist imperative to reconstruct a form of community and to harness the commitment associated with community to the interests of increased production and consumption. On the other hand, there is a more hidden tradition of radical communities that refuse the transcendent imperatives of efficiency and accumulation and insist upon a more democratic form of mutual accountability.

Both these forms of community have something in common. Association in most of the forms of community discussed in this chapter except in Tönnies's original formulation of *Gemeinschaft*, are voluntary. Despite this voluntarism, the very idea of a community presents a challenge to the individualism that has characterized mainstream organizational behaviour with its theories of motivation, leadership and personality types. The discourse of community implicitly, and sometimes explicitly (Lave and Wenger, 1991; Muniz and O'Guinn, 2001) recognizes that the subject does not exist independent of, or prior to, their social relations. Subjectivity is an inherently social process, even when the end result of subjectivization is a sovereign 'individual' because humans never actually exist in some abstract 'state of nature', free from social ties and relationships. In this sense the apparent sovereignty of the modern subject – the independent consumer or worker – is both part and product of a wider set of social relations. Whilst community is sometimes rejected as an affront to individuality, in its more radical forms it can open on to an active recognition and conscious, collective engagement with the social relations that constitute us as subjects. The commercial discourses of community outlined in this chapter do not follow through on this self-conscious and collective shaping of subjectivity but seek rather to insert the market and capital into subjectivization, subordinating it to an external logic. The more radical experiments conducted in communes and on board pirate ships, on the other hand, offer a distinctly collective ontological and political basis for processes of subjectivization that may not fall into the trap of modernist meta-narratives of authenticity and alienation. Either way, what is certain is that community in both of these forms offers a fertile ground for critical studies of organization and for re-imagining the possibilities of a 'corporate' life.

8

IDENTITY

Nick Llewellyn

Introduction

This chapter examines the relationships between work, organization and identity. The nature of these relationships has been a perennial concern for social scientists, dating back to the very beginnings of industrial capitalism. Of particular interest has been the matter of how organizations shape the identities of members, sometimes as a result of conscious planning and design (Alvesson and Willmott, 2002; Pratt, 2000). But people's identities are also shaped before they enter the workplace as well. The matter of how people are prepared for work has always fascinated social scientists. Most famously, in *The Protestant Ethic and the Spirit of Capitalism*, Max Weber (1930/2001) linked the motivational basis of work in capitalism to religious beliefs associated with Protestantism, especially Calvinism. For Weber religious doctrine, aside from any corporate interventions, prepared the individual for a steady life of labour. In *Learning to Labour*, Paul Willis (1978/2003) asked how working-class boys were prepared for working-class jobs. Willis described how class-based attitudes, rather than religious beliefs, prepared people for work, instilling specific orientations to authority and hard work. Chris Grey (1994) considered long running efforts, stretching back into childhood, to accumulate and document non-academic skills, dispositions and achievements. Before entering the labour market, trainee accountants described how they had managed their lives in order to secure their future employment prospects.

This chapter asks how young people are encouraged manage themselves as subjects of work, before entering the labour market. One way this is done, it will be argued, is via the 'discourse of transferable skills'. A 'discourse' is a framework of thought and action people use to talk about, understand and manage conduct (Clarke and Newman, 1997; Miller and Rose, 1990). The discourse of transferable skills allows people to forge meaningful connections between seemingly separate areas of society. For example, it might be argued that sport teaches teamwork and teamwork is relevant for work. Sport and work are linked, via teamwork. It might be argued that yoga teaches self-discipline and self-discipline is relevant for work. Yoga and work are thus connected, via self-discipline. This simple framework is powerful because virtually all aspects of experience, across diverse areas of life, can be made relevant for work, via the idea of generic transferable skills.

Such discursive possibilities do not just hang around. They tend to emerge from and find their way into the plans and material practices of different institutions, most obviously the state institutions like schools and careers advice centres as well as parts of hiring organizations like personnel functions. Hiring organizations have occasion to examine individuals to see whether they have accumulated the right mix of employable attributes, skills and dispositions. In order to evidence their possession of these skills and dispositions, candidates typically talk about extra-curricular activities, such as playing sport, playing music, sitting on organizing committees, travel, etc. Having the right pool of experience to draw upon is critical in a tight market for graduate labour, where large numbers of people graduate each year with 'good degrees' from 'good universities'. At school, and through the family, individuals are encouraged to accumulate such skills and attributes by participating in appropriate activities and pastimes. The discourse of transferable skills, it is argued below, may have similar effects in contemporary society as over-arching formations have previously had. Through this framework of 'transferable skills', individuals can manage themselves – and be managed – as subjects of work before entering the labour market.

Changing 'the Subject'?

To frame the discussion at the broadest level it is necessary to explore what is meant by 'identity'. This is a daunting task, because every major social science perspective has something to say on the matter. Rather than attempting the impossible, this chapter begins by briefly exploring Stuart Hall's (1996) useful delineation between three 'strategic points in modernity' at which the sense of *the subject* shifted. According to Hall, over-arching identities associated with religion and class have given way to more individual and idiosyncratic identities. This means the question of crafting an individual and unique sense of self becomes a challenge for us all.

The Sovereign Individual

What does it mean to be an individual? For most people perhaps the matter of their own *individuality* appears to be a massive and undeniable fact. It is very common for people to say that they are not being true to themselves.

Such utterances trade on taken-for-granted assumptions; that people are unique and that they have a stable or 'true' character that allows for 'false' displays. Two points are relevant here. First, this view of the subject as unique and indivisible is not natural but is only a fairly recent historical invention. Second, this is not the only way of thinking about 'the subject'. A great many social scientists have argued that this view of a unique, unified and coherent individual is problematic. This section works through these ideas briefly and simply. We will start by asking where assumptions of uniqueness and indivisibility come from and, more importantly for this chapter, where they still persist.

The individual has a long history, but only relatively recently did a decisive form of individualism become enshrined in the institutions, mentalities and practices of society (Hall, 1996). In traditional society, prior to the Renaissance and the Enlightenment of the eighteenth century, people came to know themselves and their place in the world through religion and feudalism. An individual's place in the world was thought to be divinely ordained and thus by definition 'not subject to fundamental change' (Hall, 1996). In a relatively short period of time tradition started to give way to a new 'spirit' of individualism (Weber, 1930/2001). This was bought about by the birth of science, logic and mathematics, the movement against feudalism and the Protestant Reformation (Hall, 1996). People began to be released from 'traditional' attachments as society came to privilege individual reason and rational argument above dogma and superstition (Giddens, 1991).

In the sphere of economics and management, actions were understood to flow from 'reason' which was bound up with an essential or *identical* 'human nature'. For example, on the 'division of labour' Adam Smith wrote:

> Whether this propensity be one of those original principles in human nature of which no further account can be given; or whether, as seems more probable, it be the necessary consequences of the faculties of reason and speech ... It is common to all men, and to be found in no other race of animals. (Smith, 1776/1970: 119)

For Smith, economic action, 'justice and morality are expressions of man's nature' (Skinner, 1970: 27). What might be seen as a political intervention, the division of labour into increasingly small and repetitive tasks, is understood by Smith as something essentially human and thus unquestionable.

In the sphere of ethics and moral philosophy, the autonomous, free-thinking rational subject was thrust centre stage and contrasted with actors and actions governed by tradition. 'The human faculties of perception, judgment, discriminative feeling, mental activity and even moral preference are exercised only in making a choice. He who does anything because it is the custom makes no choice' (Mills, 1859/1991: 74). The notion of a rational, discriminating sovereign individual, bestowed with a nature held in common, or *identically*, with other people comes to the fore. Identity is equated with human faculties which are 'within' each individual and unfold throughout the course of a life.

The notion of society is not ignored. But social influences upon character are understood in a particular way (Mills, 1859/1991: 76; Smith, 1776/1970: 120). In Mills's work, society imposes constraints upon free choice, either through force or coercion. For Smith, society is understood as a break upon the actor's ability to know their own essential human nature. Smith famously argued that differences between 'philosophers and common street porters' derive not 'so much from nature as from habit, custom and education' (Smith, 1776/1970: 120). People start with identical attributes and human faculties and social factors stop them knowing their true human selves.

It is worth raising one point about 'the sovereign individual' at this point. Whilst most philosophers and social theorists have consigned the sovereign individual to history, not all social institutions have followed suit. The law, for example, still starts and ends with 'the individual' (Williams, in Hall, 1996). The business of the criminal court is to know the person, their motivations and their sense of remorse. Appearances can be seen through; motivations can be known; character can be measured. The HRM practices considered latter in this chapter also place the individual candidate centre stage. The business of recruitment involves knowing, assessing and measuring a candidate's individual dispositions and attributes: 'The individual is the basic unit of analysis underpinning many HRM practices, that is, an essential human subject whose nature is to be discovered or uncovered and who is to be motivated through the exercise of correct procedures of recruitment, selection, appraisal …' (Townley, 1993: 522). The point here is that organizational practices – and not just 'theories' – are posited upon particular ways of knowing the subject. Whilst the sophisticated analyst might suggest HRM practices create the illusion of a unified subject, the practices roll on regardless because there are 'good organizational reasons' (Garfinkel, 1967) for such assumptions; they provide for apparently rational, reasonable and impartial decisions.

The Social Self

The second 'strategic point' in Hall's (1996) account is the emergence of the 'social self' in light of the massive social and institutional transformations of the nineteenth and twentieth centuries. Modern industrial society established complex social groupings, along the lines of work, occupation, class, region, gender and ethnicity. Efforts to understand identity simply in terms of a generic set of human faculties unfolding from within each person seemed to overlook the reality of complex urban society; that it was awash with different 'ways of being'. These differences came to define key political fault-lines of the twentieth century, such as class politics, trade unionism and feminism. Identity came to be viewed as the product of the individual's engagement with society and thus became thoroughly politicized as a site of struggle and contestation.

Of course, scholars differed sharply on how best to theorize the 'social' basis of identity and this was nowhere more apparent than in discussions about work. In their study of a car plant in the UK, Goldthorpe et al. (1968) described three different orientations to work, 'instrumental', 'bureaucratic' and 'solidaristic'. These orientations, it was argued, were independent of the social specifics of the workplace. They did not arise from within the 'enclosed sphere of work' (Townley, 1993). To understand work identities, they argued, we need to consider the 'structures and processes of the wider society'. In the 1960s Britain was becoming increasingly consumerist and the relative affluence of the workers that Goldthorpe and his colleagues studied was increasing. The dull work in factories and offices was simply an instrumental means to an end for them; work enabled them to participate in the more exciting domain of consumption.

At first glance, Paul Willis's (1978/2003) account stands in sharp contrast. But like Goldthorpe and colleagues, Willis also describes how working identities are constructed outside the workplace. Willis considered how a group of teenagers ('the lads') participated in a school counter-culture whose central motifs were class based. 'The lads', rejected the official aims of the school and tormented teachers and 'the earols' (the name 'the lads' gave to the 'swots') alike, assuming a heroic status for themselves right up to the point where they – like their fathers before them – passed through the factory gates.

In both these studies, working identities are established aside from specific corporations. For Willis the important matters were class and the implicit (misogynistic) masculinity of the lads; for Goldthorpe and colleagues, the focus was on changing urban society. Authors such as Goldthorpe et al., however, did not study work practices, say ethnographically. In contrast, authors such as Erving Goffman and Michael Burawoy did and say ethnographically they came to stress the importance of organizational practices for the identities of members.

Burawoy (1979) took the opposite view to those expressed above, arguing that shopfloor culture is a 'relatively autonomous' domain. For Burawoy, employee identity and consent are manufactured at the point of production. The important matter is how an individual is positioned with respect to: formal and informal rules, colleagues, the flow of materials, supervisory and higher management and necessary skill levels. Wider issues such as race, age and religion are secondary. At most, Burawoy concedes 'consciousness moulded in practices outside the factory do affect, although within narrow limits, the way operators respond' (Burawoy, 1979: 152).

Erving Goffman also examined how identity is produced in organizational practices and arrangements. Indeed, Goffman (1961) specifically chose to study organizations which aimed to shape individual identity, such as asylums and prisons. He explored processes including admissions procedures, which deprived people of their name and property and the imposition of degrading postures, uniforms and restrictions on self-determination, such as choices about when to eat and rest. These processes strip the individual of normal supports and attachments and pave the way for identities to be fleshed out in light of institutional aims.

Goffman brings into view a 'disturbed and disturbing picture of the subject' (Hall, 1996) as dominated by what he calls 'organizational logics'. In one of the most powerful sections in Goffman's work the conniving logic of the asylum is revealed. In asylums, forms of resistance, such as throwing furniture, ripping clothes and establishing collections were treated as *further evidence of why the person should be confined*, that is as irrational, dangerous and inexplicable acts, rather than entirely understandable responses to harsh forms of domination. Organization comes to rule the individual; efforts to resist just make matters worse.

In these studies, 'rational individualism' is strongly rejected. They show how identity is forged with respect to class (Willis, 1978/2003), the consumer society (Goldthorpe et al., 1968), the organization of production (Burawoy, 1979) and practices specifically designed to craft identities (Goffman, 1961). The centrality (or irrelevance) of organization for forging identity becomes a point of debate with strong arguments on either side.

The Decentred Subject

As with all tragic heroes, in the final act of Hall's account the modern subject is finally killed off. In the work of the aforementioned authors, traces of this subject remained. In Burawoy priority is given to labour as 'humankind's constitutive activity' (Du Gay, 1996: 17); everything else is only relevant within 'narrow limits'. As such, Burawoy might be accused of drawing upon some notion of an essential human condition realized through work. In much of Goffman's work there also remained a tense and ambiguous distinction between the social self and the interior self, who is writing the script for self-as-performer. The nature of this relation and questions about the origins of the inner self were rarely explicitly addressed by Goffman.

The next move was to finish the job. There are a large number of suspects. These include authors such as Garfinkel, Lacan (via Freud), Althusser (via Marx) and Foucault. These authors differ radically in how they approach identity. But they share a common theoretical drift. They reject any assumption that identity is fixed, stable and somehow aside from politics and power. They share the belief that identity always has to be brought into being, via ideology, through unconscious psychic processes and disciplinary practice. They agree that identity is never 'finished' but is an ongoing project. They all suggest identities are rife with tensions and contradictions – in Freud between the good and bad parts, masculine and feminine, and love and hate for the father (Hall, 1996).

The rest of this section further elaborates Foucault's role in the final de-centring of the subject. The argument is not that Foucault's work is somehow the most important or influential, though it has shaped Organization Studies substantially (see Knights and Willmott, 1989). The point is more pragmatic: these ideas are deemed the most relevant for exploring the practices and techniques considered later in this chapter, through which extra-curricular activities are accumulated and assessed.

In a series of historical studies Foucault moved beyond the notion of 'the individual as reducible to an internal core of meaning' (Townley, 1993: 522) by examining how a series of modern subjects was brought into being, these modern subjects including the 'criminal', the 'insane' and the 'sexual pervert'. In each case, Foucault asked how such identities were generated through a complex of institutional arrangements (asylums, factories, barracks, prisons), forms of expertise (criminology, psychotherapy, psychology) and mundane practices (examinations, schedules, charts, inspections).

Foucault described three main ways in which modern societies produced subjects. In the first two, subjects are constituted by others, perhaps against their will. This would apply to students being graded by academics or employees being graded by 'accurate and objective HR practices' administered by suitably trained individuals (Townley, 1993: 522). To track these modes of objectification, the research is encouraged to examine systems of 'classification, codification, categorisation, precise calibration … tables and taxonomies' (Townley, 1993: 522) through which trained professionals assess and rank members of a population, such as job applicants or employees.

In the third mode, individuals are more active in turning themselves into subjects 'by becoming objects to themselves' (Metcalfe, 1993: 623). Here Foucault emphasizes practices through which actors write about and assess self. These include the confessional, the autobiography, the mediation and the diary. In the workplace, the equivalent practices would be the CV, the interview, the application form and the annual report. The individual is invited to apply frameworks of classification, codification and assessment to themselves, as a way of producing knowledge about themselves. Systems of power even require the actor to actively participate in their own individualization (Metcalfe, 1993).

For instance, academic assessment is a good example of a hierarchical system of 'normalizing judgement'. It creates homogeneity by establishing norms for the whole population. At the same time it individualizes 'by establishing minute distinctions between people according to their variation from the norm' (Metcalfe, 1993: 623). But academic assessment is also something students do to themselves. Through prolonged exposure to academic assessment, students routinely begin to assess themselves in these terms. Those who regularly get beyond 70 per cent begin to think of themselves as 'a first-class student'. For them, a grade of 58 per cent would not only be disappointing; it would be 'out of character'. This sense of self and the anxiety it produces, sometimes leads students to work excessively. The focus is on practices and techniques that are productive of identities ('the first-class student'); power is not purely negative – rather, in part, it is constitutive of ways in which people might think about and act upon themselves.

Identity and Organization Theory

Over the last 20 years, researchers studying organizations have become increasingly interested in identity. This is the result of different observations about the changing nature of society including: (a) the fragmentation of class groupings (see Hanlon, 1998); (b) the recognition of different orientations *within* occupational groupings (Ezzamel and Willmott, 1998; Knights and McCabe, 2000); (c) the recognition that 'gender' had been largely overlooked in accounts that privileged masculine labour (such as Willis, 1978/2003); and (d) the refusal to treat 'the point of production' (Burawoy, 1979) as *the* site for the constitution of identities (Du Gay, 1996). These points, and others besides, have led to a problematization of identity, which organization theory has pursued with vigour.

At the same time authors have noted that organizations, perhaps more than at previous times, are seeking to explicitly manage the identity of employees. Some examples of such attempts to manage identity include culture management initiatives (Fleming, 2005c; Grugulis et al., 2000), corporate induction and training programmes (Alvesson and Willmott, 2002: 622; Pratt, 2000); and even the construction of organizational histories (Rowlinson and Hassard, 1993). The expansion and formalization of such practices has been conceptualized by Alvesson and Willmott (2002: 622) in terms of broader social changes, whereby 'The relatively stable aesthetic of Fordist modernism has given way to all the ferment, instability and fleeting qualities of a post-modern aesthetic that celebrates difference, ephemerality, spectacle, fashion, and the commodification of cultural forms' (Ezzamel et al., 2000 in Alvesson and Willmott, 2002: 622–3).

In organization theory then, as elsewhere, those transformations sketched so clearly by Stuart Hall have been discussed. The stable subject of Fordism gives way to the de-centred postmodern subject. Previously secure relationships between identity, meaning and employment are no longer 'presumed or taken-for-granted', but 'have to be actively engendered or manufactured' (Alvesson and Willmott, 2002:623) through a variety of practices.

Where they have been studied in detail, these practices look familiar but different from those examined at previous historical points. Consider two illustrations. In their study of a team-based reorganisation at a car manufacturing plant, Knights and McCabe (2000) describe a remarkable level of attentiveness to meaning and identity. This includes the use of psychologists, the re-labelling of employees – irrespective of rank – as 'associates', the distribution of firm-based uniforms, 'hypnotic propaganda' in company training documents, the articulation of a new mission statement and the construction of an in-house learning centre. These practices are familiar enough. Many were described by Erving Goffman nearly half a century ago. The difference being, of course, that Goffman studied asylums and prisons and not car manufacturers.

Second, consider personnel counselling at Hawthorne. For an extended period at Hawthorne, each employee had access to a trained counsellor and the opportunity to break from work to discuss matters with them. Often these discussions were very personal in nature. Perennial concerns for the reproduction of an efficient workforce – sex and alcohol – featured often. Wilensky and Wilensky (1951) have argued that personnel counselling was simply clever management; it diffused conflict, weakened trade unions and established trust in the employment relationship. Even so, employees' files were confidential and counsellors at least seemed to believe they were using their expertise to help individuals. It was a professional service aside from management, although how far *is* debatable (see Wilensky and Wilensky, 1951).

Initiatives like personnel counselling are familiar but different from contemporary developments, such as those described by Pratt (2000), through which Amway 'agents' were encouraged to identify with the organization. In Pratt's study, psychological expertise is deployed in a more nakedly aggressive way, to engender 'cult-like' levels of commitment to the 'cause' of the corporation. The form of expertise is familiar, but the locus of power has shifted to solve, not personal problems, but 'problem employees' who are unenthused by the mission of Amway.

Studies in the tradition of those mentioned above (Alvesson and Willmott, 2002: 622; Casey, 1995; Collinson, 2003; Du Gay, 1996; Ezzamel and Willmott, 1998; Fleming, 2005c; Gabriel, 1995; Grugulis et al., 2000; Knights and McCabe, 2000) have tended to focus on people who are already in work. However, the impulses, rhythms and styles of corporate life also permeate and shape lives more broadly, beyond the legal or geographical boundaries of workplaces. Indeed, many people are familiar with practices of workplace control before they even enter the workplace. They develop this familiarity in a range of ways. One is through developing 'transferable skills'. These are not expressed in an explicit manual, but are a broad framework through which it is possible to talk about, plan and evidence individual experience. Via this framework, it is possible to draw connections between seemingly disparate activities and domains. Such connections are fluid, they have to be accomplished a new each and every time and there are no set rules. Nevertheless, there are familiar ways of going about establishing such connections. Consider an example from a Department for Education and Skill's (DfES) publication. This is a hypothetical example of a personal statement of someone applying to university.

> Practising Yoga in my leisure time has taught me to be more self-disciplined and motivated. I also enjoy singing and hope to be able to use this skill to generate extra income for the university. Currently I am continuing to build on my word processing skills, learning to drive and planning to travel to Greece next year. (DfES, 2002: 62)

The imaginary candidate trawls their everyday life for sources of value. They find familiar connections and associations. It is not just that the candidate can drive, but that they are 'learning' to drive; they are not simply going on holiday, they are 'planning' to 'travel' to Greece. They do not just sing; they will use this 'skill' – somewhat unbelievably – to earn money for the university. It is not just that they practise Yoga, Yoga has enabled them to be more 'self-disciplined' and 'motivated'. Everyday activities are made relevant for an entirely different domain (Higher Education) via the idea of *generic skills*. The assumption of generic skills is that, for example, 'planning' can be separated from what is being planned. People can be good or bad at planning *per se*. Nothing can escape this type of reasoning. Even buying a pair of trainers can become an impressive feat of decision-making (DfES, 2002: 36).

This has a comic aspect; but there is a serious element too. The market for graduate labour is very tight in the UK. With increasing numbers of people passing through Higher Education each year, this looks set to continue. Large numbers of people are graduating each year with good degrees from good universities. In the UK a 2:1 is fast becoming a base requirement but not something to distinguish the candidate from others in a very competitive labour market. In this context these rather ambiguous skills and attributes become a key source of differentiation and value. This is reflected in the practices of hiring firms. In the graduate recruitment processes considered later in this chapter, candidates were scored out of 30. Only 10 points were for educational attainment. Twenty points were allocated for personal qualities and depth; extra-curricular activities and achievements.

Many of my own tutees routinely spend anything up to a third of each week on extra-curricular activities, such as working (often in a voluntary capacity), chairing committees and helping run university societies, playing for and helping to organize sports teams, and so on. There is a growing market now for the acquisition of transferable skills. Companies such as World Challenge offer experiences designed to develop transferable skills, such as team-working, leadership skills and perseverance. There is evidence that people do take such matters seriously and act on themselves in the light of such considerations.

I approached job hunting very seriously in terms of thinking what I really wanted and what I had been working towards since I was about 14 ... I always wanted a good career, that's why I did economics, because it would give me good career options, and I went very early to the careers office, at the start of my second year ... and of course I tried to make sure I didn't work all the time because I knew that they want more than just a good academic record ... so I did things like running the golf team. It all shows that you can take responsibility for things. (Grey, 1994: 483)

Managing one's identity this way is not entirely straightforward. One matter concerns the character of the skills and attributes being assessed. Some skills, such as being able to fit a new clutch or re-wire a house, can be empirically demonstrated. Business skills and qualities such as 'creativity' or the candidate's 'business sense' are less easy to practically demonstrate; it would be like trying to prove someone was nice or reasonable. All that can be done, in the absence of any direct measure, is to describe specific occasions where the quality or skill in question may have been demonstrated. The candidate needs a list of 'suitable' experiences to draw on and the ability to spin a good yarn.

A second related matter concerns the individual's ability to know their own abilities and skills. In contrast to music abilities, for instance, where individuals can practise graded pieces, there is no standard or national test for 'creativity' or 'teamwork'. There are numerous psychological measures and books which tell candidates how to score these tests. These form part of this discourse. But there is no single scale. People cannot know whether they have done enough, compared to others. Perhaps these are the uncertainties which can propel some students to manage themselves fairly strictly, as Weber (1930/2001) suggested.

To summarize, at certain points some people are located within the ambit of a system of power–knowledge that renders their lives and experiences amenable to observation, classification and assessment in terms of the presence or absence of employable skills, qualities and attributes. Such possibilities arise from the assumption of generic skills, which transcend specific domains. Around this idea, a whole body of knowledge and expertise has been produced, which has opened the way for new forms of assessment and evaluation: psychological scales that measure 'leadership skills'; books that tell candidates 'how to' demonstrate specific skills; assessment schedules of hiring firms that rank individuals against desired corporate standards. These are technologies and instruments that position the individual as a subject of a particular historically specific discourse. Of course, there are lots of different ways of having an identity; in the same way that 'fashion' gives rise to lots of different ways of dressing. The discourse of transferable skills gives rise to *possibilities* for new forms of self-management.

Such discursive possibilities do not just hang around. They are made concrete in the plans, strategies and practices of different institutions, most obviously the institutions of the state and of hiring organizations. Let's look at two illustrative examples, the first is the progress file for school children, the second is the application process for gaining a graduate job.

Progress File

Progress File (DfES, 2002) was developed by the Department for Education and Skills (UK) and is literally a file, divided into four sections entitled: 'getting started', 'moving on', 'exploring pathways' and 'widening horizons'. Each is around 50–70 pages long and consists of a great many exercises, logs, quizzes and tests. It is aimed at school children and is administered via schools, on a voluntary basis. The individual author (the pupil) is encouraged to record and develop their skills and qualities via Progress File over the course of numerous years. It is an example of a 'technology of the self' (Miller and Rose, 1990), a set of practices administered by the self, about the self, designed to produce employable selves. A small number of features of Progress File are considered below to illustrate themes discussed above.

First, Progress File trades on the image of the sovereign individual. It claims to gradually reveal the self of the author, to the author, through a series of exercises, logs and charts. The self of the author is already formed but opaque. The exercises, logs and assessments are thus akin to technologies (Miller and Rose, 1990) for casting light on something that was previously in the gloom.

Second, Progress File is not a hierarchical system of assessment and grading, although the individual's work is occasionally considered by their 'team of supporters' ('Getting Started' DfES, 2002: 13), which includes parents, family, teachers, tutors, personal advisers, careers advisers and friends. For the most part, the individual is asked 'what kind of person are you?' ('Moving On' DfES, 2002: 31) and has to produce and retrospectively assess their own answers over time. Progress File is understandable in terms of Foucault's third mode of objectification; individual authors are actively invited to turn themselves into objects of conscious reflection and analysis (Metcalfe, 1993: 623). The file is akin to an extended diary.

Third, Progress File is an evidence-based system. It is committed to the idea that personal qualities can be demonstrated: 'it is easy enough to say that you are like this or that, but when you need to get it across to someone else.....they will want proof' ('Getting Started' DfES, 2002: 45). The sheer weight of evidence that is demanded is remarkable. Progress File demands constant writing. Within one stretch of 12 pages, there are exercises, tables and charts which invite authors to record

- all their achievements (p. 30), in each case presenting both *'what I did'* and the *'evidence'* of that achievement
- general activities undertaken in their private lives, and evidence of the skills used (p. 37)
- instances (up to two for each) where the author used one or combinations of the seven key skills (pp. 40–1)
- their possession of personal qualities *'that make you an individual'*, with appropriate evidence (p. 43).

Fourth, Progress File trades on the idea of generic transferable skills and teaches the author how to make mundane activities relevant for work; 'having a party' is conceptualized in terms of planning, organizing, budgeting, shopping and communication. The idea of generic transferable skills is not exposed as an assumption or a point of view. It is embedded in the text: 'I turned up to football training every week and did not miss a match *which shows I'm reliable*' and 'I wrote to every supermarket in town until I got a weekend job, *which shows I'm persistent*' ('Widening Horizons', DfES, 2002: 41).

Fifth, Progress File has an obvious disciplinary zeal. Individuals are asked to look at their lives and find areas to improve. In one case the reader is told about an imaginary character 'Sam' who enjoys 'snack meals at home, likes being with friends but spends a lot of time watching TV and is sporty but cannot be bothered to train hard'. Sam is clearly a problem; he is idle and eats badly. Under the heading 'Improving and Developing Sam' the author is asked how Sam might change his life at school and 'in other areas' ('Getting Started', DfES, 2002: 25). Matters including diet and watching TV are brought under the disciplinary gaze. On the next page the author is invited to reflect on how *they* might 'Improve and Develop' themselves.

Following on, Progress File clearly privileges some qualities and characteristics over others. Skills associated with 'adapting to change', 'creativity', 'influencing others' and 'risk taking' are emphasized throughout (e.g. see 'Widening Horizons', DfES, 2002: 38). This is not subtle or implicit. Authors are asked directly 'how enterprising are you'? They are challenged to name an entrepreneur and state whether they are willing to take risks and respond to change ('Moving On', DfES, 2002: 55). The central problem is the author's possession of employable skills and dispositions.

Progress File nicely illustrates a number of points raised above. It can be understood as a disciplinary technology that, rather than passively revealing the self of the author, actively seeks to generate some types of subject and not others. It enables young people to talk about, think about and manage themselves as a bundle of employable skills and attitudes. It is a quintessentially modern technique, though the individual author has to apply a set of Victorian values – against idleness, poor diet and lacking endeavour – to themselves, through continual writing and self-reflection. The values promoted are familiar ones, bound up with contemporary discourses of work (Du Gay, 1996), such as risk, creativity, dynamism and entrepreneurship. Clearly corporations are not the only conduits for the reproduction of privileged organizational and managerial categories and values. Well before they enter the labour market, young people are confronted with materials that ascribe ontological priority to such ideas. Connections are forged between the everyday lives of children – playing sport, eating snacks, buying trainers, watching TV – and the world of work.

Recruitment and Selection: HR Practices

When people apply for a job, they face the full force of such systems. This second illustration looks at how candidates for graduate jobs are assessed in terms of their possession of employable skills and attributes. The materials come from the graduate recruitment process of a large multinational firm.

First, these recruitment processes are also based upon assumptions of an inner self that can be revealed through inspection 'an essential human subject whose nature is to be discovered or uncovered ... through the exercise of correct procedures' (Townley, 1993: 522). The candidate is measured, not their social performance. Their performance is 'seen through' in order to get to their character. Whilst the candidates' ability to play the 'interview game' may be the most important factor, the practices themselves cannot be explicit about this.

Second, this is a system of hierarchical observation and normalizing judgement. The candidate is broken down into various categories which both homogenize, whilst allowing for minute distinctions to be drawn. In Figure 8.1, for example, 30 points are allocated for academic ability (higher and secondary education), experience and activities (travel and work) and qualities, depth and breadth (responsibilities, hobbies, achievements). Each is allocated a maximum of 10 points, resulting in a total possible score of 30. The candidate needs to score 18 or more to progress through to the final phase of recruitment. In the example in Figure 8.1, the candidate scored 19. Even though there is no agreed science of 'depth', points are allocated nevertheless.

Third, this is a system of assessment based on recounted experience, rather than proof. During the job interviews, individuals were asked to recount occasions where they 'motivated a team', displayed 'leadership abilities' and 'overcame a challenge'. Candidates often admitted, in post-interview comments, to exaggerating and simply lying, that is, drawing on things friends had done. It is thus a fairly loose system of assessment. Candidates must know how to make everyday experience relevant for workplace categories and have a suitable list of experiences to draw upon.

Fourth, despite the semi-scientific character of the form, the interviewer is also 'making it up on the spot'. Filling out the form is a social achievement.

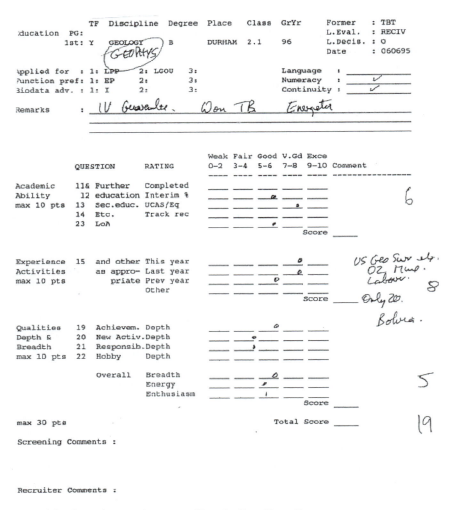

Figure 8.1   Assessing experiences, qualities, depth and breadth

Human Resources professionals do not have manuals that rank, for instance, yoga above Grade 3 on the piano, or captaining the football team above organizing a holiday to France. On each and every occasion the interviewer has to 'find' a score of five rather than six, or six rather than seven. The interviewer's reasoning is made concrete through the classification system of the form. All that is left of the candidate are these numbers. Facts about the candidate are actively manufactured by the very processes that claim to be passively revealing the candidate's actual essence.

During the period of the interview at least, the individual is caught within a complex web of techniques, expectations, categories, scales, and expertise that take their everyday activities, interests and hobbies and rank them with respect to some desired corporate standard. For the candidate there is no way out, assuming they want the job. The gaze of the corporation is extended backwards in time. The list of relevancies is familiar enough, for example, washing-up rotas and domestic arrangements, the issue of mid-week drinking, the individual's interest in healthy outdoor pursuits, girlfriends. The genius of such practices is their ability to lend arbitrary options a veneer of fact and objectivity. Even though there is no science of 'hobbies', such features of every-day life can be easily brought within a bureaucratic logic of codification, measurement and control.

Discussion

The materials discussed above help to illustrate the idea that corporate identities might be forged, not simply by specific corporations, but in and through the individual's engagement with frameworks of thought and action which cut across organizational boundaries and social systems. Corporate life extends beyond the boundaries of specific corporations; this is one of the defining features of an organizational society. In late modern society, boundaries between work and non-work blur or even dissolve. Famous examples have large corporations attempting to control employee conduct beyond the boundaries of the workplace via such initiatives as the 'sociology department' at Ford, which was founded on the idea that a good corporate culture arose from appropriate home conditions.

> The enquiries conducted by the industrialists into workers' private lives and the inspection services created by some firms to control the morality of their workers are necessities of the new methods of work ... [this] is the biggest collective effort to date to create, with unprecedented speed, and with a consciousness of purpose unmatched in history, a new type of workers and of man. (Gramsci, 1971: 302)

On other occasions, employees remain at work, but the scope of corporate 'inspection' extends to the very soul of the employee (Rose, 1989). By 1945 Jacoby suggests over 20 per cent of US psychologists were engaged in efforts to sustain employee morale (Jacoby in Grint, 1998: 123).

The present chapter has considered one further way in which boundaries between work and non-work may be becoming increasingly unclear. It has pointed to techniques that make watching TV, eating snacks, playing sport, buying trainers, practising yoga, having a party, going on holiday and domestic cleanliness relevant for work. Such connections are forged by the idea of 'generic transferable skills'. Around this idea a world of knowledge, expertise and technique has been produced in recent years. This has smoothed the way for new forms of assessment and self-management. Children as young as 12

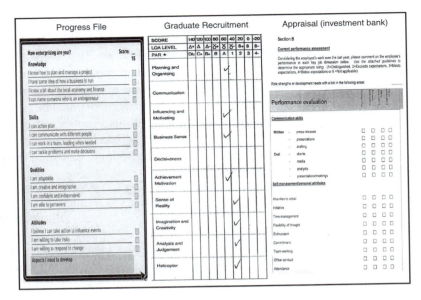

Figure 8.2   Three examples of assessment frameworks

can be encouraged to imagine themselves in relation to privileged managerial categories, such as risk-taking, innovation, entrepreneurship and even 'change'.

By exploring such matters further, previously un-examined connections and overlaps might be revealed that would raise questions about the preparation of subjects of work. Corporate systems of assessment and classification don't exist in isolation, but dovetail with other comparable frameworks aside from the world of work, both in terms of form and content. Figure 8.2 considers just three examples. In each case, the techniques for assessment are familiar, even though they target different groups: school children, graduates and investment bankers. Intangible skills, attitudes and qualities are numerically scored on single scales. Each relies on an element of self assessment. Each produces facts about the individual. Even the layout and style are familiar. More importantly perhaps, each is similar in content. The categories resonate with each other. Children and graduates are asked to evidence their leadership skills and business sense. School children and investment bankers are quizzed about their orientation to risk and even change. By the time they find themselves at work, people are very used to talking about themselves using privileged corporate categories.

It is clear why Giddens (1991) suggests the late modern subject is, perhaps above all else, a subject that reflexively knows itself. When writing personal statements, job applications, CVs, performance appraisals and annual reports, the individual is propelled to take a reflexive stance towards themselves as a subject of work. This is, according to Giddens, utterly characteristic. He argues that whatever the topic – body size and shape, parenting, looks, business acumen or various other abilities (sporting, culinary, DIY, sexual) – there has been a massive expansion in opportunities to talk about and rate 'self'. In each topic area discussed above, there are an array of TV shows, magazines, websites, discussion groups/forums, clubs and qualifications. Through participation in such diverse networks, people learn how to assess and manage their self in relation to what is normal, excellent or avant-garde.

Consider these points in relation to the matters discussed above. Whilst the state was traditionally the key conduit for careers advice, today a multiplicity of actors, technologies and bodies of knowledge combine to deliver on-the-spot advice. How to get the 'dream job' is a stock question addressed by glossy magazines, reality TV series (e.g. *Who Would Hire You*, BBC Three, UK), prescriptive bestsellers (e.g. *How to Master Personality Questionnaires* and *101 Best Resumes*) and endless websites (mycvbuilder, instantcv, skillsstudio). Different media and forms of expertise and knowledge are combined. In the series *Who Would Hire You*, occupational psychology overlaps with reality TV; in the same BBC online article about recruitment entitled 'Getting the Job', the views of Angela Baron, from the Chartered Institute of Personnel and Development are intertwined with those of Caroline Baxter, fashion editor of *Cosmopolitan*. In this domain, there has been a characteristic expansion of discourse and a 'dispersion of centres from which discourse emanates' (Foucault, 1976/1998: 34). Whilst the present chapter has considered formal interventions, by schools and hiring firms, the spread of discourse about individual performance at work is clearly much broader than this.

Conclusion

This chapter has considered links between identity, work and organization. The main aim has been to discuss a broad shift in thinking about identity. Rather than treating the sense that people have that they are unique and indivisible, as natural and unproblematic, it can be viewed as something that has to be achieved or accomplished. Once this is assumed, numerous avenues of research open up and these are reviewed by way of conclusion.

First, the researcher can examine where assumptions of a stable inner-self (Townley, 1993) persist and then attempt to explain why. This can help reveal core features of organizational life. Consider the matter of graduate recruitment. Suppose an interviewer were to state that they were assessing, not character, achievement or truth but performance and style. Decisions between equally qualified candidates would be made on the basis of 'artistic merit'. Most likely, this would offend organizational requirements for rational decision-making and candidates' desire to be treated seriously and fairly. The 'sovereign individual' is thus a happy and convenient myth for the purposes of recruitment. Some organizational practices cannot be entirely reflexive.

Even though candidates do lie and even though there is no system for ranking 'hobbies', the business of recruitment demands that such matters are kept under the surface.

Second, such a shift directs attention to how frameworks of thought and action find their way into the plans and practices of *different* institutions. The focus on 'employability' has highlighted this well. It has become apparent how a contemporary discourse of transferable skills cuts across boundaries of age, sector and institution. Moreover, whilst the state might traditionally have been the key conduit for 'careers advice', in the contemporary period knowledge and expertise has been de-coupled from traditional sources of authority (Giddens, 1991); the medium has come to reflect the message. The individual is no longer a passive recipient of state-approved knowledge, but an active and discerning consumer of diverse forms of expertise. Of interest is thus both: (a) how 'employability' is broken down, assessed and rendered manageable; and (b) how individuals consume such knowledge. On both counts, the analyst is able to grasp important social changes.

Finally, the analyst is able to locate organizational practices historically, by exploring shifts in discourse underpinning organizational practices. Such matters are well beyond the scope of this chapter, but it is possible to imagine questions about hegemony and contradiction. In the present chapter, for example, an individualizing logic of assessment was used to distinguish between candidates who, nevertheless, came from institutions (Oxford, Cambridge and Durham) steeped in tradition and class privilege. How the discourse of transferable workplace skills maps onto broader, seemingly contradictory, social formations would be an interesting matter to explore. It might be argued that characteristic middle-class activities and forms of self-understanding – that one 'travels' (rather than goes on holiday), that one's children should play musical instruments from an early age, etc. – allow some to effortlessly accumulate a long list of suitable experiences. Perhaps technologies such as Progress File are best understood in this light; as optimistic attempts to enable those without such advantages to 'enterprise themselves up' (Du Gay, 1996). In this sense, it would be a classically Thatcherite intervention; quasi-Victorian, pro-enterprise and anti-class privilege.

9

KNOWLEDGE

Jacky Swan and Maxine Robertson

Introduction

Nowadays, in what is often referred to as 'knowledge based' economies, corporations are giving serious attention to managing and exploiting knowledge, perceiving it to be the most important strategic resource. Commentators and researchers claim that if corporations are going to sustain competitive advantage in the knowledge economy then they must continually innovate, and this requires the development of a more strategic approach to 'knowledge management' (Hansen, 1999). However, the notion that knowledge can (or should) be managed, in much the same way that other corporate resources (e.g. finance, labour) are managed, has been subject to significant critique in recent years (Alvesson et al., 2002; Fuller, 2002; Newell et al., 2002; Swan and Scarbrough, 2001). In this chapter, we will build on these earlier critiques by outlining the treatment of 'knowledge' in corporate life and by reviewing what actually happens when organizations attempt to 'manage' knowledge and what assumptions underpin these attempts. In particular, the chapter will explore the implications of the recent vogue in 'knowledge management' for the appropriation by corporations of the personal network relationships and friendship ties of their employees in order to satisfy their increasing hunger for knowledge.

We start by considering the emergence and hype surrounding 'knowledge management' and trace a brief history of key developments within this field. In so doing, we discuss the implications of managerial approaches to 'knowledge management' for work organization and relationships. This discussion suggests that, regardless of more academic debates on the manageability (or otherwise) of knowledge, corporations are increasingly attempting to introduce a host of mechanisms to handle and deal with knowledge – mechanisms that may have profound (and sometimes unintended) consequences for the working lives and roles of those involved.

We then consider the implications of different management responses to the 'knowledge management' problem. In particular, we note that, as the intensity of 'knowledge work' increases, and the boundaries around what it means to be 'an organization' become increasingly blurred, corporations are increasingly looking towards intra- and inter-organizational alliances and networks as major vehicles for acquiring and exploiting knowledge. Networks, including personal and friendship-based networks, are now on many corporate agendas as forums that require active management intervention. The chapter on 'community' in this book directly speaks to this issue, highlighting the way in which many firms are currently trying to create and manage communities-of-practice as part of the approach to 'knowledge management'. On the one hand, this could be seen as another example of the ways in which managerialism further encroaches upon personal life. On the other hand, the deployment of personal friendships to source information and get work done could also be seen as an everyday aspect of working life, combining personal and work objectives. We consider these possibilities by examining the ways in which people working in the biotechnology industry – often described as 'knowledge workers' – are apparently willing to exploit their interpersonal relationships and friendship ties to achieve corporate objectives. We conclude by considering the implications of this both for corporations, in terms of their ongoing quest to manage knowledge and the risks associated with promoting this activity, and also for the individual in terms of the blurring of professional and personal relationships.

The 'Knowledge' Discourse and the Emergence of 'Knowledge Management'

The term 'knowledge' can be broadly defined as the ability to discriminate within and across contexts (cf. Tsoukas and Vladimirou, 2001). It encompasses the ways in which individuals in particular social situations and contexts understand, and make sense of, where they are and what they are doing. The problematizing of 'knowledge' as an asset that needs to be nurtured, protected and exploited by corporations in order to ensure survival is one that is certainly not new. The development of American patenting systems of the eighteenth century, and Tayloristic attempts to redesign work in the early twentieth century, both sought to reduce variations in production by managing and controlling the craft-based skills of workers and the organizations' knowledge base.

What does appear to be distinctive in recent decades, however, is an increased intensity of knowledge in the production process, fuelled by significant developments in information technology and the growth of the service sector in developed economies. As Castells notes:

> What characterises the current technological revolution is not the centrality of knowledge and information but the application of such knowledge and information to knowledge generation and information processing/communication devices, in a cumulative feedback loop between innovation and the uses of innovation . . . For the first time in history, the human mind is a direct productive force, not just a decisive element of a production system. (1996: 32)

Knowledge, it is claimed, is now acting upon itself in an accelerating spiral of innovation and change. Consultancy work, and the growing importance of the consultancy sector to economic change (Armbruster, 2006), is a good example of this in so far as what consultants do is to apply knowledge to existing knowledge to circulate and commodify new (arguably sometimes not so new) knowledge.

Mirroring these trends in the organization of work, recent decades have seen an explosive growth in the attention and status afforded to 'knowledge' in relation to innovation and economic growth by academe, industry and policy groups alike. Studies tracking the emergence of 'knowledge management', for example, demonstrate exponential growth in academic articles, practitioner texts and websites on the subject since the term first started to appear in the mid-1990s (Scarbrough and Swan, 2001). This explosion of interest in 'knowledge as an asset', which needs to be proactively managed by corporations, also reflects trends seen in the management literature – with consultants and management 'gurus' such as Peter Drucker, Erik Sveiby, and Peter Senge, their own networks of publishers and the media, further fuelling the fire (Greatbach and Clark, 2005). 'Knowledge', has come to occupy an important discursive space – a space that has, of course, existed since Socrates ('The only good is knowledge and the only evil is ignorance'), but that has, it is claimed, been opened yet further by post-industrialism and associated shifts in the organization of work. Knowledge has become an imperative for economic growth amongst political leaders – 'We know what the twenty-first century needs. A strong civic society. A knowledge based economy. A confident place in the world. Do that and a nation masters the future. Fail and it is the future's victim' (Tony Blair, speech, 1999) – and one that shows few signs of abating – 'In the last decade Britain's knowledge intensive sector has grown twice as fast as the overall economy' (Gordon Brown, speech, 2005).

In this overly hyped environment, it is easy to dismiss 'knowledge management' as just another management fashion, not worthy of any further serious attention by those interested in really understanding organizations. Yet, beneath the hype there lies something quite enduring – a positioning, by researchers across many academic disciplines and practitioners, of knowledge as *the* most critical asset that corporations, and societies as a whole, have. Regardless of the different ontological and epistemological debates around 'intellectual and social capital' (Nahapiet and Ghoshal, 1998), 'the knowledge economy', 'knowledge work', 'knowledge intensive firms', and the growth of, 'knowledge-worker occupations' (Drucker, 1993), they are all typically underpinned by one central assumption – knowledge is a critical resource, and the more there is of it, the more advantageous for individuals, corporations and economies as a whole.

In sum, as with other significant management discourses, the emergence of 'knowledge management' can be linked to both an internalist, or intellectual argument (i.e. the development of a world-view which sees knowledge as the defining characteristic of a new age) and also to an externalist account (i.e. through its ability to 'generate a resonance with popular opinion' – Grint, 1996). Moreover, even if the term 'knowledge management' does turn out to be ephemeral, this does not mean that it is a 'non-issue'. 'Management fashions are not cosmetic and trivial. Management fashions shape the management techniques that thousands of managers look to in order to cope with extremely important and complex managerial problems and challenges' (Abrahamson, 1996: 279). In short, employees in corporations do things, and sometimes do things differently, in the name of 'knowledge management'. The next sections consider, in more detail, what those things might be.

Approaches to Knowledge and 'Knowledge Management'

It was the 'resource-based view' of the firm which emerged in the strategic management field at the start of the 1990s (Barney, 1991) that initially alerted corporations to the importance that should be afforded to their employees (or human resources). This, it was argued, was what made corporations unique and could not be replicated by competitors. This view placed an emphasis on the corporation's human resources as the prime source of sustainable competitive advantage. It directed corporate attention to the need to manage the knowledge that employees were considered to have. The 'knowledge based view' therefore emerged, a few years later, as an extension and development of this. Strategies to develop and sustain 'dynamic capabilities', for example, address, what Schultze and Stabel (2004) refer to as, 'the double-edged' nature of knowledge in corporate life, with too little resulting in inefficiencies and too much resulting in core rigidities that prevent much needed innovation and change in turbulent environments (Grant, 1996; Leonard-Barton, 1992; Teece et al., 1997). Similarly, other widely cited models focus on firms balancing the tensions between re-using existing knowledge to ensure efficiencies (i.e. exploitation), and creating new knowledge to generate innovation and change (i.e. exploration – March, 1991). Whilst there is consensus, at least in these more normative accounts, that knowledge should be managed, precisely how corporations could do this practically has been the subject of considerable debate. Approaches have tended to be polarized around two broad camps – one which views knowledge as something that people have (an 'epistemology of possession'), and one which treats knowledge (or, often the preferred term is 'knowing') as something that people do (an 'epistemology of practice' – Cook and Brown, 1999).

Knowledge as Possession

The 'epistemology of possession' sees knowledge as something that, fundamentally, individuals possess but that organizations need to harness in order to ensure success. This emphasizes the cognitive aspects of knowledge – knowledge is seen as a possession of the human mind – a mental capacity, or 'high value' form of information. 'Knowledge management' therefore became interpreted as a means to increase the quantity, circulation and exploitation of knowledge so that it could be deployed more easily for corporate objectives, premised on the basis that this knowledge would otherwise remain unexploited within the heads of individuals. With this came a corresponding strategy by organizations to attempt to capture and store 'stocks' of knowledge. Accordingly, 'knowledge management' systems – for example large corporate intranets – were developed by, and sold to, corporations as a means to capture the knowledge (often tacit) possessed by employees, and then to objectify and codify it, hence making it accessible for re-use as an organizational resource. Global consultancies (e.g. IBM), for example, being heavily reliant themselves on the knowledge of their workers, developed their own KM technology-based systems and saw this as a business opportunity to be exploited across sectors in the late 1990s. Organizations' initial attempts to manage knowledge were thus grounded in a strongly functionalist tradition that treated knowledge as an object, or 'thing', that could be captured and moved around in corporate intranets and shared resources. It was thought that by using this approach corporations were free from the risk that it was individuals and not the corporation that controlled the firms' most valuable, strategic resource.

Clearly these initiatives could be interpreted (and possibly resisted) as the latest in a long line of management attempts to exert direct control over an increasingly disenfranchised workforce – the emphasis, much as in Taylor's attempts at job redesign, being on capturing, almost literally, the minds, thoughts and skills of employees (Fuller, 2002). At the same time, however, the notion that knowledge is a critical resource *and* that it is possessed by people, supports the edict that 'people are our greatest resource', so circumventing concerns about whether this approach is indeed desirable from the point of view of employees. Knowledge management, then, had a natural appeal to a broad spectrum of professionals including both information management specialists and technologists, and personnel managers (Scarbrough and Swan, 2001).

These 'cognitive' approaches to 'knowledge management' also assumed a positive relationship between the 'stockpiling' of knowledge and improvement in organizational performance (see discussion in Newell et al., 2002). Yet, this relationship is rarely examined. More often than not, knowledge is treated as valuable in its own right – divorced from the social actions, tasks and practices that actually generated changes in performance. Knowledge as possession accounts have focused on different 'types' of knowledge, most commonly separating 'tacit' from 'explicit' knowledge, and focusing on the conversion of the former (which is localized to individuals) to the latter (which can be made into a corporate good – e.g. Nonaka, 1994). However, in so doing, the 'essential tacitness' of knowledge, evident in Polanyi's original work is lost (Polanyi, 1962; Tsoukas and Vladimirou, 2001). The idea instead – and one that many corporate 'knowledge management' initiatives reflected at this time – is that individual knowledge (albeit not all of it) can indeed be objectified, abstracted from the social context where it is produced, and captured as an organizational resource through the use of IT systems.

Perhaps not surprisingly, many IT-based 'knowledge management' initiatives have failed. Sometimes there was active resistance from those whose knowledge was being 'managed' and sometimes there were problems with the technology or employees' willingness to engage with it, but mostly the systems simply stood outside of the day-to-day practices of work life and were soon ignored or discarded.

Knowledge as Practice

Dissatisfaction with the knowledge as possession view has prompted a general mood swing in theory and practice on knowledge and on the possibilities for 'knowledge management'. In particular, the premise that knowledge could be extracted from social context to be possessed by corporations has been widely criticized by proponents of what can be termed an 'epistemology of practice' (Cook and Brown, 1999). Theorists adopting this position come from very diverse traditions, including social philosophy, social and organizational theory, cultural theory and ethnomethodology. As such then no unified social theory practice exists, nor is it likely to (Gherardi, 2006). However, proponents of an epistemology of practice share a position that knowledge is constructed socially, and is embedded in, and emerges from, the day-to-day practices that groups are engaged in. It is not something that stands meaningfully on its own outside of those practices.

According to this view, the knowledge enacted by different groups is inextricably bound up with the way these groups work together and develop shared identities and practices. Accounts vary in terms of how social practice is viewed but definitions include 'action informed by meaning drawn from a particular group context' (Cook and Brown 1999: 387), 'socially recognized forms of activity, done on the basis of what members learn from others, and capable of being done well or badly, correctly or incorrectly' (Barnes, 2001: 19) and 'a mode, relatively stable in time and socially recognised, of ordering heterogeneous items into a coherent set' (Gherardi, 2006: 34). What these definitions have in common is that practice is socially recognized – that is embedded in wider 'fields' of practice or systems of meaning (Schatzki, 2001).

Knowing in practice accounts emphasize, then, knowledge as both an individual and a collective phenomena. Thus, they highlight the embodiment of individual practice (e.g. an action or activity) in a broader field of collective practice (e.g. professional practices) which is both constituted by, and constituent of, that practice (Schatzki, 2001). For example, the knowledge of a scientist is part of a broader field of scientific practice, including epistemic practices that determine how knowledge is produced (e.g. via the scientific method) and what is considered legitimate (Knorr-Cetina, 1999). Scientists have come to negotiate norms around what counts as 'good' science. However, knowledge claims are not set in stone – they vary across socio-historical contexts.

Empirical support for a 'knowing in practice' view, is now widespread (e.g. Carlile, 2002; Gherardri, 2006; Nicolini, 2006; Nicolini et al., 2003; Orlikoswki, 2002, 2006; Orr, 1990). These studies have shown, that social groups, as diverse as photocopier technicians, shipbuilders, tailors and alcoholics, do not spend their time converting tacit knowledge into explicit knowledge, but rather share norms, stories, representations and technical artefacts which allow individuals' experiences to be related to the knowledge base of the wider community (Orr, 1990). The 'knowing in practice' view emphasizes this interweaving of human activities with non-human, material configurations. This is why the term 'knowing' is often used in preference to 'knowledge' precisely to emphasize the interweaving of what people do, with what they know and who they are. Knowledge is seen in processual terms as an 'ongoing social accomplishment' not an independent objective entity (Orlikowski, 2002). Studies in this area tend to focus on different aspects of practice including:

- work practice – actions taken in the transformation of work tasks, processes and material objects (e.g. developing a work plan)
- discursive practice – linguistic acts such as speech and narratives that allow people to interact with, and make sense of, work processes (e.g. discussing the plan with others)

- aesthetic practice – perceptive faculties, feelings and sensibilities (e.g. having a feeling for who, and on what, you can trust)
- morality practice – actions around what is acceptable and legitimate and linked to the power of different groups (e.g. helping a novice (Gherardi, 2006).

The 'knowing in practice' view has clearly had a major role to play in implicating social relationships as core to knowledge and learning, and furthering the view that knowledge cannot be directly managed or captured in IT systems, but that fostering social relationships and 'communities of practice' is the major means of cultivating knowledge benefits for the corporation (Wenger, 2000).

Networks and Knowledge

It is worth mentioning here other branches of academic work – for example in studies of innovation and strategic alliances – that have continued to reinforce the power of collaborative relationships and networks, within and across organizations, for knowledge and innovation (e.g. Alter and Hage, 1993; Child et al., 2005; Hakannson et al., 1999; Maurer and Ebers, 2006; Swan and Scarbrough, 2005). For example, there has been a surge of interest in 'social capital' in recent years – a notion that directly links the development of a firm's 'intellectual capital' (its knowledge base) to the exploitation of social networks amongst individuals (Nahapiet and Ghoshal, 1998).

The role of networks in knowledge has been examined in many different ways. Some have focused on networks as *organizational forms* for dealing with complex and uncertain transactions (Alter and Hage, 1993). Others have focused on networks as *structures*, relating the structural properties of networks (e.g. strong versus weak ties) to the transmission of different kinds of knowledge (Ahuja, 2000; Hansen et al., 1999; Powell, 2005). Empirical studies have also demonstrated that in sectors where knowledge develops rapidly, such as biotechnology, intense inter-organizational network activity is vital for promoting innovation (Owen-Smith and Powell, 2004).

Some studies have focused on the processual features of networks showing how knowledge and innovation 'crystalizes' around networks and leads to the development of further networks and networking relationships. For example, Kreiner and Schultz's study of informal university–industry networks highlights the importance of 'accidental encounters' and exploratory trust-building through interpersonal networks, especially in the early stages of idea creation (Kreiner and Schultz, 1993). These accounts assume varied epistemological positions (e.g. structural accounts tending towards knowledge as possession, and processual accounts learning towards knowledge as practice) but all have served to fuel the notion that networks, social relationships and practices are the roots of knowledge and innovation and, so, organizations should seek to manage them.

'Knowledge Management' – a New Generation

A new generation of 'knowledge management' has been proclaimed. It is one that stresses knowledge as being inextricably linked to social practices which are developing through, and within, social relationships and context. Following this new wave, global corporations have recently begun to incorporate the building of social relationships and networks into their 'knowledge management' agendas and initiatives. The reasoning here is that if knowledge is sourced through social networks, then the corporation needs to build and foster these relationships in order to better exploit them for corporate success. On the back of this, initiatives such as 'learning communities', 'communities of practice' and 'peer assists' have started to become central within the corporate 'knowledge management' strategy (Brown and Duguid, 2001; Von Krogh et al., 2001; see also Chapter 7, this volume). Some corporations (notably, those in relatively knowledge-intensive industries such as biomedical and oil), have also started to appreciate that knowledge is highly distributed and, in many instances, politically contested. The management of knowledge is, therefore, far more complex and problematic than originally conceived. Corporate attention is thus shifting from attempts to manage knowledge as an entity in its own right, to attempts to manage social relationships, networks (intra- and inter-organizational as well as personal) and social spaces with a view to developing and applying knowledge through practice improvements.

One important implication of this new wave of thinking is that employees throughout the corporation are expected to incorporate their personal networks (both internal and external, including friendship ties) into their working lives and to exploit these networks specifically for the benefit of the corporation. This is reflected in changes in work spaces (atrium-type work spaces, for example) and, importantly, the discursive practices of organizations and policy makers which now legitimate networking as measurably productive corporate activity – 'social events' being replaced by 'networking opportunities', 'coffee breaks' by 'networking breaks', etc. The idea is that working together is more productive that working apart.

The impetus for workers to engage in networks and networking is sometimes quite explicit (e.g. bonus incentive systems for contributions to workplace communities at companies such as Buckman Labs and Shell Oil). More often however, it is quite insidious with, for example, visibility in networks and exploitation of networks being discretely encouraged for career development. Clearly, networks have long been seen as important to individual employees as vehicles for career development and status building (the 'old boys' network, for example, cf. Ibarra, 1993). However, informal networking across organizational boundaries has not, in the past, been directly sanctioned by management (Kreiner and Schultz, 1993). We suggest, then, that this situation is changing and what is new is the ways in which personal and professional relationships are becoming increasingly incorporated into the organization's formal agenda as a means of profiting from the 'social capital' of individual employees. The more transient nature of employment in many organizations may further fuel a perceived need to strategically exploit these relationships, since traditional, informal opportunities for the building of friendship ties through organizational tenure and longer-term commitment are becoming more limited. Increasingly, then, employees are expected to deliberately construct and exploit their interpersonal relationships in order to fulfil specific corporate objectives (Bouty, 2000).

These shifts have led to heated debate around the manageability of networks and communities of practice. Thus, critics argue that notions such as 'communities of practice' have been appropriated from their original emancipatory, voluntaristic roots and incorporated into the managerial landscape as a legitimate target for management intervention for purposes of improving corporate performance (Contu and Willmott, 2000; Fox, 2000). In so doing, concerns with power, conflict and politics, present in the original, have almost entirely disappeared, being 'safely tucked away in the footnotes' (Fox, 2000:857).

Whilst useful as a riposte to managerialism, these debates have tended to focus attention on managerial intentions – either benign or manipulative – rather than actual practices. This risks ascribing to an overly unified view of management with managers being depicted as uniformly powerful in acting out their intentions, either to facilitate networks and communities, or to exploit them. However, power does not simply reside with the management group, especially in knowledge-intensive sectors, such as biotechnology, which are populated by expert groups such as scientists, regulators, etc., where the role responsibilities are blurred (e.g. scientists are also managers) and where work practices span organizations, and so resist hierarchical power. In these contexts 'management' needs to be viewed not as monolithic and all powerful, but, rather, as encompassing a distinctive array of provisional, fragmented and sometimes contradictory practices, for example primary practices aimed at the development, of new products, say, and secondary practices, such as project management practices which aim to coordinate those primary practices (Harris, 1987; Reed, 1984, Tsoukas, 1994). Networking, in this sense, comprises activity that spans both primary and secondary practice. In the example that follows, then, of 'knowledge work' in the biotechnology industry, we try to highlight the varied ways in which people, engaged in different forms of practice, deploy their own networks, including friendships, as a way of accomplishing works tasks.

Translating scientific knowledge into new drugs as quickly and cost-effectively as possible is the basis on which biotechnology and pharmaceutical corporations compete. A single drug can now take over $1.2bn to develop due to the complexity and uncertainty of the work required, with failure rates as high as 85 per cent Firms in this sector are also experiencing rising costs and higher probability of failure than ever before (CMR, 2004). Even the largest pharmaceutical corporations do not possess all of the resources to develop a drug through to market. Instead they must create networks with a myriad of other firms (e.g. other large pharmaceutical firms, smaller biotechnology firms, clinical research organizations, the regulatory bodies, etc.) during the development and commercialization process if they stand any chance of success.

This example, taken from a larger study of biomedical innovation,[1] centres on the development of a radical new drug treatment to fight an inflammatory disease. In this case a medium-sized biotechnology firm in the US (Immutec)[2] was beginning early Phase I and II human clinical trials. The project was being coordinated by a project team, which comprised a product development manager plus managers from several sub-teams dealing with different aspects of the development process (e.g. pre-clinical research, clinical trials, regulation, finance, manufacturing). The project team met every two weeks and took advice from each of the sub-teams represented. On the whole, the sub-teams operated fairly autonomously but there was considerable informal personal contact ongoing across the different teams. The networking example given here focuses, in particular, on the work involved in clinical trials design.

Immutec had little experience of conducting clinical trials and so (as is common in the industry) needed to contract an external clinical research organization (CRO) to conduct the trials and recruit patients. The clinical group had detailed discussions around the choice of CRO. Most of this centred, not on the contractual arrangements, or even on the scientific expertise of potential partners, but, rather, on whether the CRO had networks with clinicians specializing in the disease who could help them recruit the right kinds of patients in sufficient numbers (as yet undecided) to the timescales (as yet unknown) involved and, second, whether the CRO team would be 'the type' of people that Immutec could collaborate with. This was seen as particularly crucial. The scientific expertise that was involved in the development of this particular drug was so specialized that the Immutec managers who had years of experience, needed to feel confident that the CRO they ultimately contracted to conduct the trials, would have a team of people available with similar expertise as ultimately Immutec were responsible for the design of the trials and the safety of the patients, as well as for the commercial success of the product – 'No-one else understands the technology as we do' (project manager).

All human clinical trials are also heavily regulated so Immutec needed to acquire knowledge about the regulatory environment and the hurdles this particular kind of drug might encounter, in order to design trials that had any chance of getting approval. Since the firm had limited experience in this area, they recruited a specific individual to be responsible for all regulatory affairs to do with the development of this drug. The person recruited observed:

> Somebody who knew me had done some work for another biotech and said I should apply. It was sort of an informal route because it wasn't for an advertised position. I have to say it's quite incestuous in this business. It's not that big an industry. Especially in regulatory where there aren't that many people, you get to work with the same group of people all the time. You use a lot of consultants and get to know people who work in a number of different companies.

As the drug was so novel, there was no particular precedent or source this individual could turn to in order to anticipate which trials would be best or would be deemed acceptable. He pointed out:

> You rely a lot on people you know and their information that they can give you on other projects – things that worked and didn't work. Top Pro is an organization of regulatory affairs professionals worldwide. They have regular meetings and I'm doing a diploma course with them, so there's a lot of interaction with different people and you get to know people. They ring you up and say, 'we've got this general issue'. You talk to them about projects and products, but the issues are the same. A lot of knowledge is transferred that way.

Moreover, direct contact with the regulators might have led to too many, as yet unanswerable, questions being asked of Immutec and their product:

> When we were considering whether to conduct the trial in Canada, it would've been helpful to contact the Federal Drug Agency, but they would have wanted too much information, we could have ended up giving too much away and been stopped so I contacted a friend and I'm fairly confident that their advice is sound. We could go ahead in Canada.

When discussing the networking that went on more generally outside of the firm:

> I think we all interact in different sorts of ways. In regulatory affairs it's quite issue based. I have lots of friends – I would call them – in the industry who do regulatory affairs. I

know them either because I've worked with them and we have a very good social bond, or I know them through Top Pro. They're all on the same diploma course with me. Sarah, for instance, sits on the biotech working party. That's a group. We know various people and we'll think, so-and-so had a similar problem. I'll go and talk to them. But that's not to say within the team … Gez for example, has lots of interactions with academic groups. Gez is in our biology group, so we have lots of academic collaborations, where people use our science in studies and we use the data. That's how we keep up-to-date with the latest models. We have a specialized expertise that other academics draw on. He collaborates a lot. We all do it in different ways. It depends on the issue and what they're doing. But for a company of our size those interactions are key.

All of these detailed quotes illustrate the ways in which individuals deployed personal networks and friendship ties as an accepted part of their daily work practice in order to 'get the job done'. They highlight the role of networking practices and 'accidental encounters' in the kinds of 'know-how' trading associated with early development (Kreiner and Schultz, 1993). They also highlight the ways in which networks (e.g. attending the Top Pro diploma course) act as a 'centre of gravity' for the development of further networks and trust-based relations between individuals. Yet, it is also clear from these quotes, that boundaries between 'friendships' and 'colleagues', between science and the management of science, and between personal and corporate incentives, are extremely blurred, with friendship ties, for example, simultaneously providing individuals with a point of contact for their own career enhancement, as well as acting as a way of knowing in product development.

The career enhancement benefits of networking were reflected in the performance management system in Immutec. Somewhat ironically, given that it takes anywhere from between eight to 12 years to bring a drug to market, time – 'saving' time – was of the essence. The time imperative was emphasized by such stories as 'each day lost in bringing a potential block-buster drug to market costs about $1 million' and individual objectives were aligned with organizational goals via time targets that needed to be met by any means. The Human Resource Director commented:

The way that we articulate our goals (at an individual level) are as goals, measures and targets. You have three columns. The operating goal for a particular drug may be to develop it through to Phase II in the coming year … then the measures at the highest level could be achieving regulatory submission or approval. Then the target (for the regulatory affairs person) will be a date by which to achieve that approval.

In turn, effective collaborations were seen by employees as indispensable and imperative if targets were to be met to time.

Whilst these examples indicate the felt benefits for innovation of openness and collaboration, other examples from the same project revealed inherent 'conflicts of collaboration' in enacting networking within a work, as opposed to a purely social, context. For example, at the same time as Phase I trials were being designed, Immutec was in the process of attempting to negotiate a deal to partner with a large pharmaceutical firm that would have the resources to be able to license the product and take it through the, much larger scale and therefore much more costly, Phase III trials that would be required. Partnering can typically take 12 to 18 months before a deal is signed due to the very complex legal and financial arrangements involved. In the meantime however, Immutec needed to keep the Phase I clinical trials on course in case the partnering deal went, as they put it, 'belly up'. This meant that the future partners' plans about Phase III trials further down the road had a direct bearing on Immutec's decisions about the design of their current Phase I/II trials and also vice versa. Recognizing that their programmes of work were mutually dependent, Immutec managers' discursive and work practices reflected an emphasis on open communication, knowledge sharing and full disclosure with the potential partner, since this would be crucial for the future success of the product. As the project leader put it, 'it's very much been a team effort'. Work practices involved informal collaboration and frequent meetings between counterparts in the two organizations, joint training exercises, and a formalized two-way 'due diligence', conducted so that each side 'put all the cards on the table'.

Simultaneously, however, the formal partnering arrangement was not yet finalized. Therefore a major issue for Immutec managers and the clinical team was in estimating what risk to absorb (in terms of committing resources to a trial that may or may not work out) for an expected return from a partnering arrangement that was yet to be agreed. In particular, the more robust the evidence for the efficacy of the product, the better the financial deal they would be able to negotiate with the partner. However, there was also a risk that the results of the Phase I/II may not be ideal, which could then put the entire partnering process at risk. There was really no way of resolving these conflicts since, as is typical of these kinds of biologic drugs, the outcomes of human trials, however well designed, can never be predicted precisely in advance from animal models. Immutec managers, therefore, went with their *'best guess'* as to who to talk to, when, and how far they were able to share information with their colleagues in the partner company as well as within Immutec itself. Since these colleagues were sometimes also friends, tensions often arose between the need to get (and give) enough information to be able to *'get the job done'* without jeopardizing the partnering deal, and the desire not to compromise working relationships and/or friendships by retaining confidential company information.

Final Comments

The Immutec example highlights, to some extent, some of the deeply embedded practices and day-to-day challenges of working in the biotechnology sector.

As the knowledge as practice view highlights, knowledge (knowing) is a process of 'social accomplishment', enacting and making sense of practices as they unfold (Orlikowski, 2002, 2006). Market forces and regulations continually change, outcomes of trials are uncertain and unpredictable, costs and risks of failure are high, and competition in terms of first-to-market is intense. In these situations, therefore, knowledge is highly distributed, formative (little is yet 'known') and partial (it depends what angle you look at a problem from).

In such contexts, there are few reliable, stable, more codified sources of 'knowledge' upon which to draw. As Kreiner and Schultz put it, 'frontier', rather than 'historical' knowledge (that might be sourced from more typical, codified, sources, such as journals) is required (Kreiner and Schultz, 1993). Network relationships, then, including personal friendships, are drawn upon as a routine part of daily work, necessary to test understandings and resolve problems at work as and when they arise. At the same time, one of the main issues, as far as individuals are concerned, is knowing who to trust and what to 'give away' since, in the majority of instances, this informal exchange is also occurring between potential competitors both within and across firms (Bouty, 2000). Managers and scientists therefore engage 'aesthetic practices' (best guesses, hunches and feelings) in judging who to trust, and precisely how much to reveal.

The example also illustrates how different, and sometimes competing, 'logics of action' collide in the process of knowing (Gherardi, 2006). For example, a scientific logic (around what constitutes 'good science') and a financial/business logic (around what constitutes a robust partnering model) meet, sometimes quite uncomfortably, in the practice of designing clinical trials. Superseding these different logics, however, is a broader ideology around developing a new (life saving) drug and getting it to market as quickly and as safely as possible. This, to some extent, allows these semi-autonomous professionals to reconcile the joint pursuits and goals of science and commerce, mobilizing action, despite the different logics that underpin action (Brunsson, 1982; Swan et al., 2002). Thus, although the professionals involved manage their own practices to a large extent, they also have significant incentives to align these practices with corporate ends. Power, then, is best explained, not so much as a property that individuals (top managers) possess and choose to exercise or not, rather, as Gherardi puts it,

[obedience to authority] is explained by the alignments of all the people concerned; and the likelihood that it will be modified in the process depends on those who seek to achieve their own goals in the meantime. The question of power, then, is the question of what holds people and things together. (2006: 60).

By focusing on informal networking in relation to the processes of knowing, the issues raised in this chapter have hopefully acted as a counterfoil, both to the numerous studies of formal network structures in knowledge and learning, and to the underlying position, assumed by many in the field of knowledge management, of 'knowledge as possession'. Of course, the importance of informal networks has long been established – the importance of 'weak ties' being an example (Granovetter, 1973). However, as the intensity of knowledge work increases and knowledge is both the main product and the means of production, it can be argued that today's corporations are more dependent than ever on the activities of individuals in deploying their own interpersonal networks, including friendships, in order to accomplish tasks. As far as the corporation is concerned, this poses a quandary. On the one hand, they rely heavily on the 'social capital' of employees to produce knowledge and to get work done. On the other hand, if they attempt to generate more social capital by, for example, facilitating the networking activities of individual employees, then they are more at risk of losing it because, as seen here, personal networks are also deployed in order to progress in careers, which may involve leaving the corporation.

This chapter also raises a number of questions with broader implications. First, it underlines the point that, whilst variations in social and organizational context – including organizational structures, roles, routines, physical spaces, technologies, incentive systems, and so forth – certainly shape flows and transformations of knowledge (or knowing), in sometimes unpredictable ways, 'knowledge' cannot be directly managed by corporations, any more than personal relationships can be managed. At best corporations might be able to provide a context for the development of practices that might encourage knowledge sharing. Second, debates around managerialism and the weakening of professional power, whilst worthwhile in their own right, do not adequately describe the coming together of different forms of practice managerial, professional and social) in everyday life for the accomlishment of corporate or personal objectives. Third, if, in a 'knowledge based society', friendships are being increasingly instrumentally exploited for corporate and career purposes, then this raises some perplexing questions for the individual around the blurring of colleague-based relationships and friendships in work and home life. For example, who, then, might be considered a 'genuine' friend and how big are the favours that can be asked?

Notes

1 This example is taken from a study of 'The Evolution of Biomedical Knowledge' conducted by the authors with colleagues, Sue Newell, Mike Bresnen, Anna Goussevskaia, Demola Obembe, Miriam Mendes, and Markus Perkmann, and supported by the ESRC and EPSRC.
2 Immutec is a pseudonym and details are withheld to ensure anonymity.

10

EMOTION[1]

Emma Surman and Andrew Sturdy

Introduction

In the West, there is a tradition of splitting emotion and reason, of seeing the two as irreconcilable opposites. Within the workplace, the latter has undoubtedly dominated, at least in terms of managerial and organizational procedures and initiatives (Barbalet, 1998). Indeed, the modern work organization, and bureaucracy in particular, has long been seen as the bastion of rational thinking, where the prevailing view has been that the application of logical thought will lead to efficient and profitable operation (Weber, 1978). This view emerged or, at least, prospered, during the industrial revolution when, as the burgeoning factory system increasingly centralized production, the home became distanced from paid employment and sentimentalized by the middle classes (Gerth and Mills, 1953). If the head dominated the workplace, the home was seen as a place for the heart. As a result, the private sphere was portrayed as a place that was altogether more wholesome than the public, a haven from what was seen by many as the alienating or serious world of paid work (Hochschild, 1997).

However, this focus on the rational hasn't been totally at the expense of the emotional. There have been some attempts to channel emotions such as those associated with motivation, and suppress others, such as anger, for organizational ends (Stearns and Stearns, 1986). In particular, *human relations* initiatives recognized the need to treat workers as more than just machines if output was to be maximized (Rose, 1989). In recent times, such programmes have intensified, with an increasing acknowledgement of the emotional dimension within the workplace. Hence, rather than seeking to eliminate emotions from the processes of organization, both scholars and practitioners are encouraged to see them as inextricably linked to their production (Fineman, 2000a). One result of this is that, along with physical and intellectual capabilities, emotions are now seen very much as a resource and something to be managed. This may be in terms of emotional labour, such as demonstrating an emotional attachment to the organization or customer (Hochschild, 1983; Sturdy, 1998) or mastering the skill of managing one's own and others' emotions more generally (e.g. emotional intelligence) (Fineman, 2000b).

Much of this activity has been directed at achieving *organizationally defined* emotions. Increasingly, however, the management of emotion seeks not only to redirect, but to appropriate the emotional world of everyday life for organizational purposes. Here, emotions are defined more broadly and from employees' wider experiences, but brought into the organization and transformed or redefined (Deal and Kennedy, 1999). In particular, culturally based gender patterns and (stereotypical) assumptions of emotion are evident and utilized even more than previously. As a consequence, management can be seen as becoming more 'feminized', with regard to its practice – 'soft capitalism' – even if not in terms of a significantly increased level of participation of women at senior levels (Thrift, 2005: 121). Thus, for example, prescriptive accounts call for change agents to become feminized and leaders to be emotionally intelligent (cf. George, 2000; Ross-Smith et al., 2005). In part, this reflects a more general breaking down (or re-defining) of organizational boundaries, including that between home and paid employment. This can be linked to a number of social and political processes, including the design and use of new technologies, making it possible and even desirable for people to work within new temporal, geographical and emotional contexts (Brocklehurst, 2001; Hodson, 1996).

By drawing on various studies of emotion within organizations and some of our own research on the work of call centre teleworkers, this chapter will focus on a particular aspect of these changes taking place in corporate life. It will consider the emotional challenges, opportunities and boundaries that emerge from managerial attempts to appropriate emotional experiences still largely thought of as the preserve of everyday life beyond paid employment. We describe this emotional arena as *fun and friendliness*. Here, rather than largely focusing on the consumer interface with the organization, managerial efforts have turned to the emotions generated within organizations and between colleagues. For example, we see the sort of activities one might engage in outside of working hours with friends or family, on days out or in the pub, etc. (games, quizzes, dressing up, raffles, etc.). While there has been a wider trend in seeking to establish work as a 'fun' and 'friendly' place to be, distinct from the rational traditions of organization (see 'Best Employers' literature, e.g. Leary-Joyce, 2004), such initiatives are especially evident in call centres. Here, there are typically intense regimes of work surveillance and the designed tasks and output requirements, including expectations of emotional labour with customers, are often experienced as highly routine and stressful (cf. Sturdy and Korczynski, 2005). Thus, managerial attempts to introduce fun and friendliness aim to mitigate such experiences and generate an environment in which people want to work, and, of course, thereby to improve their retention and performance as a result. Indeed, such regimes may also serve as a medium for sharing the emotional pressures of work with colleagues – collective emotional labour (Korczynski, 2003).

We shall focus on the nature and experiences of such initiatives in an effort to reveal some of the emotional complexities and contradictions of contemporary corporate life. In particular, we show how 'fun' initiatives in the workplace can be highly managed and monitored activities. Furthermore, whilst managers might be willing to allow, and even encourage, *friendliness* to develop, they do not always sanction the development of *friendship* and, on occasion, take steps to prohibit it, along with other collective forms of emotion which might be deemed negative for the organization. First however, we introduce some of the literature which explores emotion management and, in particular, the development of recent managerial programmes and the emotionality of organizations in terms of fun, friendship and collective emotional labour.

Feelings, Emotion and Emotional Labour/s

While there is little scope here to chart a history of the varying cultural conceptions of emotion, it is worth noting, however, that it has been long and widely regarded as demonic and/or mystical (e.g. see Bendix, 1956). Accordingly, in the 'age of reason', it not only became marginalized, but subject to, albeit imperfect, regimes of exclusionary control (e.g. Elias, 1978; Stearns and Stearns, 1986), notably through bureaucracy (Weber, 1978: 225), patriarchy and psychoanalysis (Gabriel 1999; cf. Carr, 1999). '[T]he dominance of rationality in Western (masculinist) thought ... has led to the relative neglect or dismissal of emotions as "irrational", private, inner sensations which have been tied, historically, to women's "dangerous desires" and "hysterical bodies"' (Williams and Bendelow, 1996: 150–1).

The empirical neglect of emotion in organizational theory as well as the problematic nature of its separation from rationality are now quite well known and beginning to be addressed, albeit gradually. New topics, texts, connections, conferences and courses are unfolding (see e.g. Bolton, 2005; Fineman, 2003; the *International Journal of Work, Organization and Emotion*). Emotion, like gender before it, is coming to be recognized as a central feature of organizations, including their rational domains. Indeed, it has been claimed that 'we are on the brink of relocating feelings as a focal point for organizational studies' (Albrow, 1997: 95). However, here we are primarily concerned with the related domain of emotions, that is, emotions and feelings are considered conceptually, if not always empirically, distinct. The former is associated with display while the latter is linked to what is subjectively felt (see Fineman, 2000a). This is not to say that what is felt is somehow independent of socio-political processes or, indeed, what is expressed – both emotions and feelings are cultural *and* corporeal/embodied (Burkitt, 1997). Rather, it is simply that we are concerned with emotion, its management in organizations and employees' responses to such processes.

Emotion has become a particular target of management control in the service economy, where the production of the 'right' (organizationally specified and acceptable) emotions are seen as central to the act of consumption and to distinguishing between similar service 'products' (Du Gay, 1996; Sturdy, 1998). A key concept here is that of emotional labour. This is now quite a common term, but gained currency from the pioneering study by Hochschild (1983) which shows how the emotion work or self-management associated with everyday life is extended and transformed for commercial ends, such as in the service smile of flight attendants or the frown of debt collectors. This is important for her analysis and is based explicitly on a distinction between emotion work and emotional labour. The former refers to our 'own' (i.e. cultured and gendered) control of displayed feelings in various contexts outside of the formal workplace, such as showing concern at a friend's misfortune, while the latter is the management of our emotions as an integral part of tasks in paid employment. Thus, it is not so much the appropriation of particular activities or feelings from everyday life that Hochschild was concerned with, as the emotion management process itself; that is, with who was in control of the display of feelings (cf. Hochschild, 1997). Clearly, the distinction is not so clear cut, as we can bring into being feelings through displaying them as much as we can by suppressing their display (e.g. anger). Moreover, management efforts to secure high levels of customer service are not always only concerned with the display of feelings, but their subjective experience too – being 'genuinely' committed to the customer/organization (Sturdy, 1998). Finally, emotional labour is not simply concerned with expression (or suppression) of one's own emotion to effect positive feelings in others, but other techniques designed to control employees' emotions, such as when handling angry customers or 'irates' (see e.g. Fineman, 1993; Sturdy, 1998).

Hochschild's *The Managed Heart* (1983) has positively influenced almost all studies of emotion in organizations since its publication. However, it has also been subject to critique. For example, Bolton (2005) draws on a growing stream of emotion literature to distinguish other forms of emotional expression and management in the workplace. This recognizes Hochschild's emotional labour, but also the role of emotion rules which are not simply derived from managerial prescription, but also from other forms of socialization, occupational norms or social etiquette, pointing to, for example, how employees draw on their emotional skills in other (non-managerially prescribed) ways. These may, however, be congruent with the interests of their customers or clients, but at the expense of organizational performance, such as through ethics of care. For example, service workers can empathize with and advise customers in a way which goes against managerial pressures to limit organizational liability or to make a sale – 'philanthropic emotion' (see also Taylor and Tyler, 2001; Wray-Bliss, 2001). Indeed, it is important to recognize that there are numerous forms and motives of workplace emotion and that these can often not easily be distinguished from those of other social contexts.

An example of this is the case of what has come to be known as *collective emotional labour*. In another article which seeks to elaborate on Hochschild's (1983) work, Korczynski (2003) draws attention to work that takes place within call centres, this time not between employees and customers, but between colleagues. Often the subject of abuse from frustrated or unhappy customers, Korczynski found that after dealing with a call from an irate customer, customer service advisors frequently found other colleagues to be a source of support and refuge as they recounted, and sought to cope with, the abuse they had received. In doing so, Korczynski looks beyond the confines in which emotional labour has more usually been seen, to a form of collective emotional labour between colleagues, something he refers to as 'communities of coping' (Korczynski, 2003). Whilst not forming part of the formal labour process, he still refers to this as emotional labour as these acts can be seen to have a functional, pecuniary value, albeit indirectly. For, it is argued, it is only through sharing and discussing such customers with colleagues that the customer service advisors can continue taking calls. 'By providing a way for service workers to survive the systematic tensions of their working days, communities of coping may help preserve the "fragile social order" of the service workplace' (Korczynski, 2003: 58). Unlike the emotional labour identified by Hochschild, Korczynski reported that staff saw communities of coping as a positive aspect of their working day. However, unlike managerially defined emotional labour, and as we shall see shortly from our own cases, this collective work was not always valued by managers. This 'hidden' emotional labour (Surman, 2004) that takes place *between* colleagues is largely invisible and, despite its positive impact for the organization, may be actively discouraged by management. As it does not form part of the visible labour process and thus, is not recognized as having a direct effect on the production of the service or, therefore, on the financial performance of the organization, it is unlikely to receive any recognition or be attributed any value (cf. Hochschild, 1983).

In a way, this is surprising, for there is a long history of managerial tolerance or 'indulgency' towards informal workplace activities which employees create to cope with the pressures and routines of work and control (Gouldner, 1954). For example, games might be constructed out of the work in ways which formally break the rules, but are allowed to continue since they diffuse tension and do not fundamentally disrupt output (Burawoy, 1979;

Sturdy, 1992). Likewise, other games or activities might be played in work time (e.g. football on the factory floor), but in space created by completing formal requirements in other ways. Such activities not only helped to relieve boredom and low autonomy, but often were pleasurable and satisfying and thus led to the formation of close personal relations and friendships which otherwise might have been the preserve of 'everyday', rather than work, life. However, in the cases reported by Korczynski at least, such activity was frowned upon by management. One possible reason for this is that, even this emotional realm – mutual and unmanaged support and 'fun' – is now being targeted as an object of control. We now introduce this recent development in the management of emotion before exploring it empirically.

Fun and Friendliness Regimes

As already noted, while emotion may have been sidelined explicitly, in the name of rationality, there is a long tradition of employers seeking to shape the values (and therefore also feelings) of employees to encourage organizational attachment and, more recently, customer orientation. However, such *normative control* has been criticized in terms of the problems rigidly strong cultures bring in dynamic market environments (Brown and Starkey, 2000) as well as the resistance provoked from employees who may cynically distance their 'real' selves from managerially prescribed corporate values and emotions (Kunda, 1992). While the importance of a customer orientation remains almost sacred, organizational loyalty and attachment and homogenous corporate culture initiatives are more vulnerable and even seen as self-defeating in contexts where rapid changes (e.g. downsizing) in staff numbers, task requirements or location are more commonplace (Kunda and Ailon-Souday, 2005).

As part of this critique, among the ranks of some management gurus (e.g. Peters, 2003), it is argued that recruits should not share the organization's values (and should even oppose them), but, in effect, be existentially 'empowered' (and exposed) (Fleming and Sturdy, 2009). Moreover, a central way in which they should express more of their true selves is by 'having fun' at work (Florida, 2004; cf. Collinson, 2002). For example, popular writers like Deal and Key (1998) argued that managers should encourage workers to express their fun and playful side, rather than suppress it in the name of sober productiveness and a 'bottom-line mentality' (1998: 6). If, as Deal and Kennedy suggest, the 'Fun Quotient' is high in a firm, then employees will be more committed to their tasks and everyone will benefit (1999: 234). Here, fun is a licence to 'be oneself' in a way that leads workers to love being *in the* company rather than love *the* company (see also Ross, 2004). Indeed, such instrumentality is implied in managerial efforts to become an 'employer of choice' or 'best place to work', especially when tasks are predominantly routine, mundane and repetitive, such as in call centres, and fun is primarily directed at compensating for limited job discretion rather than fostering innovation. Indeed, while many of the prescriptions of gurus can be treated sceptically in terms of their translation into organizational practice, there is considerable evidence that the management of 'fun' has now become quite widespread, at least in documented cases of the 'best companies to work for'. For example, Kwik Fit, a car servicing chain in the UK, has a full time 'Minister of Fun' managerial position (*Sunday Times*, 2005, 2006).

While both bureaucracy and normative control are not supplanted through such initiatives, a shift in employer practices is clearly evident. The managerial and guru exhortations resonate both with earlier human relations interventions concerning the appropriation of employees' informal involvement in the organization (Rose, 1975) as well as with contemporary (Western) political discourses of individualism, equal opportunities and multiple identities/difference – especially in relation to sexuality and lifestyle (see Fleming and Sturdy, 2009, for a fuller discussion). At the same time, the notion of celebrating the emotional expressions associated with fun and other aspects of everyday life is explicitly seen by its protagonists as blurring the traditional work–home boundary. Thus, the idea associated with normative control regimes, that employees must adopt an *organizational* persona at work (e.g. Hochschild, 1983; Kunda, 1992) is reversed – people can express their 'authentic' and explicitly emotional selves at work rather than repress the intrinsic desire to be playful and curious (Peters, 2003). Indeed, in *Happy Mondays* (2004), Reeves argues that organizations now provide purpose, fun, creativity, friendship networks and love (see also Hochschild, 1997; Ross, 2004).

Such managerial initiatives may be presented as and appear to be liberating and empowering, perhaps at the deepest level. Indeed, they are often welcomed in workplaces which hitherto have sought to suppress and discriminate against people 'being themselves'. As we shall see from the following discussion, however, whilst call centres are frequently keen to increase their fun quotient – often through the introduction of specific activities such as 'fundays' – this does not necessarily provide a vehicle by which employees can express what they might see as their true, private or authentic selves. Instead, in practice, there are often limitations as to what kind of 'fun' is permitted and the activities that are encouraged under the 'fun' banner can, therefore, be seen as simply another organizational practice with which employees are forced to conform. Therefore, whilst fun becomes officially sanctioned and encouraged, rather than banished or tolerated, this is only done if the fun is manifested in ways arranged and deemed appropriate by the organization itself. Thus, whilst we can witness these new domains of everyday life and their feelings, emotions and associations being brought into the workplace, they are being transformed and constructed in a particular, commercialized and/or managerial form (see also Janssens and Zanoni, 2005).

This is the case not only for 'fun', but, as intimated in the reference to Reeves (2004) above, to friendship too. Here, a different trajectory of control is evident, but one which, as we shall see, comes to connect with the context of emotional labour in call centres. As was once the case with emotion generally, the emotional attachment of friendship rarely enters the Organizational Behaviour (OB) literature despite the fact that many friends are made in and through work, and organizations may even be formed through friendship (Grey and Sturdy, 2007). Typically, the term is subsumed under catch-all concepts such as social capital and trust, seen only in terms of how it is functional or dysfunctional for organizational performance. However, there has been some recognition of *friendliness*, most notably by Carnegie in his classic prescriptive text – *How to Win Friends and Influence People* (1937/1990) and more recently *as a tactic* in coalition-building (Handy, 1985), organizational politics (e.g. Buchanan and Badham, 1999) and 'relationship management' (Dawson, 2000). In talking about friendliness, therefore, there is a suggestion that a friendly persona is adopted, not necessarily in response to any sincere liking of the other person, but in order to facilitate a particular agenda, whether that be seeking to progress one's career, making a sale, fostering a more productive working environment, etc. There is thus a degree of 'fakeness' or, at least, instrumentality about it.

Drawing distinctions between types of relationships is notoriously difficult (Pahl, 2000). For example, in sociology and social psychology, friendship has long been identified through its apparent difference to kinship, sexual and work relations (Argyle, 1988; Carrier, 1999; cf. Foucault, 2000). But this is far from straightforward, not least because of historical, cultural and situational shaping of what it is to be a friend (see Grey and Sturdy, 2007). Nevertheless, here we take friendship to be conceptually distinct from friendliness in much the same way as we have distinguished feelings and emotions. Friendship involves feeling towards another rather than simply emotional display or acting in a certain manner with the purpose of achieving a specific end. Thus, as opposed to a superficial level of smiles and politeness, there is a willingness to share the difficult as well as the fun times. The relative spontaneity and unregulated nature of friendship is also important, although this is largely neglected in accounts emphasizing *friendliness*. Friendship then, which has long been part of the workplace (but largely ignored or suppressed in formal controls), may now be rendered more visible as management control enters further into the emotional domains once seen as the preserve of everyday life. While friendliness might be seen as functional for co-worker relations as part of an overall arena of managed fun, much as it is seen as functional for business deals more generally (Ingram and Roberts, 2000; Sturdy et al., 2006), friendship might be altogether more problematic. This is largely because of the relative strength of the bond between individuals that it typically involves, the cultural strength of its location outside of the remit of management and therefore the threat this poses for regimes of control. We shall begin to explore this emergent domain of corporate life further in our account of the management of emotion and fun in call centres.

Fun and Friendliness in the Call Centre

Our exploration of the everyday emotions of fun, friendliness and friendship is conducted by drawing on data from our own and others' research (see e.g. Fleming and Spicer, 2003; Sturdy and Fleming, 2003; Surman, 2004) into two different call centres. The first is a UK high street bank (Any Bank) (a pseudonym). Here, the data is taken from interviews with individuals at all levels of the organization (directors, managers, supervisors, staff) involved with two pilot home-working projects. These projects enabled a small number of customer service advisors to leave the central office and, utilizing information and telecommunications technologies, still operate as part of the call centre whilst working from their own homes. In the course of discussing their own experiences of home working it was inevitable, therefore, that comparisons were made with the call centre environment and thus many of the interviews about the experience of working away from the call centre office revealed a great deal about their particular experience of working within it.

The second organization from which data is drawn is Sunray (a pseudonym) – an American owned call centre with around 1,000 employees based in Australia. Sunray deals with communication functions outsourced by banks, airlines, insurance firms and the like and thus puts much emphasis on the customer service skills of its employees, within a demanding working environment. We draw on data collected in research by Fleming (2005b). Among other methods used, one-to-one interviews were held with 33 (15 male) employees at various intervals over eight months. The average age of telephone agents interviewed was 23 (which had significance for the research findings, as will be discussed shortly).

At Any Bank, the fun element was introduced to generate competition between both individuals and teams. All customer service advisors were assigned into teams which were given names in accordance with a particular theme. For example, they were named after properties on the *Monopoly* board or after animals. Each team then competed against the rest on a number of sales-based parameters, with prizes awarded to the top performers. This theme of *competitive fun* was periodically reinforced through the hosting of specifically named 'fun days' within the call centre. On such days a specific theme was chosen, for example, Halloween or Christmas and, instead of wearing the required corporate uniform to work, on these days employees, their supervisors and managers were encouraged to come to work in appropriate fancy dress. Staff would then compete to win various (often very modest) prizes throughout the day.

The fun element was consciously and openly introduced as direct compensation for the nature of the work which the staff had to undertake and in an effort to reduce the high levels of turnover which the bank experienced. The work was recognized as being stressful, high pressured and not all that stimulating, as this quote from Stella, one of the supervisors in the call centre, reveals:

> We have quite a lot of fun days, what we call them in-house, and because we're in a selling environment, it's to actually make, rather than make the job monotonous, it's to have like a fun day, a fun element, because the line of work they're doing, they can't generally sit and chat. They have like dressing up days, or theme days, things like that.

The work is target driven and staff are constantly monitored and become subject to formal disciplinary procedures if their personal performance does not consistently meet the required standards. Thus, within this highly disciplined environment, the company permits little room for fun within the everyday working environment, except on the days which it specifically allocates for this purpose.

Although similar in many respects, such as fun names for teams and regular 'dressing up' days, prizes and other competitive 'fun' events, Sunray management went to even greater lengths to make fun a central element of the everyday working life of the organization. Firstly, the recruitment strategy was to select people who had recently completed high school. Aside from cost considerations, the employment of young people is typically associated with the relative ease with which an organizational culture can be incorporated or inculcated. However, the managerial rationale given here reversed this logic in that, it was claimed that, 'young people find [the] … culture very, very attractive because they can be themselves and know how to have fun'. In other words, rather than being perceived as impressionable, young people were seen as more likely to be emotionally expressive and playful and were therefore targeted as potential employees. This is suggested in the rhetoric observed in a staff induction session where workers were encouraged to sing the words 'open up [and] so express [your] inner child' from the children's programme, *The Muppets*.

While such practices might be seen as simply infantilizing employees more than existentially empowering them, the company also encouraged practices which incorporated the expression of explicitly adult identities under the theme of partying. In particular, employees were openly encouraged to drink alcohol. Job advertisements were headed with the phrase 'Do you know how to party?' and management often said that Sunray life is similar to a 'party' because of the energy and 'good times' that distinguished the firm from other call centres.

Responding to Fun and Friendliness

Many, but by no means all, the employees at Sunray appeared to experience the activities in a positive manner and value the emphasis that the company placed on 'having fun': 'It's like this: when you leave work you don't feel drained – the fun allows you to focus not only on your work but yourself as well – you come out feeling fantastic and you like coming to work'. This seems to fit with managerial objectives of securing motivation and retention from such an approach. However, the activities extended beyond the 'fun' activities of Any Bank. At Sunray, the expression of sexuality and flirting was encouraged among employees. This was not simply confined to parties nor can it be seen simply as a reflection of workplace life or, even, the demographics of the employees. Rather, it was openly condoned. As one team leader, said 'we like to think of ourselves as fun, sexy and dedicated'. In keeping with the notion of 'being yourself', the sexual dimension of the Sunray culture did not conform to the heterosexist norm, but also had a strong gay focus. Rather than hiding their homosexual identities at work, Sunray was perceived by some workers as 'very gay' (see also Clair et al., 2005). For example, agents, claimed that 'they [gays] like it 'cause they can be themselves' and that 'Sunray definitely promote it [open homosexuality] ... well, not promote it but, say, you are what you are and you are allowed to be that way'. Thus, consistent with the literature in this area, the responses of employees at Sunray would appear to indicate that the introduction of 'fun' into the workplace served as a vehicle for the expression (and transformation) of at least some aspects of their 'private' (non-work) selves.

However, the response of the customer service advisors to the 'fun days' at Any Bank (as well as that of a number of employees Sunray) was more mixed. A small number of the home workers again reported that they valued this aspect of their working lives and were less likely to feel isolated on these days. However, the overwhelming majority claimed that escaping from participation in 'fun days' was one of the key reasons that they wanted to work from home. In this sense then, they served as a kind of self-selected sample of those more likely to be negative about the workplace regime.

All the home workers at Any Bank were women, and the majority had families. Unlike many of the staff at Sunray, these women felt that such activities were infantile and that their forced participation in this 'fun' demeaned them. They also saw and resented it is a 'cheap trick' by the company to increase their sales performance, one which they felt they did not need or welcome.

It is just horrible, they have these stupid fun days [...] people dressing up and [...] you've got managers running around dressed as fairies. Primary school type thing, basically it's like being at school [...] And it's just pathetic, it's the only way to sum it up I'm afraid. I mean it really does not motivate people to get a Quality Street [a type of chocolate] or something. You're not going to be that excited about it really are you [laughs]? You're not are you really? Especially when your manager's running around dressed up as Robin Hood or something [...] It's just a primary school type thing, you can do without it. It's bad enough being called teams named after animals, it's like being in the Rainbow class or something [...] There are some people you don't want to see dressed as fairies [laughs], there really are. (Sally)

Some of the Sunray workers were similarly cynical:

Working at Sunray is like working for *Playschool* [a children's television programme]. It's so much like an American kindergarten ... a plastic, fake kindergarten. The murals on the wall, the telling off if I'm late and the patronising tone in which I'm spoken to all give it a very childish flavour.

Thus, overall we see two different types of response, reflecting a concern with the appropriation or 'falseness' of 'fun' or a more active engagement with it. The latter appeared to be associated with positive orientations towards the organization and remaining there, while the former prompted and legitimated the decision to work away from the company office and its direct regime of control, as home workers. This position was reinforced by the stance taken by the Any Bank management towards the related phenomenon of friendliness, in that its instrumentality was rendered especially visible by attempts taken to prevent friendships from developing, as one advisor, Margaret, explained:

Margaret: I mean when we were in the office they don't let you settle anywhere [...] you've got all your different teams and you'll be allocated a team to go on and then once you actually get settled [...] they'll suddenly say 'right okay you're not going to be a cheetah anymore, you're going to be a jaguar' [laughs] [...] and of course the whole team, nobody knows anybody, so you think 'oh' and of course that upsets the apple cart.
Emma: Why do they move you? [...]
Margaret: You're not allowed to sit with your friends.
Emma: Why?
Margaret: I think they think you'll sit there talking [...] when everybody starts getting to know one another and they start chatting they go 'right okay, we're changing the rota again' [laughs].

While the bank accepts organizationally orchestrated fun and the friendliness that is required in order for this to run smoothly, they are not willing to permit this to extend to the development of more sustained and less managed friendships. This is not so much a concern with friendship *per se* as with a perceived danger of being distracted and the implications of this for conventional managerial concerns with individual and company performance. Thus, the data from Any Bank would indicate that far from being the liberating experience portrayed by gurus of fun and friendship, there are distinct limits imposed on the possibility of the 'genuine' or non-work selves being brought into the office.

The seemingly more liberal approach of Sunray was also reflected in the approach they took to employees' problems. In addition to breaching the division between home and work by bringing the fun element of people's everyday lives into the workplace, the home–work divide was also challenged in relation to more formal psychological support for employees in that staff were encouraged to bring their problems into work, as a team leader explains:

> We have a situation here where an agent can feel comfortable enough to say the reason why they've been coming late is because they have a serious problem at home ... We try to deal with them in a very caring way – and ask them how to fix the problem so they can be really great at what they do.

Thus, we see a form of formalized or managed collective emotional labour – of colleagues sharing issues – that is very similar to the aspirations of human relations and normative control more generally. But unlike in Korczynski's (2003) study of communities of coping, this sharing of issues has gone beyond work/task related stresses and has been extended to personal issues as well. This then moves the relationships beyond friendliness into a more conventional role associated with friendship as well as other 'non-work' social domains such as the family, as one agent admits:

> I've had some personal problems and because of the way things are here I've had so much support I've overcome these. And I see it as my family, I don't see it as Sunray the company I work for – I come in and do more than I would normally do because of that.

There was evidence of a similar, but less formal approach at Any Bank. Although this was referred to in terms of an American soap opera, it reflects an openness for individuals' personal/home problems to be brought into and shared in the workplace:

> Christine: This department's known as Dallas [...]
> Emma: By whom?
> Christine: By all of us, you walk into this department. I mean you walk into it, we've had so many break ups of marriages and bits and pieces like that, it is just not true. I'm divorced myself and you know I've seen it in my, what's happened to me, I've seen it in my staff. We've had people who have lost

children, we've, my father died quite recently and again we've had people whose parents have died, very suddenly like my own did. And I was able to help with that.

While this exchange reveals the attitude of one manager at Any Bank, it is interesting to note that she was not responsible for the call centre, but another department. No references to such communities of coping were made by managers responsible for the call centre. Moreover, the collective emotional element, where it did happen (although unauthorized by management) did not appear to be valued by all staff. Instead, what is revealed is a desire to escape from the kind of collective emotional labour which the subjects in Korczynski's (2003) study found to be so beneficial.

I just like being here [at home] doing my job rather than ... It might sound a bit selfish, but I don't really want to hear of everybody else's problems and things, you know. There were enough problems, there were enough things happening with work things and with customers, you know for me to be living with. I don't want others' problems as well [...]

Thus, while for the subjects in Korczynski's study this form of collective emotion work was presented as a positive counter to the more harmful emotional labour, for some teleworkers at Any Bank it was seen as so unpleasant and undesirable that it was an important reason for wanting to leave.

Once again, however, there was some ambivalence evident. While working from home had released them from the drudgery of providing hidden emotional labour to others, it also removed a source of support for themselves. For example, a number of them recalled events that had occurred when they would have appreciated some support from their colleagues. One recounted a night when she received bad news regarding the health of her son while another missed the empathy of colleagues when she was feeling unwell herself.

I felt like if I'd been in the office [...] then other people would say, 'Oh Suzanne, I've got some really good tablets', you know, 'you need to take these' or 'you need this', or 'Oh, I've had that' and a bit of sort of camaraderie, sort of feeling for me [...]

This ambivalence suggests that instrumentality is not restricted to regimes of friendliness, but is also part of what might be seen as friendship or, at least emotional support. However, in this case at least, the relief that they felt from not having to engage in this form of emotion work with colleagues seemed to be worth the loss of some of their own sources of emotional support.

Thus, overall, we see not only some variation between the reactions of staff at Any Bank and Sunray with regard to their particular managerial regimes of 'fun' and friendliness, but some variation or, rather, ambivalence among those at Any Bank who opted to work at home. Here, they both welcomed and missed the new-found freedom from the demands and satisfactions of collective emotional labour as well as, in some cases at least, finding a new 'dual burden' of emotion work and emotional labour in the home (cf. Hochschild, 1983).

Discussion and Conclusion

In this chapter we have focused on some particular aspects of emotion in corporate life, those which have long existed in the workplace, but which, until recently, have been largely tolerated, ignored or gladly received by management, but have been generally absent from their formal interventions to increase productivity and efficiency. Fun and friendliness have been, and to a large extent remain, culturally in an existentially protected and protective sphere of everyday life and everyday (unmanaged) working life. But we have seen how, in the call centres we explored as well as elsewhere, they have come to be appropriated by management into their control regimes. This extends the seemingly progressive encroachment of management in the appropriation of everyday life and its emotional dimensions, moving on from emotional labour with customers to collective emotions between colleagues (cf. Korczynski, 2003). In a sense, such initiatives parallel the development of emotional intelligence (i.e. social skills) as a management or 'self-development' tool (Fineman, 2000b) and the channelling of friendliness as social capital in inter-organizational relations (Uzzi, 1997).

The promotion of fun and friendliness in organizations can also be seen as management of what were once considered indulgency patterns, the informally sanctioned 'free' zones for workers, or as an extension of human relations initiatives towards, not just appropriating work group norms, but their emotions (or collective emotional labour) too, for productive ends. These 'free' zones served a contradictory or ambivalent role. They both challenged managerial authority, in terms of formal rules, and allowed it to go uncontested in facilitating the achievement of work tasks and output. Thus, it is perhaps unsurprising that combined with its persistent, yet changing cultural status as 'beyond management', intervening in fun and collective support produces complex and contrary effects. How are we to make sense of these?

We have seen how both the regimes at Sunray and Any Bank and the staff's responses to them were similar in some respects, but also different. Also, we have drawn on data from non-equivalent groups. In the former case, we referred to a sample of telephone agents working in the call centre while in the latter, we relied on accounts from those who had reflected on their position and chosen to leave the call centre and work from home. As noted earlier, this methodological difference is important when considering the data. For example, at Any Bank, it is unlikely that these workers would be especially positive about their time in the call centre as this would make their decision to leave it more difficult to deal with. At the same time, however, they were interviewed away from the call centre, in their homes for the most part, and this may also influence how they talked of their work – less distanced from home, but also more able to speak freely about work and the regime.

Given these issues, what insights can we gain? First there appeared to be qualitative differences in the scope of the 'fun' regimes between the sites. Sunray's was more extensive and, perhaps, consistent, in terms of the frequency of events and the inclusion of an apparent celebration of lifestyle freedom, with regard to sexuality for example. By contrast, at Any Bank regime activities were more directly and explicitly focused on output and this instrumentality for direct control was rendered most visible by the hypocrisy or contradiction of a deliberate suppression of the formation of friendship groups (Brunsson, 1989). There was a clear contrast between managerial words and deeds (Sturdy and Fleming, 2003). This was also the case at Sunray, although less so, where some staff reported their concerns at the instrumentality, hollowness and limits of the espoused messages of fun and freedom.

It is also important to consider the staff themselves and where they were coming from. Here, we are forced to be more speculative in drawing conclusions and yet it is probably no coincidence that the greater criticality of the Any Bank staff arises not only from the difference in regime and their particular position with regard to working at home, but from their greater age and experience. This informs expectations of what work *should* be like such that the managerial intrusion into what are deemed to be private or personal features of life is unlikely to be welcomed. Rather, more experienced staff retain what might be seen as a positive bureaucratic outlook in the sense of maintaining the separation of work and non-work/ emotion. This is somewhat paradoxical in that they have decided to work from home.

By contrast, the staff at Sunray were on average less experienced, perhaps had fewer or less established expectations of work life and were more open to what might be seen as a post-bureaucratic mentality where lifeworlds and work boundaries are more fluid (cf. Hochschild, 1997). This is not to say that the Sunray managerial view of young staff as being more open and free is correct nor the opposite, that they are more malleable. Rather, they have been constituted as, or become, different people with different expectations and experiences. Likewise, some of the views of the Any Bank staff suggest that gender/life-stage are also important here. Many of them had family as well as work responsibilities – the 'dual burden' – and as a consequence were more ambivalent about what

Korczynski (2003) terms 'collective emotional labour' in the office – some had too much emotion work to deal with in their everyday lives already, without this extra, triple burden.

Finally, we should comment more critically on the nature of the regimes. For many, the issue might be the managerial intrusion on, and appropriation of, what can be seen, and felt, as genuine or authentic selves, to re-construct or direct them for productive ends. This can be seen most clearly in the artificiality of fun events and the instrumental way in which they are designed and, at Any Bank especially, the prevention of friendship, in favour of fake friendliness. The latter certainly seems to have had the effect of reinforcing the cultural space of friendship as being beyond managerial intervention. At the same time, a liberal view of the Sunray regime might support the fact that once proscribed behaviour associated with sexuality is now accepted – people can be their true selves and many welcome this. However, and as many others have argued (see Fineman, 1993), the notion of having one's own real self, is important in terms of how one might experience identity, but is more problematic empirically and politically. A more dynamic and pluralistic view of identity suggests that we acquire and transform our senses of self from different experiences over time and enact it differently according to situation. This means that the 'selves' who come to work and the associated expectations (e.g. of boundaries) are already partially produced through various means such as education and the media. They may be no less real because of this, but by no means exist independently.

In addition, even where these identities appear to be fostered (rather than suppressed), as is seemingly the case at Sunray, they are also necessarily transformed in the process. As Janssens and Zanoni (2005) argue, identities such as sexuality are not only enabled, but produced and transformed through diversity management. In other words, what it means to be, say, homosexual or heterosexual or simply, 'yourself' is shaped by corporate employment practices. In this way, control turns into self control in much the same way that corporate advertising has been critically portrayed for some time. The question therefore becomes, not how can we prevent identity being interfered with, but what are the different agencies involved in the co-production of identities; do some have more influence than others; and what forms of identity are more desirable and acceptable than others.

Thus, the issue is the relative power of organizations in managing how we see ourselves and how we feel as well as the particular forms of identities and feeling rules which are encouraged. This is not a new issue in that employers have been involved in seeking to shape subjects, by design or default, and how they think and feel since the industrial revolution at least (e.g. see Thompson, 1967). Indeed, one could argue that with the return, for some, of paid work in the home, employers are once again seeking to control how people feel at home as well as in the workplace. As we have seen however, such efforts may always have effects, but never exactly those which are intended.

Note

1   Empirical examples in this chapter are taken from a number of different papers and articles: Fleming and Sturdy, 2009; Grey and Sturdy, 2007; Sturdy, 2003; Surman, 2004).

CONCLUSION

André Spicer

It is supposed to be the most rational place in the world. When you walk through the big revolving doors of a large corporation, you are supposed to be moving from the disorder, chaos and unreasonable world of street life into an altogether more reified environment. The expensive marble beneath your feet, the sleek black leather chairs, and the cool lighting are all supposed to remind you this is a different universe. The security barrier staffed by guards and the speedy lifts that race you towards the heavens of the executive quarters are all there to remind you that this is not normal life. This is corporate life.

In this book, we have tried to take you inside this corporate life. As you probably know, it is a life that many aspire to lead. It is a life that looks attractive, well paid, and very exciting from the outside. It seems to be life doing important things with important people. And, as many texts books about management remind us, it is. But instead of trying to paint a picture of corporate life as one that is bursting with satisfaction and rationality, we have tried to let you in on a few of the dirty secrets. In this book, we have tried to provide the reader with a picture of corporate life that is at once inspiring as well as insipid. It is hyper-rational as well as completely crazy. It is moving and leaves you cold at the same time. It showers you with information but makes no sense.

In order to let you into this world, we have gathered together a series of essays that each look at one aspect of corporate life. Instead of looking at the topics you would usually encounter in a textbook (like motivation, groups, structure), we tried to focus on the most immediate and obvious aspects of corporate life. We looked at how people use knowledge in organizations. We asked what kinds of space people dwell in and how they use them. We considered how people experience time during their day at work. We investigated the ways people seek to build an identity in the workplace. We uncovered the effects that globalization is having on everyday life at work. We traced through the ways in which technology is used and played with in the workplace. We deliberated on the aesthetics of corporate life. And finally, we asked whether community might be built within organizations. With all these questions, we have tried to lead you into some of strange corners and back allies of corporate life which are always there, but rarely visited. In doing so, we hope to have opened your eyes to some of the aspects of this world that you have either never thought about, or recognized, but never been able to talk about.

Cross-cutting Themes

Reading across the text, we hope to have drawn out three cross-cutting themes. The first is the importance of *understanding*. Too often, we simply take corporations at their word. We assume that what their CEOs say is a matter of truth. If we are a little cynical, then we might suspect they are misleading us, but also think that we can do very little about such deception. Too often the words and sweet phrases of management gurus and grand plans associated with corporate change are too seductive to ignore. But we know all too well that when such advice is implemented, at best it can often only lead to fairly minor improvements in performance. At worst, it can lead to disastrous failures and the kind of corporate catastrophes that are becoming only too familiar today. By seeking to *understand* corporate life, rather than taking it at face value, we hope to push our readers beyond the corporate hype and into all the strange contradictions which plague everyday life at work. In addition, we also hope to question some of the more explicitly scientific views of the organization which hold that corporate life is a strict pattern of causality (like a giant game of billiard's). This involves realizing that, unlike the physical universe, the corporate world does not always go to plan. One may pull a 'strategic lever' and nothing happens. But it is equally possible that an entirely unexpected result will appear. This is because humans are far less predictable in their reactions than lumps of physical matter. It is just a pity that so many scientific and engineering trained managers seem to forget this, and get so confused when people do not react as they are expected to.

Understanding corporate life also allows us to expand our repertoires of ways of understanding this world. Instead of simply assuming that there is one correct model that perfectly describes the social world, we would like to suggest multiplying the ways in which we are able to look at a problem. This means that we do not have a single myopic perspective on aspects of organizational life. Rather, it means that we can look at it from a range of different and contrasting perspectives. This is vital because any good social actor must have the ability to recognize the multi-faceted nature of any problem with an organization. By doing so, it means that they are able to appreciate the often unacknowledged or unthought of aspects of an organization.

By seeking to enhance our understanding of corporate life, we are able to begin to describe and name aspects of organizational life that we already recognize but were previously not able to put into words. A proper understanding provides us with a formal language we can use to analyse, discuss and consider a particular phenomenon. For instance, by developing a proper understanding of space we are able to develop a language and set of terms that we can use to describe the office space which we work in now. It means we can talk sensibly about this space, describe it in some detail and perhaps compare it to other spaces. Instead of it just being there, it becomes something that has a degree of meaning for us. No longer are we mute about the things that happen to us and around us. When we seek to understand corporate life we gain the ability to actually make sense of this world which we accepted as just 'there' before.

By seeking to develop an understanding of corporate life, we become far more able to intervene in it. An understanding of a phenomenon gives us a language that we can play with, talk about, and possibly use to suggest alternatives. For instance, once we begin to gain a language for talking about aesthetics in the workplace, it means we are able to talk about the horrible décor or oppressive architecture. It also means that we might be able to pick out what exactly we don't like about, and possibly begin to suggest alternatives. A proper understanding allows us to see the limitations of our existing understandings. It also allows us to play with alternative ways of understanding a phenomenon. This begins to provide us with different ways of engaging with it. Ultimately, we hope that understanding will become a central plank in identifying what we would like to change about a situation and then having the ability to set about changing it.

The second theme that we hope cuts across the book is reviewing various aspects of the *corporation*. We hope that each of the chapters reminds the reader that corporations have become increasingly dominant institutions within our society. Indeed, they often infuse more and more aspects of our lives. Corporations have shaped our most intimate behaviour, such as how we experience time and how we move about in space. They also seek to forge a specific sense of identity and self within us. Furthermore, they build communities for us and offer us a sense of belonging in the increasingly faceless cities in which we dwell. Finally, we have tried to highlight that corporations shape even the broadest and most systematic aspects of social behaviour. For instance, in the chapter on globalization, we discussed how corporations have been instrumental in forging links between individuals and societies throughout the world.

In addition to seeing how corporations shape aspects of lives, we hope that the chapters that are contained in this book remind us of another meaning of corporate life – that is a life lived in a corpus, or body. By reminding readers of this dimension, we hope to highlight the highly embodied aspects of corporate life. After all, we take our bodies to work, we drag them through the time of the work-day, our knowledge and skill is often inscribed into our bodies. Indeed, the corporation is in many ways a collection of bodies. But at the same time as being a group of actual bodies, it is also an abstract person – a person with a legal reality but without any body. So it seems that the corporation requires the bodies of the people who work for it to carry out all the tasks that it can't do. In some ways it is a kind of a body snatcher.

The final aspect that cuts throughout these chapters is a reminder that corporate life is not like 'normal' life. Rather, life in the corporation involves a whole series of constraints that would not be tolerated in most aspects of our lives. Attempts to control where we move in space, how we use our time, the kind of knowledge we acquire, would be shocking to us in other circumstances. However, when we enter into the workplace, we merely take these aspects as a given in the workplace. Moreover, the kind of rights that the corporation has over our time, space and knowledge differs quite radically in different national contexts. For instance, *Karoshi* (or death by overwork) is a common consequence of the extreme demands on employees' time in Japan. However, this would not be tolerated in most European companies, because a corporation's claim on an individual's time is thought to be highly circumscribed to the working day. By thinking through these different constraints, we begin to understand why corporate life is so different in different national contexts.

And yet these chapters also illustrate the fact that the time we do in corporations is after all part of our *life*. We hope to have shown the reader that there is no strict demarcation to be drawn between the corporation and life. Rather, much of our lives take place within corporations. We increasingly eat, are entertained, make friends, meet romantic partners, play sports and even sleep within the corporation. Even when we leave for the night, the corporation follows us home with the Blackberry we keep in our pockets. Further, forms of life and living seem to have become increasingly incorporated. This has happened as the most basic details of what we eat, how we sleep, how we make love, how we develop our sense of identity and our sense of time are governed and shaped by corporations. Recall that some corporations own the copyright for certain words, DNA structures, and even various routine behaviours. Indeed, some would argue that life is increasingly becoming the next big zone for corporations to do their trade in. Companies increasingly sell 'life itself' in the form of our human genome, our patterns of eating and sleeping, and our biorhythms. We live a life incorporated. And to understand it, we must understand the corporations that shape it.

In the march to quantify and commodify, corporations often come up against a barrier, something that they find very difficult to deal with. Bodies are messy things that cannot be fitted into corporate life that easily. Our bodies demand sleep, they cannot be effectively disciplined, and they have biological needs. Some people have bodies that are not accepted by large corporations because they do not fit into their criteria for the perfect worker. More than this, humans in corporations also demand a life. We want a sense that we can live a normal life. In fact, we often want a good life, something that is attractive and sustainable. And we are likely to say no to corporations when that good life is threatened, when we feel we risk our health, or when stress invades every pore of who we are. The result is that life continues to fight against being incorporated.

Future Corporate Life

The chapters in this book provide a compelling and interesting exploration of corporate life. Corporate life, as it has been lived for the past two decades, is very specific. It is has been a life where corporations have been rapidly expanding, where they have been increasingly flexible, where they have sought to incorporate people into them through a whole range of ideological mechanisms, where they have developed increasingly short-term commitments, where they have focused on speeding up and innovation. Underlying this new form of corporate life has been an emphasis on neo-liberal economic models which mean that the individual has to be available for the marketplace 24/7.

However, this model of corporate life is now under serious threat – the recent financial melt-down has resulted in many of the most advanced corporations in the financial, manufacturing and service sectors coming under severe strain, and in some cases collapsing. Some of the basic principles that lie behind the contemporary corporation, such as short-term flexibility, control by financial institutions, increasing incorporation of all aspects of people's life-world are now being questioned. Some see the financial melt-down and the mass company failures associated with it as evidence that the kinds of principles developed by large companies have not been applied rigorously and strenuously enough. Others, however, argue that it is precisely these principles which have precipitated such a melt-down. Indeed, the increasingly short-term orientation of corporations has meant that they engaged in increasingly risky behaviours, did not undergo adequate due process when considering the issues associated with their undertakings, and so on. Indeed, many would argue that the forms of corporate life which we describe in the chapters in this book in fact laid the very groundwork for the economic tragedy which we now see unfolding before us.

If we are indeed faced with the prospect that the theories we used to understand corporate life have utterly failed us, then we are faced with some very tough decisions. In particular, there is the question of how it is possible to sustain these kinds of ways of organizing and of living in the future. It is a question of exactly how we might actually make our way in the world and deal with many of these questions – how we might begin to forge a new kind of organizational life? There are many open questions about what it would actually look like. For instance, how would knowledge be developed, shared and transformed into innovations? How would these new corporate spaces look? Would they still be the same kind of skyscrapers in downtown areas which we see today, or would they be quite different? How about time? Would we see a consistent concern and obsession with clock time? Or would some other way of marking time emerge? Would we find the need to develop new kinds of rhythms, and what would these be? What about speed? Would we continue with our obsession with increasingly accelerating the pace and circulation of commodities and people? Or might the gigantic financial coronary that the world economy is now suffering actually provide an opportunity, and indeed a reason, to slow down? What about globalization? Are we witnessing a deepening global connection?

Or might we actually be seeing a de-linking as some companies seek to protect themselves from the financial maelstrom? What will this mean for identity? Will people continue to invest significant aspects of their identity in the workplace? Or will this identity actually be something which changes? Will people find their identities in new places? Where will these be? And what of people who find themselves out of work following this collapse? How will they craft an identity in a workless present? What will the new corporate aesthetic look like? Will it still be one of unceasing blurring and modern slickness? Or will it be something altogether different? A cosier aesthetic? Or maybe an aesthetic of rubble and junk? Perhaps one of the hardest questions that we need to ask ourselves is what the revolutions and crises of our time might mean for communities? Will corporations still be able to provide the promise of community to employees? Or has that promise disappeared into ash and smoke? Are we going to witness quite another form of coming together to work in time to come? These are all question that must be answered in the future if we want to understand and indeed remake corporate life into something that is more fruitful, engaging and beautiful. These are the questions that we hope that you might begin to answer.

REFERENCES

Abrahamson, E. (1996) 'Management fashion', *Academy of Management Review,* 21: 254–85.

Ackroyd, S. and Crowdy, P.A. (1990) 'Can culture be managed?', *Personnel Review,* 19: 3–13.

Adam, B. (1990) *Time and Social Theory.* Cambridge: Polity.

Adam, B. (1995) *Timewatch: The Social Analysis of Time.* Cambridge: Polity.

Adam, B. (2002) 'The gendered time politics of globalization: of shadowlands and elusive justice', *Feminist Review,* 70: 3–29.

Adam, B. (2004) *Time.* Cambridge: Polity.

Adam, B., Whipp, R. and Sabelis, I. (2002) 'Choreographing time and management: traditions, developments and opportunities', in R. Whipp, B. Adam and I. Sabelis (eds), *Making Time: Time and Management in Modern Organizations.* Oxford: Oxford University Press.

Adorno, T. (1970/1997) *Aesthetic Theory,* trans. R. Hullot-Kentor. London: Athlone Press.

Ahuja, G. (2000) 'Collaboration networks, structural-holes, and innovation: a longitudinal study', *Administrative Science Quarterly,* 45: 425–55.

Albrow, M. (1997) *Do Organizations Have Feelings?* London: Routledge.

Alferoff, C. and Knights, D. (2003) 'We're all partying here: target and games, or targets as games in call center management', in A. Carr and P. Hancock (eds), *Art and Aesthetics at Work.* Basingstoke: Palgrave.

Alter, C. and Hage, J. (1993) *Organizations Working Together.* Newbury Park, CA: Sage.

Alvesson, M. and Willmott, H. (2002) 'Identity regulation as organizational control: producing the appropriate individual', *Journal of Management Studies,* 39: 619–44.

Alvesson, M., Karreman, D. and Swan, J. (2002) 'Departures from knowledge and/or management in knowledge management', *Management Communication Quarterly,* 16: 282–91.

Anderson, B. (1991) *Imagined Communities: Reflections on the Origin and Spread of Nationalism,* revised edition. London: Verso.

Anderson, B. (2002) *Doing the Dirty Work: The Global Politics of Domestic Labour.* London: Zed Books.

Anderson, B. (2006) 'A very private business: migration and domestic work', *Working Paper 26.* Centre on Migration, Policy and Society, University of Oxford.

Argyle, M. (1988) 'Social relationships', in M. Hewstone, W. Stroebe, J-P. Codol and G.M. Stephenson (eds), *Introduction to Social Psychology.* Oxford: Blackwell.

Armbruster, T. (2006) *The Economics and Sociology of Management Consulting.* Cambridge: Cambridge University Press.

Armitage, J. (2000) 'Paul Virilio: An Introduction', in J. Armitage (ed.), Paul *Virilio: From Modernism to Hypermodernism and Beyond.* London: Sage.

Armstrong, P. (1984) 'Competition between the organisational professions and the evolution of management control strategies', in K. Thompson (ed.), *Work, Employment and Unemployment: Perspectives on Work and Society.* Milton Keynes: Open University Press.

Armstrong, P. (1985) 'Changing management control strategies: the role of competition between accountancy and other organisational professions', *Accounting, Organizations and Society*, 10: 129–48.

Arthur, M.B., Hall, D.T. and Lawrence, B.S. (1989) *Handbook of Career Theory*. Cambridge: Cambridge University Press.

Augé, M. (1995) *Non-places: Introduction to an Anthropology of Supermodernity*. London: Verso.

Bachelard, G. (1958) *The Poetics of Space*. Boston: Orion Press.

Bain, P., Watson, A., Mulvey, G., Taylor, P. and Galf, G. (2002) 'Taylorism, targets and the pursuit of quantity and quality by call centre management', *New Technology, Work and Employment*, 17: 102–21.

Baldry, C. (1999) 'Space – the final frontier', *Sociology*, 33: 535–53.

Barbalet, J.M. (1998) *Emotion, Social Theory and Social Structure – A Macro-sociological Approach*. Cambridge: Cambridge University Press.

Barker, J. (1993) 'Tightening the iron cage: concertive control in self-managing teams', *Administrative Science Quarterly*, 38: 408–37.

Barker, J. and Downing, H. (1985) 'Word processing and the transformation of patriarchal relations of control in the office', in D. MacKenzie and J. Wajcman (eds), *The Social Control of Technology*. Milton Keynes: Open University Press.

Barnes, B. (2001) 'Practice as collective action', in T. Schatzki, K. Knorr Cetina and E. von Savigny (eds), *The Practice Turn in Contemporary Theory*. London: Routledge.

Barney, J.B. (1991) 'Firm resources and sustained competitive advantage', *Journal of Management*, 17: 99–120.

Baruch, Y. (2000) 'Teleworking: benefits, and pitfalls as perceived by professionals and managers', *New Technology, Work and Employment*, 15: 34–48.

Bauman, Z. (1998) *Globalization. The Human Consequences*. Cambridge: Polity.

Bauman, Z. (2000) *Liquid Modernity*. Cambridge: Polity Press.

Bauman, Z. (2001) *Community: Seeing Safety in an Insecure World*. Cambridge: Polity.

Bayley, C.A. (2004) *The Birth of the Modern World, 1780–1914*. Oxford: Blackwell Publishing.

Beck, U. (2000) *What is Globalization?* Oxford: Polity Press.

Becker, F. (1981) *Workspace: Creating Environments in Organizations*. New York: Praeger.

Becker, H. (1982) *Artworlds*. Berkeley, CA: University of California Press.

Beechey, V. (1982) 'The sexual division of labour and the labour process', in S. Wood (ed.), *The Degradation of Work? Skill, Deskilling and the Labour Process*. London: Hutchinson.

Bell, D. (1915) *Art*. London: Chatto and Windus.

Bell, E. and Tuckman, A. (2002) 'Hanging on the telephone: temporal flexibility and the accessible worker', in R. Whipp, B. Adam and I. Sabelis (eds), *Making Time: Time and Management in Modern Organizations*. Oxford: Oxford University Press.

Bendix, R. (1956) *Work and Authority in Industry*. Berkeley, CA: University of California Press.

Bennis, W.G. (1966) *Changing Organizations*. New York: McGraw-Hill.

Berg, P.O. and Kreiner, K. (1990) 'Corporate architecture: turning physical settings into symbolic resources', in P. Gagliardi (ed.), *Symbols and Artifacts: Views of the Corporate Landscape*. Berlin: de Gruyter.

Bessant, J. (1991) *Managing Advanced Manufacturing Technology*. Oxford: Blackwell.

Bijker, W. (1995) 'Sociohistorical technology studies', in S. Jasanoff, G.E. Markle, J.C. Peterson and T.J. Pinch (eds), *Handbook of Science and Technology Studies*. Thousand Oaks, CA: Sage.

Bloch, M. (1967) *Land and Work in Medieval Europe*. London: Routledge.

Bloomfield, B., Coombs, R., Cooper, D. and Rea, D. (1992) 'Machine and manoeuvres: responsibility accounting and the construction of hospital information systems', *Accounting, Management and Information Technology*, 2: 197–219.

Blyton, P. and Turnbull, P. (eds) (1994) *Reassessing Human Resource Management*. London: Sage.

Böhme, G. (2003) 'Contribution to the critique of the aesthetic economy', *Thesis Eleven*, 73: 71–82.

Boltanski, L. and Chiapello, E. (2005) *The New Spirit of Capitalism*. London: Verso.

Bolton, S.C. (2005) *Emotion Management in the Workplace*. Houndmills: Palgrave.

Boorstin, D.J. (1983) *The Discoverers*. New York: Random House.

Boudon, R. (1986) *Theories of Social Change*. Cambridge: Polity.

Bouty, I. (2000) 'Interpersonal and interaction influences on informal resource exchanges between R&D researchers across organizational boundaries', *Academy of Management Journal,* 43: 50–65.

Braverman, H. (1974) *Labor and Monopoly Capital: The Degradation of Work in the Twentieth Century*. New York: Monthly Review Press.

Brecht, B. (1957) *Schriften zum Theater*. Berlin and Frankfurt: Suhrkamp.

Brigham, M. and Corbett, J.M. (1997) 'Email, power and the constitution of organisational reality', *New Technology, Work and Employment*, 12: 25–35.

Brocklehurst, M. (2001) 'Power, identity and new technology homework: implications for new forms of organising', *Organization Studies*, 22: 445–66.

Brown, A.D. and Starkey, K. (2000) 'Organizational identity and learning: a psychodynamic perspective', *Academy of Management Review*, 25: 102–20.

Brown, G., Lawrence, T.B. and Robinson, S.L (2005) 'Territoriality in organizations', *Academy of Management Review*, 30: 577–94.

Brown, J.S. and Duguid, P. (2001) 'Knowledge and organization: a social-practice perspective', *Organization Science*, 12: 198–213.

Brunsson, N. (1982) 'The irrationality of action and action rationality: decisions, ideologies and organizational actions', *Journal of Management Studies*, 19: 29–44.

Brunsson, N. (1989) *The Organization of Hypocrisy: Talk, Decisions and Actions in Organizations*. Chichester: Wiley.

Buchanan, D.A. and Badham, R. (1999) *Power, Politics and Organizational Change*. London: Sage

Buchanan, D.A. and Boddy, D (1983) *Organisations in the Computer Age*. Aldershot: Gower.

Burawoy, M. (1979) *Manufacturing Consent: Changes in the Labor Process Under Monopoly Capitalism*. Chicago: University of Chicago Press.

Burkitt, I. (1997) 'Social relationships and emotions', *Sociology*, 31: 37–55.

Burrell, G. (1992) 'Back to the future: time and organization', in M. Reed and M. Hughes (eds), *Rethinking Organization*. London: Sage.

Burrell, G. (1997) *Pandemonium: Towards a Retro-Organization Theory*. London: Sage.

Callon, M. (1986) 'The sociology of an actor-network: the case of the electric vehicle', in M. Callon, J. Law and A. Rip (eds), *Mapping the Dynamics of Science and Technology*. London: Macmillan.

Cappetta, R. and Gioia, D. (2006) 'Fine fashion: using symbolic artifacts, sensemaking, and sensegiving to construct identity and image', in A. Rafaeli and M.G. Pratt (eds), *Artifacts and Organizations: Beyond Mere Symbolism*. Mahwah, NJ: Lawrence Erlbaum.

Carey, A. (1967) 'The Hawthorne Studies: a radical criticism', *American Sociological Review*, 32: 403–16.

Carlile, P. (2002) 'A pragmetic view of knowledge and boundaries: boundary objects in new product development', *Organization Science,* 13: 442–55.

Carnegie, D. (1937/1990) *How to Win Friends and Influence People.* New York: Vermilion.

Carr, A. (1999) 'The challenge of postmodernism and the casting of psychoanalysis as mere hermeneutics', in Y. Gabriel (ed.), *Organizations in Depth: The Psychoanalysis of Organizations.* London: Sage.

Carr, A. (2003) 'Art as a form of knowledge: the implications for critical management', in A. Carr and P. Hancock (eds), *Art and Aesthetics at Work.* Basingstoke: Palgrave.

Carrier, J. (1999) 'People who can be friends: selves and social relationships', in S. Bell and S. Coleman (eds), *The Anthropology of Friendship.* Oxford: Berg.

Carroll, D. (1987) *Paraesthetics: Foucault, Lyotard, Derrida.* London: Routledge.

Carter, P. and Jackson, N. (2000) 'An-aesthetics', in S. Linstead and H. Höpfl (eds), *The Aesthetics of Organization.* London: Sage.

Carter, P. and Jackson N. (2005) 'Laziness', in C. Jones and D. O'Doherty (eds), *Manifestos for the Business School of Tomorrow.* Truku: Dvalin Books.

Carty, V. (1997) 'Ideologies and forms of domination in the organization of the global production and consumption of goods in the emerging postmodern era: a case study of Nike Corporation and the implications for gender', *Gender, Work and Organizations,* 4: 189–201.

Casey, C. (1995) *Work, Self and Society: After Industrialism.* London: Routledge.

Casey, E. (1999) *The Fate of Place.* Berkley, CA: University of California Press.

Castells, M. (1996) *The Rise of the Network Society.* Oxford: Blackwells

Caulkin, S. (2007) 'How ICI settled on the wording of its epitaph', *Observer,* 24 June, at: http://observer.guardian.co.uk/business/story/0,,2109728,00.html

Chanda, N. (2007) *Bound Together: How Traders, Preachers, Adventurers and Warriors Shaped Globalization.* New Haven: Yale University Press.

Child, J. (1997) 'Strategic choice in the analysis of action, structure, organizations and environments: retrospect and prospect', *Organization Studies,* 18: 107–41

Child, J. (1972) 'Organisation structure, environment and performance: the role of strategic choice', *Sociology,* 6: 1–22.

Child, J., Faulkner, D. and Tallman, S. (2005) *Cooperative Strategy: Managing Alliances, Networks and Joint Ventures.* Oxford: Oxford University Press.

Chrisafis, A. (2003) 'Fiascos that haunt 'cando' company', *The Guardian* 15 February, at: http://www.guardian.co.uk/environment/2003/feb/15/london politics.congeston charging

Clair, J.A., Beatty, J.E. and MacLean, T. (2005) 'Out of sight but not out of mind: managing invisible social identities in the workplace', *Academy of Management Review,* 30: 78–95.

Clark, J. (1995) *Managing Innovation and Change: People, Technology and Strategy.* London: Sage.

Clarke, J. and Newman, J. (1997) *The Managerial State.* London: Sage.

Clark, T. and Mangham, I. (2004) 'From dramaturgy to theatre as technology: the case of corporate theatre', *Journal of Management Studies,* 4: 37–59.

Clegg, S., Kornberger, M. and Pitsis, T. (2008) *Managing & Organizations: An Introduction to Theory and Practice.* London: Sage.

CMR International (2004) *Centre for Medical Research International R&D Compendium 2004.* London: CMR.

Cockburn, C. (1983) *Brothers: Male Dominance and Technological Change.* London: Pluto Press.

Cohen, M.D., March, J.G. and Olsen, J.P. (1971) 'A garbage can model of organizational choice', *Administrative Science Quarterly*, 17: 1–25.

Cohen, S. and Taylor, L. (1992) *Escape Attempts*. Harmondsworth: Penguin.

Collins, M. (2005) 'The (not so simple) case for teleworking: a study at Lloyds of London', *New Technology, Work and Employment*, 20: 115–32.

Collinson, D. L. (1992) *Managing the Shopfloor: Subjectivity, Masculinity and Workplace Culture*. Berlin: Walter de Gruyter.

Collinson, D. L. (2002) 'Managing humour', *Journal of Management Studies*, 39: 269–88.

Collinson, D. L. (2003) 'Identities and insecurities: selves at work', *Organization*, 10: 527–47.

Collinson, D.L. and Collinson, M. (1997) '"Delayering managers": time–space surveillance and its gendered effects', *Organization,* 4: 375–407.

Contu, A. and Willmott, H. (2000) 'Comment on Wenger and Yanow. Knowing in practice: a delicate flower in the organizational learning field', *Organization*, 7: 269–76.

Contu, A. and Willmott, H. (2003) 'Re-embedding situatedness: the importance of power relations in learning theory', *Organization Science*, 14: 283–96.

Cook, S.D.N. and Brown, J.S. (1999) 'Bridging epistemologies: the generative dance between organizational knowledge and organizational knowing', *Organization Science,* 10: 381–400.

Cooley, M. (1987) *Architect or Bee?: The Human Price of Technology*. London: Hogarth Press.

Cooper, R. (1992) 'Systems and organizations: distal and proximal thinking', *Systems Practice*, 5: 373–7.

Cooper, R. and Law, J. (1995) 'Organization: distal and proximal views', *Research in the Sociology of Organizations*, 13: 237–74.

Corbett, J.M. (2003) 'Sound organisation: a brief history of psychosonic management', *ephemera: critical dialogues on organization*, 3: 261–72.

Crace, J. (2002) 'Making a drama before the crisis', *The Guardian*, 5 January.

Cully, M., Woodland, S., O'Reilly, A. and Dix, G. (1999) *Britain at Work*. London: Routledge.

Currie, G. and Proctor, S. (2005) 'Impact of MIS/IT upon middle managers: some evidence from the NHS', *New Technology, Work and Employment*, 20: 115–29.

Dale, K. and Burrell, G. (2003) 'An-aesthetics and architecture', in A. Carr and P. Hancock (eds), *Art and Aesthetics at Work*. Basingstoke: Palgrave.

Danius, S. (2002) *The Senses of Modernism: Technology, Perception and Aesthetics*. Ithaca, NY: Cornell University Press.

Danto, A. (1964) 'The artworld', *Journal of Philosophy*, 61: 571–84.

Darley, G. (2003) *Factory*. London: Reaktion.

Davenport, T. and Prusak, L. (1998) *Working Knowledge: How Organizations Manage What They Know*. Cambridge, MA: Harvard Business School Press.

Davidow, W.H. and Malone, M.S. (1992) *The Virtual Corporation*. New York: Harper Business Press.

Dawson, R. (2000) *Developing Knowledge-Based Client Relationships*. Woburn, MA: Butterworth.

de Geus, A. (1997) *The Living Company*. Boston, MA: Harvard Business School Press.

De Grazia, V. (2005) *Irresistible Empire: America's Advance through 20th Century Europe*. Cambridge, MA: The Belknap Press of the University of Harvard.

De Monthoux, P.G. (2004) *The Art Firm: Aesthetic Management and Metaphysical Marketing*. Palo Alto, CA: Stanford University Press.

Deal, T. and Kennedy, A. (1999) *The New Corporate Cultures*. London: Orion.

Deal, T. and Key, M. (1998) *Celebration at Work: Play, Purpose and Profit at Work*. New York: Berrett-Koehler.

193

Dean, D. (2005) 'Recruiting a self: women performers and aesthetic labour', *Work, Employment and Society*, 19(4): 761–74.

Delanty, G. (2003) *Community*. London: Routledge.

Delbridge, R. (1998) *Life on the Line in Contemporary Manufacturing*. Oxford: Oxford University Press.

Deleuze, G. (1992) 'Postscript on the societies of control', *October*, 59: 3–7.

Deleuze, G. and Guattari, F. (1984) *Anti-Oedipus: Capitalism and Schizophrenia*. Minneapolis: University of Minnesota Press.

Dery, K., Grant, D., Harley, B. and Wright, C. (2006) 'Work, organisation and Enterprise Resource Planning systems: an alternative research agenda', *New Technology, Work and Employment*, 21: 199–214.

DfES (2002) Progress File: 'Getting Started', 'Moving On', 'Exploring Pathways', 'Widening Horizons'. London: HMSO.

Dicken, P. (2006) *Global Shift*, 5th edn. London: Sage.

Dickie, G. (1974) *Art and the Aesthetic*. Ithaca, NY: Cornell University Press.

Dickinson, P. and Svensen, N. (2000) *Beautiful Corporations: Corporate Style in Action*. Harlow: Pearson Education.

Dobson, J. (1999) *The Art of Management and the Aesthetic Manager*. Westport, CT: Quorum Books.

Drucker, P. (1993) *Post-Capitalist Society*, Oxford: Butterworth-Heinemann.

Du Gay, P. (1996) *Consumption and Identity at Work*. London: Sage.

Du Gay, P. (2000) *In Praise of Bureaucracy*. London: Sage.

Duffy, F. (1997) *The New Office*. London: Conran Octopus.

Durkheim, E. (1893/1984) *The Division of Labour in Society*, trans. W. Halls. Basingstoke: Macmillan.

Dyer-Witheford, N. (1999) *Cyber-Marx: Cycles and Circuits of Struggle in High-Technology Capitalism*. Urbana: University of Illinois Press.

Eagleton, T. (1990) *The Ideology of the Aesthetic*. Oxford: Blackwell.

Edwards, P. and Wajcman, J. (2005) *The Politics of Working Life*. Oxford: Oxford University Press.

Edwards, R. (1979) *Contested Terrain: The Transformation of the Workplace in the Twentieth Century*. London: Heinemann.

Eliade, M. (1959) *Cosmos and History: The Myth of the Eternal Return*. New York: Harper & Row.

Elias, N. (1978) *The History of Manners – The Civilising Process, Vol. 1*. Oxford: Blackwell.

Elliot, R. (1998) 'Brands as symbolic resources for construction of identity', *International Journal of Advertising*, 17: 131–43.

Ellul, J. (1964) *The Technological Society*. New York: Vintage Books.

Elsbach, K.D. (2004b) 'Interpreting workplace identities: the role of office décor', *Journal of Organizational Behavior*, 25: 99–128.

Employers for Work–Life Balance (2007) http://www.employersforwork-lifebalance.org.uk

Entwistle, J. (2002) 'The aesthetic economy: the production of value in the field of fashion modelling', *Journal of Consumer Culture*, 2(3): 317–39.

Ezzamel, M. and Willmott, H. (1998) 'Accounting for teamwork', *Administrative Science Quarterly*, 43: 358–96.

Ezzamel, M., Willmott, H. and Worthington, F. (2001) 'Power, control and resistance in the factory that time forgot', *Journal of Management Studies*, 38: 1053–79.

Faist, T. (2000) *The Volume and Dynamics of International Migration and Transnational Social Spaces*. Oxford: Oxford University Press.

Featherstone, M. (1992) 'Postmodernism and the aestheticization of everyday life', in S. Lash and J. Friedman (eds), *Modernity and Identity*. Oxford: Blackwell.

Filipcove, B. and Filipec, J. (1986) 'Society and concepts of time', *International Social Science Journal*, 107, 19–32.

Fineman, S. (ed.) (1993) *Emotion in Organizations*. London: Sage.

Fineman, S. (ed.) (2000a) *Emotion in Organizations*, 2nd edn. London: Sage.

Fineman, S. (2000b) 'Commodifying the emotionally intelligent', in S. Fineman (ed.) *Emotion in Organizations*, 2nd edn. London: Sage.

Fineman, S. (2003) *Understanding Emotion at Work*. London: Sage.

Fleming, P. (2005a) 'Metaphors of resistance', *Management Communication Quarterly*, 19: 45–66.

Fleming, P. (2005b) 'Workers' playtime? Boundaries and cynicism in a "culture of fun" program', *Journal of Applied Behavioral Science*, 41: 285–303.

Fleming, P. (2005c) 'Kindergarten cop': paternalism and resistance in a high commitment workplace', *Journal of Management Studies*, 42: 1469–89.

Fleming, P. and Spicer, A. (2003) 'Working from a cynical distance: implications for power, subjectivity and resistance', *Organization*, 10: 159–81.

Fleming, P. and Sturdy, A. (2009) 'Just be yourself – towards neo-normative control in organisations', *Employee Relations*, October, forthcoming.

Florida, R. (2002) *The Rise of the Creative Class: And How It's Transforming Work, Leisure, Community and Everyday Life*. New York, NY: Basic Books.

Folkman, P., Froud, J., Johal, S. and Williams, K. (2006) 'Working for themselves? Capital market intermediaries and present day capitalism', *Centre for Research on Socio-Cultural Change Working Paper 25*. Milton Keynes.

Forester, T. (1985) *The Information Technology Revolution*. Oxford: Blackwell.

Foucault, M. (1976/1998) *The Will to Knowledge*. London: Penguin.

Foucault, M. (1979) *The History of Sexuality, Vol. 1*. Harmondsworth: Penguin.

Foucault, M. (1982) 'The subject and power', in H. Dreyfus and P. Rabinow (eds), *Michel Foucault: Beyond Structuralism and Hermeneutics*. Hemel Hempstead: Harvester.

Foucault, M. (2000) 'Friendship as a way of life', in P. Rabinow (ed.), *The Essential Works of Michel Foucault, 1954–1984: Ethics*. Harmondsworth: Penguin.

Fournier, V. (2002) 'Utopianism and the cultivation of possibilities: grassroots movements of hope', in M. Parker (ed.), *Utopia and Organization*. Oxford: Blackwell/Sociological Review.

Fournier, V. (2005) 'Yes', in C. Jones and D. O'Doherty (eds), *Manifestos: For the Business School of Tomorrow*. Turku: Dvalin Books.

Fox, A. (1974) *Man Mismanagement*. London: Hutchinson.

Fox, S. (2000) 'Communities of practice, Foucault and actor-network theory', *Journal of Management Studies*, 37: 853–68.

Freedman, R. (ed.) (1962) *Marx on Economics*. London: Pelican.

Frenkel, S., Korcynski, M., Shire, K. and Tam, M. (1999) *On the Front Line: Organization of Work in the Information Age*. Ithaca: ILR Press.

Friedman, T. (2005) *The World is Flat: A Brief History of the Globalized World in the 21st Century*. London: Penguin/Allen Lane.

Friesen, J. and Friesen, V. (2004) *The Palgrave Companion to North American Utopias*. New York: Palgrave Macmillan.

Froud, J., Johal, S., Leaver, A. and Williams, K. (2006) *Financialization and Strategy. Narratives and Numbers*. London: Routledge.

Fry, L.W. (1982) 'Technology-structure research: three critical issues', *Academy of Management Journal*, 25: 532–52.

Fukuyama, F. (1992) *The End of History and the Last Man*. Harmondsworth: Penguin.

Fuller, S. (2002) *Knowledge Management Foundations*. London: Butterworth Heinemann.

Gabriel, Y. (1995) 'The unmanaged organization: stories, fantasies and subjectivity', *Organization Studies*, 16: 477–501.

Gabriel, Y. (1999) *Organizations in Depth*. London: Sage.

Gabriel, Y. (2003) 'Glass palaces and iron cages: organizations in times of flexible work, fragmented consumption and fragile selves', *ephemera: critical dialogues on organizations*, 3: 166–84.

Gagliardi, P. (1990) 'Artifacts as pathways and remains of organizational life', in P. Gagliardi (ed.), *Symbols and Artifacts: Views of the Corporate Landscape*. Berlin: de Gruyter.

Game, A. and Pringle, R. (1983) *Gender at Work*. Sydney: George Allen and Unwin.

Garfinkel, H. (1967) *Studies in Ethnomethodology*. Cambridge: Polity.

Gee, J., Hull, C. and Lanshear, C. (1996) *The New Work Order. Behind the Language of the New Capitalism*. Sydney, Australia: Allen & Unwin.

George, J.M. (2000) 'Emotions and leadership: the role of emotional intelligence', *Human Relations*, 53: 1027–55.

Gereffi, G. (1996) 'Global commodity chains: new forms of coordination and control among nations and firms in international industries', *Competition and Change* 1: 427–39.

Gereffi, G. (2001) 'Shifting governance structures in global commodity chains. With special reference to the internet', *American Behavioural Scientist,* 44: 1616–37.

Gereffi, G. (2005) 'The global economy: organization, governance and development', in N.J. Smelser and R. Swedberg (eds), *The Handbook of Economic Sociology*, 2nd edn. Princeton, NJ: Russell Sage Foundation and Princeton University Press.

Gereffi, G. and Korzeniewicz, M. (eds) (1994) *Commodity Chains and Global Capitalism*. Westport, CT: Praeger.

Gerth, H. and Mills, C.W. (1953) *Character and Social Structure – The Psychology of Social Institutions*. San Diego: Harvest/HBJ.

Gherardi, S. (2006) *Organizational Knowledge: The Texture of Workplace Learning*. Blackwell.

Gibb, S. (2004a) 'Arts based training in management development; improvisational theatre', *Journal of Management Development*, 23: 741–50.

Gibb, S. (2004b) 'Imagination, creativity and HRD; an aesthetic perspective', *Human Resource Development Review*, 3: 53–74.

Gibb, S. (2006) *Aesthetics and HR: Connections, Concepts and Opportunities*. London: Routledge.

Giddens, A. (1979) *Central Problems in Social Theory*. Cambridge: Polity.

Giddens, A. (1984) *The Constitution of Society. Outline of the Theory of Structuration*. Cambridge: Polity Press.

Giddens, A. (1990) *The Consequences of Modernity*. Cambridge: Polity.

Giddens, A. (1991) *Modernity and Self Identity*. Cambridge: Polity.

Giddens, A. (1999) *Runaway World: How Globalization is Reshaping our Lives*. London: Profile Books.

Glendinning, C. (1990) *When Technology Wounds: The Human Consequences of Progress*. New York: William Morrow.

Glennie, P. and Thrift, N. (1996) 'Reworking E.P. Thompson's "Time, work-discipline and industrial capitalism"', *Time & Society*, 5: 275–99.

Goff, J. Le (1980) *Time, Work and Culture in the Middle Ages*. Chicago, IL: Chicago University Press.

Goffman, E. (1961) *Asylums*. New York: Anchor Press.

Goldman, R. and Papson, S. (1998) *Nike Culture*. London: Sage.

Goldthorpe, J.H., Lockwood, D., Bechhofer, F. and Platt, J. (1968) *The Affluent Worker: Industrial Attitudes and Behaviours*. London: Cambridge University Press.

Gordon, C. (ed.) (1980) *Michel Foucault. Power/Knowledge*. Hemel Hempstead: Harvester Wheatsheaf.

Gouldner, A.W. (1954) *Patterns of Industrial Bureaucracy*. New York: Free Press.

Gramsci, A. (1971) *Selections from the Prison Notebooks*. London: Lawrence and Wishart.

Granovetter, M.S. (1973) 'The strength of weak ties', *American Journal of Sociology*, 78: 1360–80.

Grant, D., Hall, R., Wales, N. and Wright, C. (2006) 'The false promise of technological determinism: the case of enterprise resource planning systems', *New Technology, Work and Employment*, 21: 2–15.

Grant, R. (1996) 'Prospering in dynamically-competitive environments: organizational capability as knowledge integration', *Organization Science*, 7: 375–87.

Greatbatch, D. and Clark, T. (2005) *Management Speak: Why We Listen to What the Gurus Tell Us*. London: Routledge.

Grenier, R. and Mates, G. (1995) *Going Virtual: Moving Your Organisation into the 21st Century*. New York: Prentice Hall.

Grey, C. (1994) 'Career as a project of the self and labour process discipline', *Sociology*, 28: 479–97.

Grey, C. (2003) 'The fetish of change', *Tamara,* 2: 1–19.

Grey, C. (2005) *A Very Short, Fairly Interesting and Reasonably Cheap Book About Studying Organizations*. London: Sage.

Grey, C. and Sturdy, A.J. (2007) 'Friendship and organizational analysis: towards a research agenda', *Journal of Management Inquiry*, 16: 157–72.

Grint, K. (1996) 'Re-engineering history', *Organization,* 1: 179–202.

Grint, K. (1998) *The Sociology of Work*. Cambridge: Polity.

Grint, K. and Woolgar, S. (1997) *The Machine at Work: Technology, Work and Organization*. Cambridge: Polity.

Grugulis, I., Dundon, T. and Wilkinson, A. (2000) 'Cultural control and the culture manager: employment practices in a consultancy', *Work Employment and Society*, 14: 97–116.

Guarnizo, L., Portes, A. and Haller, W.J. (2003) 'Assimilation and transnationalism: determinants of political action among contemporary migrants', *American Journal of Sociology*, 108: 1211–48.

Guillén, M.F. (2006) *The Taylorized Beauty of the Mechanical and the Rise of Modernist Architecture*. Princeton, NJ: Princeton University Press.

Hackman, J.R. and Oldham, G.R. (1980) *Work Redesign*. New York: Addison-Wesley.

Hakansson, H., Havila, V. and Pedersen, A.C. (1999) 'Learning in networks', *Industrial Marketing Management*, 2: 443–52.

Hall, S. (1996) *Modernity: An Introduction to Modern Society*. London: Blackwell.

Hamilton, G.G. (2006) *Commerce and Capitalism in Chinese Societies*. London: Routledge.

Hancock, P. (1997) 'Citizenship or vassalage? Organizational membership in the age of unreason', *Organization*, 4: 93–111.

Hancock, P. (2003) 'Aestheticizing the world of organization – creating beautiful untrue things', *Tamara*, 2: 91–103.

Hancock, P. (2005) 'Uncovering the semiotic in organizational aesthetics', *Organization*, 12: 29–60.

Hancock, P. (2006) 'The Spatial and Temporal Mediation of Social Change', *Journal of Organizational Change Management*, 19: 619–39.

Hancock, P. and Tyler, M. (2000) '"The look of love": gender, work and the organization of aesthetics', in J. Hassard, R. Holliday and H. Willmott (eds), *Body and Organization*. London: Sage.

Handy, C. (1985) *Understanding Organisations*. London: Penguin.

Handy, C. (1995) *The Empty Raincoat*. London: Arrow.

Hanlon, G. (1998) 'Professionalism as enterprise: service class politics and the redefinition of professionalism', *Sociology*, 32: 43–63.

Hannerz, U. (1996) *Transnational Connections*. London: Routledge.

Hansen, M.T. (1999) 'The search transfer problem: the role of weak ties in sharing knowledge across organizational sub-units', *Administrative Science Quarterly*, 44: 82–111.

Hansen, M.T., Nohria, N. and Tierney, T. (1999) 'What's your strategy for managing knowledge?', *Harvard Business Review*, March/April, 106–116.

Haraway, D. (1991) *Simians, Cyborgs, and Women: The Reinvention of Nature*. London: Free Association Books.

Hardt, M. and Negri, A. (2000) *Empire*. Cambridge, MA: Harvard University Press.

Harris, C.C. (1980) *Fundamental Concepts and the Sociological Enterprise*. London: Croom Helm.

Harquail, C. (2006) 'Employees as animate artifacts: wearing the brand', in A. Rafaeli and M.G. Pratt (eds), *Artifacts and Organizations: Beyond Mere Symbolism*. Mahwah, NJ: Lawrence Erlbaum.

Harris, C.C. (1980) *Fundamental Concepts and the Sociological Enterprise*. London: Croom Helm.

Harvey, D. (1974) *Social Justice and the City*. Oxford: Blackwell.

Harvey, D. (1989) *The Condition of Postmodernity*. Oxford: Blackwell.

Hassard, J. (1996) 'Images of time in work and organization', in S.R. Clegg, C. Hardy, and W. Nord (eds), *Handbook of Organizations*. London: Sage.

Hassard, J. and Law, J. (eds) (1999) *Actor Network Theory and After*. Oxford: Blackwell.

Hatch, M.J. (1997) *Organization Theory*. Oxford: Oxford University Press.

Hatch, M.J. and Cunliffe, A. (2006) *Organization Theory: Modern, Symbolic, and Postmodern Perspectives*. Oxford: Oxford University Press.

Heath, L.R. (1956) *The Concept of Time*. Chicago: University of Chicago Press.

Hecksher, C. (1995) *White Collar Blues: Management Loyalties in an Age of Corporate Restructuring*. New York: Basic Books.

Heidegger, M. (1977) *The Question Concerning Technology and Other Essays*. New York: Harper & Row.

Heptinstall, S. (2004) 'A whiff of success', *Rapport: The Magazine for Peugeot Owners*, Summer Issue: 23–5.

Hill, C. (1975) *The World Turned Upside Down: Radical Ideas During the English Revolution*. Harmondsworth: Penguin.

Hill, S. (1988) *The Tragedy of Technology*. London: Pluto Press.

Hirst, P. and Thompson, G. (1999) *Globalization in Question*, 2nd edn. Oxford: Polity Press.

Hobsbawm, E. (1998) *Uncommon People: Resistance, Rebellion and Jazz*. London: Abacus.

Hobson, J.M. (2004) *The Eastern Origins of Western Civilization*. Cambridge: Cambridge University Press.

Hochschild, A.R. (1983) *The Managed Heart: Commercialization of Human Feeling*. Berkeley: University of California Press.

Hochschild, A.R. (1997) *The Time Bind: When Work Becomes Home and Home Becomes Work*. New York: Metropolitan Books.

Hodson, P. (1996) 'Love and the teleworker', *Distans*, February.

Hollway, W. (1991) *Work Psychology and Organizational Behaviour*. London: Sage.

Honoré, C. (2004) *In Praise of Slow*. London: Ovion.

Höpfl, H. (2006) 'Post-bureaucracy and Weber's 'modern' bureaucrat', *Journal of Organizational Change Management*, 19: 8–21.

Huczynski, A.A. and Buchanan, D.A. (2007) *Organizational Behaviour,* 6th edn. London: Prentice Hall.

Humphreys, R. (1999) *Futurism*. Cambridge: Cambridge University Press.

Huntington, S.P. (1996) *The Clash of Civilizations*. New York: Simon Schuster.

Hutcheson, F. (1725/1973) *An Inquiry Concerning Beauty, Order, Harmony, Design*, ed. P. Kivy. The Hague: Martinus: Nijhoff.

Ibarra, H. (1993) 'Network centrality, power, and innovation involvement: determinants of technical and administrative roles', *Academy of Management Journal*, 36: 471–501.

Ihde, D. (1990) *Technology and the Lifeworld: From Garden to Earth*. Bloomington: Indiana University Press.

Ingold, T. (1995) 'Work, time and industry', *Time & Society,* 4: 5–28.

Ingram, P. and Roberts, P.W. (2000) 'Friendship among competitors in the Sydney hotel industry', *American Journal of Sociology*, 106: 387–423.

Jackson, P. (ed.) (1999) *Virtual Working: Social and Organizational Dynamics*. London: Routledge.

Jacobson, M. (1993) *Art and Business,* London: Thames and Hudson.

Jacques, R. (1996) *Manufacturing the Employee. Management Knowledge from the Nineteenth to the Twenty-First Centuries*. Thousand Oaks, CA: Sage.

Jahoda, M. (1972) *Marienthal: The Sociography of an Unemployed Community*. London: Tavistock.

Jahoda, M. (1982) *Employment and Unemployment: A Social-Psychological Analysis*. Cambridge: Cambridge University Press.

James, O. (2007) *Affluenza*. London: Random House.

Janssens, M. and Zanoni, P. (2005) 'Many diversities for many services: theorizing diversity (management) in service companies', *Human Relations*, 58: 311–40.

Jaques, R.S. (2002) 'What is a cryptohutopia and why does it matter?', in M. Parker (ed.), *Utopia and Organisation.* London: Blackwell Books.

Jay, R. (2004) *The Successful Candidate: How to be the Person they Want to Hire*. London: Pearson.

Jermier, J. (1988) 'Sabotage at work: the rational view', *Research in the Sociology of Organizations,* 6: 101–34.

Jones, B. (1982) 'Destruction or redistribution of engineering skills? The case of numerical control', in S. Woods (ed.), *The Degradation of Work?* London: Hutchinson.

JPC-SED (2004) *Japan Productivity Center for Socio-Economic Development.* http://www.jpc-sed.or.jp (accessed 30 April 2007).

Kant, I. (1790/1997) *Critique of Judgement*, trans. J.C. Meredith. Oxford: Oxford University Press.

Kanter, R.M. (1972) *Commitment and Community: Communes and Utopias in Sociological Perspective*. Cambridge, MA: Harvard University Press.

Kenney, M. (ed.) (2000) *Understanding Silicon Valley: The Anatomy of an Entrepreneurial Region*. Stanford: Stanford University Press.

Kenney, M. with Florida, R. (2004) *Locating Global Advantage: Industry Dynamics in the International Economy*. Stanford: Stanford University Press.

Kidd, P. (1994) *Agile Manufacturing: Forging New Frontiers*. London: Addison-Wesley.

Klein, N. (2000) *No Logo*. London: Flamingo.

Knights, D. and McCabe, D. (2000) 'Bewitched, bothered and bewildered: the meaning and experience of teamwork for employees in an automobile company', *Human Relations*, 53: 1481–517.

Knights, D. and Willmott, H. (1988) *New Technology and the Labour Process*. London: Macmillan.

Knights, D. and Willmott, H. (1989) 'Power and subjectivity at work: from degradation to subjugation in social relations', *Sociology*, 24: 535–58.

Knights, D. and Willmott, H. (2006) *Introducing Organizational Behaviour and Management*. London: Thompson.

Knorr Cetina, K. (1999) *Epistemic Cultures: How the Sciences Make Knowledge*. Cambridge, MA: Harvard University Press.

Knorr Cetina, K. and Bruegger, U. (2002) 'Global microstructures: the virtual societies of financial markets', *American Journal of Sociology*, 107: 905–50.

Knorr Cetina, K. and Preda, A. (eds) (2005) *The Sociology of Financial Markets*. Oxford: Oxford University Press.

Korczynski, M. (2003) 'Communities of coping: collective emotional labour in service work', *Organization,* 10: 55–79.

Kozinets, R. (1999) 'E-tribalized marketing?: the strategic implications of virtual communities of consumption', *European Journal of Management*, 17: 252–64.

Kreiner, K. and Schultz, M. (1993) 'Informal collaboration in R&D: the formation of networks across organizations', *Organization Studies,* 14: 189–209.

Kristeva, J. (1981) 'Women's time', *Signs*, 7: 13–35.

Kummer, C. (2002) *The Pleasures of Slow Food: Celebrating Authentic Traditions, Flavors and Recipes*. San Francisco: Chronicle Books.

Kunda, G. (1992) *Engineering Culture: Control and Commitment in a High-Tech Corporation.* Philadelphia: Temple University Press.

Kunda, G. and Ailon-Souday, G. (2005) 'Managers, markets and ideologies – design and devotion revisited', in S. Ackroyd, R. Batt, P. Thompson and P.S. Tolbert (eds), *Oxford Handbook of Work and Organization*. Oxford: Oxford University Press.

Land, C. (2007) 'Flying the black flag: revolt, revolution and the social organization of piracy in the "golden age"', *Management and Organizational History*, 2: 169–92.

Land, C. and Corbett, J.M. (2001) 'From the Borgias to the Borg (and back again): rethinking organizational futures', in W. Smith, M. Higgins, M. Parker and G. Lightfoot (eds), *Science Fiction and Organization*. London: Routledge.

Landes, D.S. (1983) *Revolution in Time: Clocks and the Making of the Modern World*. Cambridge, MA: Belknap Press.

Lash, S. and Urry, J. (1987) *The End of Organized Capitalism*. Cambridge: Polity Press.

Lash S. and Urry J. (1994) *Economies of Signs and Space*. London: Sage.

Latour, B. (1991) 'Technology is society made durable', in J. Law (ed.), *A Sociology of Monsters? Essays on Power, Technology and Domination*. London: Routledge.

Lave, J. and Wenger, E. (1991) *Situated Learning: Legitimate Peripheral Participation*. Cambridge: Cambridge University Press.

Law, J. (1992) 'Notes on the theory of the actor-network: ordering, strategy and heterogeneity', *Systems Practice*, 5: 379–93.

Layard, R. (2005) *Happiness. Lessons from a New Science*. London: Penguin.

Leadbeater, C. (2000) *Living on Thin Air: The New Economy*. London: Penguin.

Leary-Joyce, J. (2004) *Becoming an Employer of Choice*. London: CIPD.

Lefebvre, H. (1991) *The Production of Space*. Oxford: Blackwell.

Leidner, R. (1993) *Fast Food, Fast Talk: Service Work and The Routinization of Everyday Life*. Berkeley, CA: University of California Press.

Leidner, R. (1999) 'Emotional labour in service work', *Annals of The American Academy of Political and Social Sciences*, 561: 81–95.

Leonard-Barton, D. (1992) 'Core capabilities and core rigidities: a paradox in managing new product development', *Strategic Management Journal*, 13: 111–25.

Linebaugh, P. (2005) 'Charters of liberty in black face and white face', *Mute*, 2(1): 72–85.

Lorsch, A. (1954) *The Economics of Location*. New Haven, CT: Yale University Press.

Lukács, G. (1920/1978) *The Theory of the Novel: A Historico-Philosophical Essay on the Forms of Great Epic Literature*, trans. A. Bostock. London: Merlin Press.

Macho, T.H. (2000) *Hybrid*. Basel: Christopher Merian Verlag.

Mann, S. and Holdsworth, L. (2003) 'The psychological impact of teleworking: stress, emotions and health', *New Technology, Work and Employment*, 18: 196–211.

March, J. (1991) 'Exploration and exploitation in organizational learning', *Organization Science,* 2: 71–97.

Marcuse, H. (1968) *Negations*. London: Routledge and Kegan Paul.

Marcuse, H. (1978) *The Aesthetic Dimension: Towards a Critique of Marxist Aesthetics*. Boston: MA: Beacon Press.

Marglin, S. (1974) 'What do bosses do?', in A. Gorz (ed.), *The Division of Labour. The Labour Process and Class Struggle in Modern Capitalism*. Brighton: Harvester.

Martin, C.J. (1999) 'The new migrants: 'flexible workers' in a global economy', in T. skelton and T. Allen (eds), *Culture and Global Change*. London: Routledge.

Massey, D. (2007) *World City*. Cambridge: Polity Press.

Massumi, B. (1992) *A User's Guide to Capitalism and Schizophrenia: Deviations from Deleuze and Guattari*. Cambridge, MA: MIT Press.

Mathews, J. (1989) *Tools of Change: New Technology and the Democratisation of Work*. Sydney: Pluto Press.

Maurer, I. and Ebers, M. (2006) 'Dynamics of social capital and their performance implications: lessons from biotechnology', *Administrative Science Quarterly,* 51: 262–92.

McAlexander, J., Schouten, J. and Koenig, H. (2002) 'Building brand community', *Journal of Marketing*, 66: 38–54.

McGillivray, D. (2005a) 'Governing working bodies through leisure: a genealogical analysis', *Leisure Sciences,* 27: 315–30.

McGillivray, D. (2005b) 'Fitter, happier, more productive: governing working bodies through wellness', *Culture and Organization*, 11: 125–38

McGregor, D. (1987) *The Human Side of Enterprise*. Harmondsworth: Penguin.

McKinlay, A. (2002) 'Dead selves': the birth of the modern career', *Organization*, 9: 595–614.

McLoughlin, I. (1999) *Creative Technological Change: The Shaping of Technology and Organisations*. London: Routledge.

McLuhan, M. (1962) *The Gutenberg Galaxy: The Making of Typographic Man*. Toronto: University of Toronto Press.

Mead, G.H. (1932/1980) *The Philosophy of the Present,* ed. A.E. Murphy. Chicago: University of Chicago Press.

Merleau-Ponty, M. (1946) *The Phenomenology of Perception*. London: Routledge.

Metcalfe, A.W. (1993) 'The curriculum vitae: confessions of a wage labourer', *Work, Employment and Society*, 6: 619–41.

Meyerson, D. and Martin, J. (1987) 'Cultural change: an integration of three different views', *Journal of Management Studies,* 24: 623–47.

Miller, P. and Rose, N. (1990) 'Governing economic life', *Economy and Society,* 19(1): 1–31.

Mills, J.S. (1859/1991) *On Liberty in Focus*, eds J. Gray and G.W. Smith. London: Routledge.

Milojevic, I. (2003) 'Hegemonic and marginalised educational utopias in the contemporary western world', *Policy Futures in Education*, 1: 440–466.

Mirchandani, K. (2004) 'Practices of global capital: gaps, cracks and ironies in transnational call centres in India', *Global Networks*, 4: 245–374.

Montreuil, S. and Lippel, K. (2003) 'Telework and occupational health: a Quebec empirical study and regulatory implications', *Safety Science*, 41: 339–58.

Morgan, G. (1985) 'From west to east and back again: capitalist expansion and class formation in the nineteenth century', in H. Newby et al. (eds), *Restructuring Capital: Recession and Reorganization in Industrial Society*. London: Macmillan.

Mueller, F. (1996) 'National stakeholders in the global contest for corporate investment', *European Journal of Industrial Relations*, 2: 345–68.

Mueller, F. and Purcell, J. (1992) 'The Europeanization of manufacturing and the decentralization of bargaining', *International Journal of Human Resource Management*, 3: 15–31.

Mumford, L. (1934) *Technics and Civilization*. New York: Harcourt Brace.

Mumford, L. (1967) *The Myth of the Machine, Volume 1: Technics and Human Development*. San Diego: Harcourt Brace Jovanovich.

Muniz, A. and O'Guinn, T. (2001) 'Brand community', *Journal of Consumer Research*, 27(4): 412–32.

Myerson, J. and Ross, P. (2003) *The 21st Century Office*. London: Lawrence King.

Nahapiet, J. and Ghoshal, S. (1998) 'Social capital, intellectual capital and the organizational advantage', *Academy of Management Review*, 23(2): 242–66.

National Audit Office (2002) 'Individual Learning Accounts' [press Notice 60/02] www.nac.org.uk/pn/Ø1-Ø2/Ø1Ø212.35.htm

Newell, H. (2000) 'Managing careers', in S. Bach and K. Sisson (eds), *Personnel Management*, 3rd edn. Oxford: Blackwell.

Newell, S., Robertson, M., Scarbrough, H. and Swan, J. (2002) *Managing Knowledge Work*. Basingstoke: Palgrave.

Nicolini, D. (2006) 'The work for making telemedicine work', *Social Science & Medicine*, 62(11): 2754–67.

Nicolini, D., Gherardi, S., Yanow, D. (eds) (2003) *Knowing in Organizations: A Practice-Based Approach*. Armonk, NY: ME Sharpe.

Noble, D. (1984) *Forces of Production*. New York: Alfred Knopf.

Noble, D. (1993) *Progress Without People: In Defence of Luddism*. Chicago: Charles H. Kerr.

Nonaka, I. (1994) 'A dynamic theory of organizational knowledge creation', *Organization Science*, 5: 14–37.

North, J. (2005) *God's Clockmaker: Richard of Wallingford and the Invention of Time*. London: Hambledon.

Novotny, H. (1989/1994) *Time: The Modern and Postmodern Experience*. Cambridge: Polity.

Ogbonna, E. and Harris, L. (1998) 'Managing organizational culture: compliance or genuine change?', *British Journal of Management*, 9: 273–88.

Ogbonna, E. and Harris, L.C. (2006) 'Organisational culture in the age of the Internet: an exploratory study', *New Technology, Work and Employment*, 21: 162–75.

Ohmae, K. (1989) 'Managing in a borderless world', *Harvard Business Review*, 67: 52–61.

Olins, W. (1989) *Corporate Identity: Making Business Strategy Visible Through Design*. London: Thames and Hudson.

Ong, A. and Collier, S.J. (2005) *Global Assemblages: Technology, Politics and Ethics as Anthropolgical Problems*. Oxford: Blackwell Publishing.

Orlikowski, W.J. (1992) 'The duality of technology: rethinking the concept of technology in organizations', *Organizational Sciences*, 3: 398–427.

Orlikowski, W.J. (2002) 'Knowing in practice: enacting a collective capability in distributed organizing', *Organization Science*, 13: 249–73.

Orlikowski, W.J. (2006) 'Material knowing: the scaffolding of human knowledgeability',
European Journal of Information Systems, 15: 460–6.

Ornstein, R.E. (1969) *On the Experience of Time*. Harmondsworth: Penguin.

Orr, J. (1990) 'Sharing knowledge, celebrating identity: war stories and community
memory in a service culture', in D. Middleton and D. Edwards (eds), *Collective
Remembering: Remembering in a Society*. London: Sage.

Ouchi, W. (1981) *Theory Z: How American Business can meet the Japanese Challenge*.
New York: Avon.

Ouchi, W. and Johnson, J. (1978) 'Types of organizational control and their relationship
to emotional well-being', *Administrative Science Quarterly*, 23: 293–317.

Owen-Smith, J. and Powell, W.W. (2004) 'Knowledge networks as channels and conduits: the effects of spillovers in the Boston biotechnology community', *Organization
Science*, 15: 5–22.

Pahl, R. (2000) *On Friendship*. Cambridge: Polity.

Parker, M. (1997) 'Organizations and citizenship', *Organization*, 4: 75–92.

Parker, M., Fournier, V. and Reedy, P. (2007) *Dictionary of Alternatives*. London: Zed Books.

Pascoe, C. (2001) *Airspace*. London: Reaktion.

Pelzer, P. (2006) 'Art for management's sake? a doubt', *Culture and Organization*,
12(1): 65–77.

Peters, T. (2003) *Re-Imagine! Business Excellence in a Disruptive Age*. London: Dorling
Kindersley.

Peters, T. and Waterman, R. (1982) *In Search of Excellence*. New York: Harper & Row.

Petrini, C. (2001) *Slow Food: Collected Thoughts on Taste, Tradition, and the Honest
Pleasures of Food*. White River Junction, VT: Chelsea Green Publishing.

Pettinger, L. (2004) 'Brand culture and branded workers: service work and aesthetic
labour in fashion retail', *Consumption, Markets and Culture*, 7(2): 165–84.

Pfeffer, J. (1992) *Managing with Power*. Boston: Harvard Business School Press.

Piore, M. and Sabel, C. (1984) *The Second Industrial Divide*. New York: Basic
Books.

Plekhanov, G.V. (1912/1947) *Art and Social Life*, ed. A. Rothstein; trans. A. Fineberg.
London: Lawrence and Wishart.

Polanyi, M. (1962) *Personal Knowledge*. Chicago: University of Chicago Press.

Pollock, L. (2001) 'That's infotainment', *People Management*, 6: 19–23.

Portes, A., Haller, W. and Guarnizo, L. (2002) 'Transnational entrepreneurs: the emergence and determinants of an alternative form of immigrant economic adaptation',
American Sociological Review, 67: 278–98.

Poster, M. (1990) *The Mode of Information*. Cambridge: Polity.

Postrel, V. (2003) *The Substance of Style: How the Rise of Aesthetic Value is Remaking
Commerce, Culture and Consciousness*. New York, NY: Perennial.

Powell, W.W. (2001) 'The capitalist firm in the twenty-first century: emerging patterns in
Western enterprises', in P. DiMaggio (ed.), *The Twenty-First Century Firm*. Princeton:
Princeton University Press.

Powell, W.W., White, D.R., Koput, K.W. and Owen-Smith, J. (2005) 'Network dynamics and
field evolution: the growth of interorganizational collaboration in the life sciences', *The
American Journal of Sociology*, 110: 1132–205.

Pratt, M.G. (2000) 'The good, the bad and the ambivalent: managing identification
among Amway distributors', *Administrative Science Quarterly*, 45: 456–93.

Putnam, R.D. (2000) *Bowling Alone: The Collapse and Revival of American Community*.
New York: Touchstone.

Quiller-Couch, A. (ed.) (1919) *The Oxford Book of English Verse: 1250–1900*. Oxford: Oxford University Press.

Rafaeli, A. and Pratt, M.G. (1993) 'Tailored meanings: on the meaning and impact of organizational dress', *Academy of Management Review*, 18(1): 32–55.

Rediker, M. (2004) *Villains of All Nations: Atlantic Pirates in the Golden Age*. London: Verso.

Reed, M.I. (1984) 'Management as a social practice', *Journal of Management Studies*, 21: 273–85.

Reeves, R. (2004) *Happy Mondays: Putting Pleasure Back into Work*. London: Pearson Education.

Ritzer, G. (1996) *The McDonaldization of Society*, revised edn. Thousand Oaks, CA: Sage.

Ritzer, G. (2004) *The Globalization of Nothing*. Thousand Oaks, CA: Pine Forge Press.

Rivoli, P. (2005) *The Travels of a T-Shirt in the Global Economy*. Hoboken, NJ: John Wiley & Sons.

Roberts, J. and Armitage, J. (2006) 'From organization to hypermodern organization: the accelerated appearance and disappearance of Enron', *Journal of Organizational Change Management*, 19: 558–77.

Robins, K. and Webster, F. (1986) *Information Technology: A Luddite Analysis*. Norwood, NJ: Ablex Publishing Corporation.

Rose, M. (1975) *Industrial Behaviour*, 2nd edn. Harmondsworth: Penguin.

Rose, N. (1989) *Governing The Soul: The Shaping of the Private Self*. London: Routledge.

Rose, N. (1996) 'The death of the social? Refiguring the territory of government', *Economy and Society*, 25: 327–56.

Ross, A. (2004) *No-Collar: The Humane Workplace and its Hidden Costs*. Philadelphia: Temple University Press.

Ross-Smith, A., Chesterman, C. and Peters, M. (2005) '"Watch out, here comes feeling!" Women executives and emotion work', *International Journal of Work, Organisation and Emotion*, 1: 48–66.

Roth, J.A. (1963) *Timetables*. Indianapolis: Bobbs-Merrill.

Rowlinson, M. and Hassard, J. (1993) 'The invention of corporate culture: a history of the histories of Cadbury', *Human Relations*, 46: 299–327.

Roy, D.F. (1960) 'Banana time: job satisfaction and informal interaction', *Human Organization,* 18: 156–68.

Russell, B. (1935/2001) *In Praise of Idleness*. London: Routledge.

Saetnan, A.R. (1991) 'Rigid politics and technological flexibility: the anatomy of a failed hospital innovation', *Science, Technology, & Human Values*, 16: 419–47.

Sale, K. (1996) *Rebels Against the Future. The Luddites and their War on the Industrial Revolution: Lessons for the Computer Age*. London: Quartet.

Sander, C. (2003) *Migrant Remittances to Developing Countries*, prepared for the UK Dept for International Development (DFID). London: Bannock Consulting.

Sassen, S. (2006) *Territory Authority Rights: From Medieval to Global Assemblages*. Princeton NJ: Princeton University Press.

Saxenian, A. (2006) *The New Argonauts: Regional Advantage in a Global Economy*. Cambridge, MA: Harvard University Press.

Scarbrough, H. and Corbett, J.M. (1992) *Technology and Organization: Power, Meaning and Design*. London: Routledge.

Scarbrough, H. and Swan, J. (2001) 'Explaining the diffusion of knowledge management: the role of fashion', *British Journal of Management*, 12: 3–12.

Schatzki, T. (2001) 'Practice theory', in T. Schatzki, K. Knorr Cetina and E. von Savigny (eds), *The Practice Turn in Contemporary Theory*. London: Routledge.

Schein, E. (1978) *Career Dynamics: Matching Individual and Organizational Needs.* Reading, MA: Addison-Wesley.

Schivelbusch, W. (1980) *The Railway Journey: The Industrialization of Time and Space in the Nineteenth Century.* Oxford: Blackwell.

Schmitt, B. and Simonson, A. (1997) *Marketing Aesthetics: The Strategic Management of Brands, Identity and Image.* New York: Free Press.

Scholte, J.A. (2005) *Globalization: A Critical Introduction,* 2nd edn. London: Palgrave Macmillan.

Schouten, J. and McAlexander, J. (1995) 'Subcultures of consumption: an ethnography of the new bikers', *Journal of Consumer Research*, 22: 43–61.

Schultz, M., Hatch, M.J. and Larsen, M.H. (eds) (2000) *The Expressive Organization: Linking Identity, Reputation, and the Corporate Brand.* Oxford: Oxford University Press.

Schultze, U. and Stabel, C. (2004) 'Knowing what you don't know? Discourses and contradictions in knowledge management research', *Journal of Management Studies*, 41: 549–73.

Schumacher, E.F. (1973) *Small is Beautiful.* London: Blond and Briggs.

Schwartz, B. (2004) *The Paradox of Choice. Why More is Less.* New York: Harper Perennial.

Seltzer, M. (1998) *Serial Killers.* London: Routledge.

Sennett, R. (1998) *The Corrosion of Character: The Personal Consequences of Work in the New Capitalism.* New York: Norton.

Sennett, R. (1999) *The Corrosion of Character: The Personal Consequences of Work in the New Capitalism.* New York: Norton.

Sennett, R. (2006) *The Culture of the New Capitalism.* New Haven: Yale University Press.

Sennett, R. and Cobb, J. (1993) *The Hidden Injuries of Class.* New York: W.W. Norton and Sons.

Sewell, G. and Wilkinson, B. (1992a) 'Empowerment or emasculation? Shopfloor surveillance in a total quality organisation', in P. Blyton and W. Streeck (eds), *Reassessing Human Resource Management.* London: Sage.

Sinclair, A. (2007) *Leadership for the Disillusioned.* Crows Nest, Australia: Allen & Unwin.

Siriginidi, S.R. (2000) 'Enterprise resource planning in re-engineering business', *Business Process Management Journal*, 6: 376–91.

Skinner, A. (1970) Introduction, in Smith, A. *Inquiry into the Nature and Causes of the Wealth of Nations* (Books 1–3). Harmondsworth: Penguin.

Smircich, L. and Morgan, G. (1982) 'Leadership: the management of meaning', *The Journal of Applied Behavioral Science*, 18: 257–73.

Smith, A. (1776/1970) *The Wealth of Nations* (Books I–III). Harmondsworth: Pelican Classics.

Smith, A. (1776/2000) *The Wealth of Nations* (Books IV–V). Harmondsworth: Penguin.

Soderberg, A-M. and Vaara, E. (eds) (2003) *Merging across Borders: People, Cultures and Politics.* Copenhagen; Copenhagen: Business School Press.

Sorokin, P.A. and Merton, R.K. (1937) 'Social time: a methodological and functional analysis', *American Journal of Sociology,* 42: 615–29.

Spicer, A. (2002) 'Technical questions: a review of key works on the question of technology', *Ephemera: Critical Dialogues on Organization*, 2: 64–83.

Starkey, K. (1989) 'Time and work: a psychological perspective', in P. Blyton, J. Hassard, S. Hill and K. Starkey (eds), *Time, Work and Organization*. London: Routledge.

Stearns, P.Z. and Stearns, P.N. (1986) *Anger: The Struggle for Emotional Control in America's History*. Chicago: University of Chicago Press.

Strati, A. (1996) 'Organizations viewed through the lens of aesthetics', *Organization*, 3: 209–18.

Strati, A. (2006) 'Organizational artifacts and the aesthetic approach', in A. Rafaeli and M.G. Pratt (eds), *Artifacts and Organizations: Beyond Mere Symbolism*. Mahwah, NJ: Lawrence Erlbaum. pp. 23–39.

Sturdy, A.J. (1992) 'Clerical consent: "shifting" work in the insurance office', in A. J. Sturdy, D. Knights and H. Willmott (eds), *Skill and Consent in the Labour Process*. London: Routledge.

Sturdy, A.J. (1998) 'Customer care in a consumer society', *Organization*, 5: 27–53.

Sturdy, A.J. (2003) 'Knowing the unknowable? – a discussion of methodological and theoretical issues in emotion research and organizational studies', *Organization*, 10: 81–105.

Sturdy, A. J. and Fleming, P. (2003) 'Talk as technique – a critique of the words and deeds distinction in the diffusion of customer service cultures', *Journal of Management Studies*, 40: 753–73.

Sturdy, A.J. and Korczynski, M. (2005) 'In the name of the customer? Service work and participation', in P. Thompson and W. Harley (eds), *Participation and Democracy at Work*. Basingstoke: Palgrave.

Sturdy, A.J., Schwarz, M. and Spicer, A. (2006) 'Guess who's coming to dinner? Structures and uses of liminality in strategic management consultancy', *Human Relations*, 9: 929–60.

Styhre, A. (2003) 'Knowledge management beyond codification: knowing as practice/concept', *Journal of Knowledge Management*, 7: 32–40.

Sunday Times (2005, 2006) *100 Best Companies to Work For*. London: *Sunday Times*.

Surman, E. (2004) 'Out of sight and beyond control? A spatial analysis of supervisors' responses to a remote workforce', working paper, University of Warwick.

Swan, J.A. and Scarbrough, H. (2001) 'Editorial: knowledge management – concepts and controversies', *Journal of Management Studies*, 38: 913–21.

Swan, J.A. and Scarbrough, H. (2005) 'The politics of networked innovation', *Human Relations*, 58: 913–43.

Swan, J.A. Scarbrough, H. and Robertson, M. (2002) 'The construction of "communities of practice" in the management of innovation', *Management Learning*, 33(4): 477–96.

Taylor, F.W. (1911) *The Principles of Scientific Management*. New York: Norton.

Taylor, F.W. (1947) *The Principles of Scientific Management*. New York: W.W. Norton.

Taylor, P. (2004) *World City Network: A Global Urban Analysis*. London: Routledge.

Taylor, P. and Bain, P. (2004) 'Call centre offshoring to India', *Labour and Industry*, 14: 15–38.

Taylor, S. and Tyler, M. (2001) 'Juggling justice and care: gendered customer service in the contemporary airline industry', in A.J. Sturdy, I. Grugulis and H. Willmott (eds), *Customer Service – Empowerment and Entrapment*. Basingstoke: Palgrave Macmillan.

Teece, D.J., Pisano, G. and Shuen, A. (1997) 'Dynamic capabilities and strategic management', *Strategic Management Journal*, 18: 509–33.

ten Bos, R. and Kaulingfreks, R. (2002) 'Life between faces', *ephemera: critical dialogues on organization*, 2: 6–27.

Therborn, G. (2000) *European Modernity and Beyond*. London: Sage.

Thompson, E.P. (1967) 'Time, work-discipline and industrial capitalism', *Past and Present*, 38: 56–97.

Thompson, P. (1989) *The Nature of Work: An Introduction to Debates on the Labour Process*, 2nd edn. Basingstoke: Macmillan.

Thompson, P. and McHugh, D. (2002) *Work Organisations: A Critical Introduction*, 3rd edn. Basingstoke: Palgrave.

Thrift, N. (2005) *Knowing Capitalism*. London: Sage

Timmons, S. (2003) 'A failed panopticon: surveillance of nursing practice via new technology', *New Technology, Work and Employment*, 18: 143–56.

Todd, P.M. and Gigerenzer, G. (2003) 'Bounding rationality to the world', *Journal of Economic Psychology*, 24: 143–65.

Tönnies, F. (1887/1963) *Community and Society*. New York: Harper & Row.

Townley, B. (1992) *Reframing Human Resources Management: Power, Ethics and the Subject at Work*. London: Sage.

Townley, B. (1993) 'Foucault, power/knowledge, and its relevance for HRM', *Academy of Management Review*, 18: 518–45.

Townsend, K. (2005) 'Electronic surveillance and cohesive teams: room for resistance in an Australian call centre?', *New Technology, Work and Employment*, 20: 47–59.

Tretheway, A. (1999) 'Disciplined bodies: Women's embodied identities at work', *Organization Studies*, 20(3): 423–450.

Trist, E. and Bamforth, K. (1951) 'Some social and psychological consequences of the longwall method of coal-getting', *Human Relations*, 4(1): 3–38.

Trowler, P. (2001) 'Captured by the discourse? The socially constitutive power of new higher education discourse in the UK', *Organization*, 9: 183–201.

Tsoukas, H. (1994) 'What is management? An outline of a meta-theory', *British Journal of Management*, 5: 289–301.

Tsoukas, H. and Vladimirou, E. (2001) 'What is organizational knowledge?', *Journal of Management Studies,* 38(7): 973–93.

Tuan, Y.F. (1977) *Space and Place*. Minneapolis: University of Minnesota Press.

Tyler, M. (2004) 'Managing between the sheets: lifestyle magazines and the management of sexuality in everyday life', *Sexualities*, 7(1): 81–106.

Uzzi, B. (1997) 'Social structure and competition in interfirm networks: the paradox of embeddedness', *Administrative Science Quarterly*, 42: 35–67.

Veblen, T. (1964) *The Instinct of Workmanship: And the State of the Industrial Arts*. New York: Norton.

Vidich, A., Bensman, J. and Stein, M. (eds) (1964) *Reflections on Community Studies*. New York: Harper & Row.

Vielba, C.A. (1995) 'Managers' working hours', paper presented to the British Academy of Management Annual Conference, Sheffield University Management School, 11–13 September.

Virilio, P. (1991) *La Vitesse*. Paris: Editions Flammarion.

Virilio, P. (1997) *Speed and Politics: An Essay on Dromology*. New York: Semiotext(e).

Von Krogh, G., Nonaka, I., and Aben, M. (2001) 'Making the most of your companies knowledge, *Long Range Planning*, 34: 421–39.

Wajcman, J. (1991) 'Technology, patriarchy and conceptions of skill', *Work and Occupations*, 18: 29–45.

Warhurst, C. (1996) 'High society in a workers' society: work, community and Kibbutz', *Sociology*, 30: 1–19.

Warren, S. (2002) '"Show me how it feels to work here": using photography to research organizational aesthetics', *ephemera*, 2(3): 224–45.

Watson, J.L. (ed.) (1997) *Golden Arches East: McDonald's in Asia*. Stanford: Stanford University Press.

Weber, M. (1904–5/1989) *The Protestant Ethic and the Sprit of Capitalism* trans. T. Parsons. London: Unwin Hyman.

Weber, M. (1930/2001) *The Protestant Ethic and the Spirit of Capitalism*. London: Routledge.

Weber, M. (1978) *Economy and Society*. Berkeley, CA: University of California Press.

Weber, M. (1991) *From Max Weber: Essays in Sociology*, trans. H. Gerth and C. Wright Mills. London: Routledge.

Webster, F. and Robins, K. (1986) *Information Technology: Post-Industrial Society or Capitalist Control*. Norwood, NJ: Ablex.

Welsch, W. (1997) *Undoing Aesthetics*. London: Sage.

Wenger, E. (1998) *Communities of Practice: Learning, Meaning, and Identity*. Cambridge: Cambridge University Press.

Wenger, E. (2000) 'Communities of practice and social learning systems', *Organization*, 7: 225–46.

Wenger, E. and Snyder, W. (2000) 'Communities of practice: the organizational frontier', *Harvard Business Review*, 78: 139–45.

Wenger, E., McDermott, R. and Snyder, W. (2002) *Cultivating Communities Of Practice: A Guide To Managing Knowledge*. Boston, MA: Harvard Business School Press.

Wilensky, J.L. and Wilensky, H.L. (1951) 'Personnel counseling: the hawthorne case', *American Journal of Sociology*, 57: 265–80.

Wilkinson, B. (1983) *The Shopfloor Politics of New Technology*. London: Heinemann.

Williams, R. (1983) *Keywords: A Vocabulary of Culture and Society*, revised edn. London: Fontana.

Williams, S.J. and Bendelow, G.A. (1996) 'Emotions and "sociological imperialism": a rejoinder to craib', *Sociology*, 30(1): 145–53.

Willis, P. (1978/2003) *Learning to Labour*. Farnham: Ashgate.

Willmott, H. (1993) 'Strength is ignorance: slavery is freedom – managing culture in modern organizations', *Journal of Management Studies*, 30: 515–52.

Wilson, F. (2004) *Organizational Behaviour and Work: A Critical Introduction,* 2nd edn. Oxford: Oxford University Press.

Witz, A., Warhurst, C. and Nickson, D. (2003) 'The labour of aesthetics and the aesthetics of organization', *Organization,* 10: 33–54.

Womack, J.P., Jones, D.T. and Roos, D. (1990) *The Machine that Changed the World.* Oxford: Maxwell Macmillan International.

Wood, M. (1998) 'Agency and organization: toward a cyborg-consciousness', *Human Relations*, 51: 1209–26.

Wood, S. (1989) *The Transformation of Work?* London: Unwin Hyman.

Woodward, J. (1980) *Industrial Organization: Theory and Practice*. Oxford: Oxford University Press.

Wray-Bliss, E. (2001) 'Representing customer service: telephones and texts', in A.J. Sturdy, I. Grugulis and H. Willmott (eds), *Customer Service – Empowerment and Entrapment*. Basingstoke: Palgrave Macmillan.

Wu, C. (2002) *Privatising Culture: Corporate Art Intervention since the 1980s*. London: Verso.

Zerubavel, E. (1981) *Hidden Rhythms: Schedules and Calendar in Social Life*. Chicago: University of Chicago Press.

Zimbalist, A. (ed.) (1979) *Case Studies on the Labour Process*. New York: Monthly Review Press.

Zuboff, Z. (1988) *In the Age of the Smart Machine*. Harvard, MA: Harvard Business School Press.

Zucker, L., Darby, M. and Brewer, M. (1998) 'Intellectual human capital and the birth of US biotechnology enterprises', *American Economic Review*, 88: 290–306.

INDEX

Research Methods Books
from SAGE

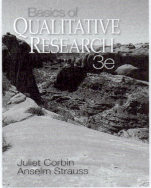

Basics of QUALITATIVE RESEARCH 3e

Juliet Corbin
Anselm Strauss

The Mixed Methods Reader

Vicki L. Plano Clark ■ John W. Creswell

DOING QUALITATIVE RESEARCH USING YOUR COMPUTER

A PRACTICAL GUIDE

CHRIS HAHN

SECOND EDITION

INTERVIEWS
Learning the Craft of Qualitative Research Interviewing

Steinar Kvale
Svend Brinkmann

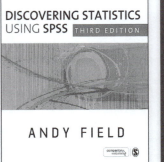

DISCOVERING STATISTICS
USING SPSS THIRD EDITION

ANDY FIELD

RESEARCH DESIGN
Qualitative, Quantitative, and Mixed Methods Approaches

SECOND EDITION

John W. Creswell

The Qualitative Research Kit

Edited by Uwe Flick

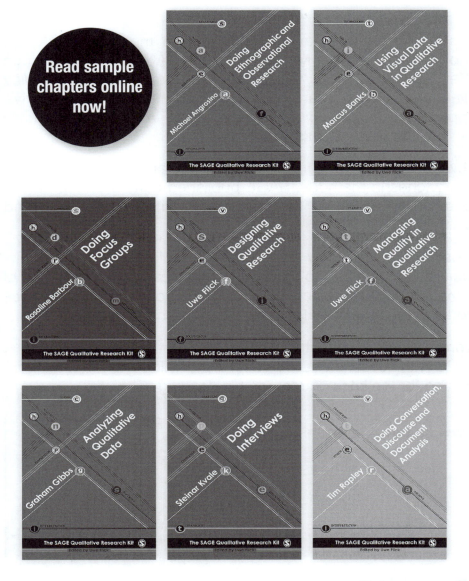

Read sample chapters online now!

Doing Ethnographic and Observational Research — Michael Angrosino

Using Visual Data in Qualitative Research — Marcus Banks

Doing Focus Groups — Rosaline Barbour

Designing Qualitative Research — Uwe Flick

Managing Quality in Qualitative Research — Uwe Flick

Analyzing Qualitative Data — Graham Gibbs

Doing Interviews — Steinar Kvale

Doing Conversation, Discourse and Document Analysis — Tim Rapley

The SAGE Qualitative Research Kit
Edited by Uwe Flick

www.sagepub.co.uk

SAGE

Supporting researchers for more than forty years

Research methods have always been at the core of SAGE's publishing. Sara Miller McCune founded SAGE in 1965 and soon after, she published SAGE's first methods book, *Public Policy Evaluation*. A few years later, she launched the Quantitative Applications in the Social Sciences series – affectionately known as the 'little green books'.

Always at the forefront of developing and supporting new approaches in methods, SAGE published early groundbreaking texts and journals in the fields of qualitative methods and evaluation.

Today, more than forty years and two million little green books later, SAGE continues to push the boundaries with a growing list of more than 1,200 research methods books, journals, and reference works across the social, behavioural, and health sciences.

From qualitative, quantitative and mixed methods to evaluation, SAGE is the essential resource for academics and practitioners looking for the latest in methods by leading scholars.

www.sagepublications.com